How the Bible Became a Book

The Textualization of Ancient Israel

WILLIAM M. SCHNIEDEWIND
University of California, Los Angeles

CAMBRIDGE UNIVERSITY PRESS
Cambridge, New York, Melbourne, Madrid, Cape Town, Singapore, São Paulo

Cambridge University Press
32 Avenue of the Americas, New York, NY 10013-2473, USA

www.cambridge.org
Information on this title: www.cambridge.org/9780521829465

First published 2004
Reprinted 2004
First paperback edition 2005

A catalog record for this publication is available from the British Library

Library of Congress Cataloging in Publication data

Schniedewind, William M.
How the Bible became a book : the textualization of ancient Israel /
William M. Schniedewind.
p. cm.
Includes bibliographical references and index.
ISBN 0-521-82946-1
1. Bible – History. I. Title.
BS445.S315 2004
220.1–dc22 2003063474

ISBN 978-0-521-82946-5 hardback
ISBN 978-0-521-53622-6 paperback

Transferred to digital printing 2008

Contents

List of Figures

Preface

"There is no end to the making of books." – Ecclesiastes

Heard across millennia of book making, these words from the preacher in Ecclesiastes ring true today. Recent technology, such as print-on-demand, e-books, e-mail, and the ubiquitous Internet, disseminate the written word more easily and more quickly than was possible in any previous era. Despite occasional laments from bibliophiles, the book is alive, well, and rapidly multiplying. Thus, the production of annual book titles in the United Kingdom rose by 72 percent during the 1990s, according to the International Publisher Association, and book production in Argentina, Brazil, Canada, Germany, the United States, and other countries also recorded significant increases.

But while books may now seem without end, they do have a more definite beginning, as the ancient preacher also may have known. His words serve as a general warning about the relatively new practice of book production. The preceding verse inveighs against any writings except the "sayings of the wise," which invite interminable study and thus "weariness of the flesh." A widespread concern for such weariness would have made sense only in a literate culture, or, more likely, in a society involved in the dangerous transition from an oral culture to a literate one. My study focuses on this transition in ancient Israel, the spread of literacy among the social classes of seventh-century Judean society. In doing so it looks at the beginnings of the making of one book – the Hebrew Bible. What follows is not an end to the question of how the Bible became a book. It does, however, offer a fresh perspective on the Bible by looking at important periods of its textualization – that is, when it was written down – alongside new ideas about the development of writing and literacy in ancient Israel.

The way the Bible emerges as a sacred text from such a context has profound implications for many religious traditions. It also has revolutionary implications for the scholarly study of biblical literature. But this book was written for a broader audience than simply biblical scholars. To this end, my technical engagement with biblical scholarship most often is relegated to the notes. I have tried to be careful, on the one hand, not to let my jousting with biblical scholarship intrude too much upon the general reader and, on the other hand, to provide enough notes to represent and engage some of the vast array of biblical scholarship. I alert the general reader to some modern biblical scholarship without burdening the book with arcane debates. Admittedly, I have simplified complex issues like the development and nature of literacy. Nor have I dealt with all the knotty issues of biblical criticism in any complete way. As a principle, I have allowed scholars to suffer at the expense of addressing a broader audience. I hope my colleagues can forgive me as the situation is usually reversed. Still, I hope that by bypassing some of the detailed scholarly issues, I can chart a general approach to biblical literature that is also useful to scholars.

This book owes much to many. In the words of the same biblical sage, "there is nothing new under the sun," and it might be said that I have not so much written this book as I have borrowed it from my teachers, friends, and colleagues. What I have borrowed, I give back in the form of this book. I hope it has come back in as good condition as what was taken. I want to especially thank Ben Sommer, who read the manuscript so carefully and improved it in so many ways. (My apologies, Ben, for being too thick to take all your suggestions to heart.) Although I am now long gone from Brandeis University, the debt to my teachers there – particularly Marc Brettler, Michael Fishbane, and Stephen Geller – lingers on in this book. Many others have read and discussed parts of the manuscript with me, including Carol Bakhos, Scott Bartchy, Tamara Eskenazi, Adriane Leveen, Bernie Levinson, Antonio Loprieno, John Monson, Michael Rosenbaum, Joachim Schaper, Tammi Schneider, Daniel Smith-Christopher, Marv Sweeney, and Ed Wright. Chapter 7 on the Torah was first presented to my friends and colleagues at UCLA's Center for Jewish Studies, and I am profoundly grateful to them for their comments, criticism, and encouragement. All these individuals showed me true friendship by patiently bearing with me while I was absorbed with this project and contributed to it in ways that the written word cannot adequately express. I wish to thank my students who patiently endured my musings and contributed much to the fermentation of this project in classes and seminars. I wish to extend thanks to Bobby Duke and Moise Isaac, who worked as my research assistants during the writing of this book. Finally, I wish to thank UCLA, which has provided me with such a stimulating place in which to engage in these intellectual pursuits. In addition, the university's Academic Senate awarded me research grants, and the dean of humanities, Pauline Yu, has also supported my research. My editor at Cambridge University Press, Andy Beck, has been one of this book's chief assets. Whatever deficiencies remain in my writing, it cannot be the fault of the living voices that have helped me along the way.

In order to make this book accessible to the general reader, I have adopted a very simplified modern Hebrew system for transcribing Hebrew words. I cite the text and versification of the English Bible (usually following the *New Revised Standard Version* or the *New Jewish Publication Society*, but sometimes adopting my own translation and adding emphasis to highlight my argument).

Although it is customary to thank one's family last, it is certainly not least that I thank my patient wife, Jeanne, and my two lovely daughters, Tori and Mikaela. They put all things in perspective and help me realize that indeed the living voice is better than written words.

Abbreviations

AB	*Anchor Bible*
ABD	*Anchor Bible Dictionary*
ANET	*Ancient Near Eastern Texts*, 3rd ed. Edited by J. Pritchard. Princeton: Princeton University Press, 1969.
AO	*Der Alte Orient*
BA	*Biblical Archaeologist*
BAR	*Biblical Archaeological Review*
BASOR	*Bulletin of the American Schools of Oriental Research*
BBR	*Bulletin of Biblical Research*
BethM	*Beth Mikra* [Hebrew]
Bib	*Biblica*
BJS	*Brown Judaic Studies*
BN	*Biblische Notizen*
BWANT	*Beiträge zur Wissenschaft vom Alten und Neuen Testament*
BZAW	*Beihefte zur Zeitschrift für die Alttestamentliche Wissenschaft*
CBQ	*Catholic Biblical Quarterly*
CD	*Cairo Geniza, Damascus Document*
CTM	*Concordia Theological Monthly*
DJD	*Discoveries in the Judaean Desert*
DSD	*Dead Sea Discoveries*
EI	*Eretz Israel*
EJL	*Early Judaism and Its Literature*
ESI	*Excavations and Surveys in Israel*
FOTL	*Forms of Old Testament Literature*
HSM	*Harvard Semitic Monographs*
HSS	*Harvard Semitic Studies*
HTR	*Harvard Theological Review*
HUCA	*Hebrew Union College Annual*
ICC	*International Critical Commentary*

IEJ	*Israel Exploration Journal*
JAOS	*Journal of the American Oriental Society*
JBL	*Journal of Biblical Literature*
JESHO	*Journal of the Economic and Social History of the Orient*
JJS	*Journal of Jewish Studies*
JNES	*Journal of Near Eastern Studies*
JNWSL	*Journal of the Northwest Semitic Languages*
JQR	*Jewish Quarterly Review*
JSJ	*Journal for the Study of Judaism*
JSNTSS	*Journal for the Study of the New Testament Supplement Series*
JSOT	*Journal for the Study of the Old Testament*
JSOTSS	*Journal for the Study of the Old Testament Supplement Series*
JSP	*Journal for the Study of Pseudepigrapha*
JSPSS	*Journal for the Study of Pseudepigrapha Supplement Series*
JSS	*Journal of Semitic Studies*
JTS	*Journal of Theological Studies*
NCBC	New Century Bible Commentary
NEAEHL	*New Encyclopedia of Archaeological Excavations in the Holy Land*, edited by E. Stern. Jerusalem/New York: Israel Exploration Society/Carta/Simon & Schuster, 1993.
OBO	*Orbis biblicus et orientalis*
OTL	*Old Testament Library*
OTS	*Oudtestamentische Studiën*
PEQ	*Palestine Exploration Quarterly*
RB	*Revue Biblique*
RQ	*Revue de Qumran*
RSR	*Religious Studies Review*
SBL	*Society of Biblical Literature*
SBLDS	*Society of Biblical Literature Dissertation Series*
SBLMS	*Society of Biblical Literature Monograph Series*
SBTSS	*Studies of Biblical Theology Supplement Series*
ScrHier	*Scripta Hierosolymitana*
SHANE	*Studies in the History of the Ancient Near East*
SJOT	*Scandinavian Journal for the Old Testament*
TA	*Tel Aviv*
TynBul	*Tyndale Bulletin*
UF	*Ugarit Forschungen*

VT	*Vetus Testamentum*
VTSup	*Supplements to Vetus Testamentum*
WTJ	*Westminister Theological Journal*
ZA	*Zeitschrift für Assyriologie*
ZAH	*Zeitschrift für Althebraistik*
ZAW	*Zeitschrift für Alttestamentlischen Wissenschaft*

[illegible] — [illegible]

[illegible] — [illegible] Testament [illegible]

[illegible] — [illegible] Theological Journal

[illegible] — [illegible]

[illegible] — [illegible]

[illegible] — [illegible]

1

How the Bible Became a Book

When was the Bible written? Why was it written? These questions strike at the heart of the meaning of the Bible as literature. They also hint at a profound transition in human culture. The Bible is a book. That seems like an obvious statement, but it is also a profound development in religion. We may take books for granted, but the ancients did not.[1] The fact that a sacred, written text emerged from a pastoral, agricultural, and oral society is a watershed of Western civilization. In the pages that follow we will explore the movement from orality to textuality, from a pre-literate toward a literate society. Along the way we will need to trace the social history of ancient Israel and early Judaism as well as the formation of the Bible as written literature. The Bible itself will be an eyewitness to this epic shift in human consciousness, the shift from an oral world toward a textual world. Central to this shift will be the encroachment of the text upon the authority of the teacher.

How did the Bible become a book? This book – the book that you hold in your hands – gives a historical account of writing in ancient Israel and of writing's role in the formation of the Bible as a book. To answer this most basic question, we need to explore a number of related questions such as what function did writing serve in ancient Israelite society during different historical periods? How is the increasing importance of writing in ancient Israel reflected in the formation of biblical literature? How does the Bible itself view its own *textuality*? What is the relationship between oral tradition and written texts? When and how does the written word supplant the authority of the oral tradition and the living voice of the teacher? When we begin to understand the answers to these questions, then we shall begin to understand how the Bible itself became a book.

These questions can be related to three basic issues. The first is a critique of the question of *who* wrote the Bible. This book contends that the question "*when* was the Bible written?" is more appropriate than an anachronistic interest in the Bible's authors. This question not only will give insight into the Bible as literature, it also will open a window into the uneasy transition of ancient Israel into a textual culture. This leads to a second issue: *how* is it that the Bible is written at all? Ancient Israel before the seventh century B.C.E. was largely non-literate. How does an oral culture like ancient Israel come to express its identity through a written text? How does the basic orality of early Israel shape the Bible as a written text? How does the authority of the written word come to supplant the living voice of the teacher and the community? This leads us to a final issue: *what* were the particular historical circumstances under which the Bible becomes a text and then Scripture?

The role of writing in the development of Western civilization is not a new topic. A few decades ago, Jack Goody, a Cambridge University professor of social anthropology, wrote the first of several articles and books dealing with the "Consequences of Literacy." This research, now summed up in his recent book *The Power of the Written Tradition* (2000), has influenced a whole generation of scholars. Goody's work was complemented by Marshall McLuhan, a professor of English at the University of Toronto, who argued in *The Gutenberg Galaxy: The Making of the Typographic Man* (1962) that the technological innovation of the printing press profoundly shaped modern humankind by bringing about the transition from an audile-tactile culture to the visually dominant age of print. Such studies have spawned scholarly work in many fields in the humanities and social sciences. For example, the linguist Walter Ong wrote *Orality and Literacy: The Technologizing of the Word* (1982), an influential outline of the impact of developments in writing upon the human consciousness. The importance of emergent literacy and the alphabet in ancient Greece during the fifth century B.C.E. was pointed out by Eric Havelock, a Yale professor of classics, in his book *Preface to Plato* (1963). Havelock argued that there was a literate revolution in ancient Greece that was inspired, at least in part, by the Greek invention of their alphabet. Havelock's research, which is summarized for the general reader in *The Muse Learns to Write: Reflections on Orality and Literacy from Antiquity to the Present* (1986), spawned vigorous debate in the field of classics. Although Havelock overstated both the significance of the Greek innovations in the alphabet and the extent and impact of literacy on Greek culture, he was certainly correct in pointing to the role of the alphabet and the spread of literacy in causing fundamental changes in Greek culture. They had an important role in ancient Israel as well, emerging there a couple centuries earlier. The importance of writing in human history is laid out nicely in a survey by Professor Henri-Jean Martin from the Ecole des Chartes in France entitled *The History and Power of Writing* (1994). All these works (and many others) testify to the transformative power of the written word for human society.

What I shall argue here is that one of the most central moments in the history of the written word occurred in ancient Israel when the written word spread from the narrow confines of palace or temple scribes to the broader society. Writing became part of the fabric of everyday life. Most importantly, written texts for the first time in human history began to have religious and cultural authority. This transference of authority from oral to written is what I refer to in the subtitle of this book, "the textualization of ancient Israel."

The Problem of Who Wrote the Bible

We tend to read the Bible through the lens of modernity. This is to say, we read the Bible as a book. Not only do we tend to think of the Bible as a single book, but we also read the Bible as if it came from a world of texts, books, and authors. We read the Bible from our own perspective of a highly literate world. Yet, the Bible was written before there were books. Let us think of this in another way. The modern "book" (in the narrow sense of that word as the pages bound between two covers) follows the invention of the codex, which had leaves of pages with writing on both sides. The replacement of the traditional scroll by the codex was a major technological development in the history of writing. Codices appeared in the first century C.E. and became common by the fourth century C.E.[2] The codex could encompass a much more extensive series of texts than a single scroll could contain and made "the Bible" as a book – the Bible as we conceive of it – a possibility. In bringing together a collection of scrolls, the codex also defined a set and order of books and made possible a more defined canon. With the codex, the Bible could be a book.[3]

But the Bible was written before there were such codices. It is helpful to remember that the Bible itself is actually a collection of books or scrolls. The English word *bible* derives from the Greek *biblia*, which may be translated as "books" or "scrolls." As a result, when we ask how the Bible became a book we are asking, in part, about a collection of books that compose our Bible. The Hebrew word *sefer*, usually translated as "book," means literally "text, letter, or scroll." In early biblical literature *sefer* could refer to any written text, although as writing became more common in later periods a more developed vocabulary begins to distinguish between different kinds of written documents.[4] A reader may remark that the title *How the Bible Became a Book* doesn't refer to a "book" as he or she recognizes it – that is, as a codex. This is true, but as the reader will discover in my second chapter, the almost magical power many continue to associate with books today is not unrelated to ancient Israel's conception of the numinous effects of writing. I chose my title because I wanted to preserve for modern readers the sense of awe and reverence that this transformation from the oral to the textual could generate. Biblical scholars, who invariably translate the Hebrew word *sefer* as "book," recognize the much broader semantic range of this word than the word "codex." It is in this broader sense of "book" as the written word and as a source of cultural authority that I speak of *How the Bible Became a Book*.

Who wrote the Bible is a fascinating question, though of debatable value. The ability of this question to captivate our attention is underscored by Richard Elliot Friedman's best-selling book, *Who Wrote the Bible?* This popular and lucidly written account of biblical criticism actually did quite a bit more than answer the facile question of who wrote the Bible, but the popularity of the work no doubt profited from being couched in this simple question and the simple answers that can be given to it. So, for example, Jeremiah is the Deuteronomist (i.e., he "wrote" Deuteronomy); or, an Aaronid priest wrote the priestly document (e.g., Leviticus).[5] Friedman suggested that biblical literature often cannot be understood without knowing something about its authors, but then he gives the sample question: "Did the author of a particular biblical story live in the eighth century B.C. or the fifth?"[6] The real import of this question is not *who* is the author, but rather *when* was the text written. Friedman actually gives rich insight into biblical literature through his adroit historical contextualization. In some ways, it is unfortunate that the book is reduced to the facile question of who wrote the Bible. Yet, it is exactly this question that captures the modern fancy.

One interesting question posed in literary circles is whether the author makes a difference in the meaning of the literature. In an enormously influential book called *Is There a Text in This Class?* Stanley

Fish argued that the interpretative community was ultimately more important than the author because the reader – much to some authors' chagrin – ultimately defines the meaning of a text.[7] The problem is quite stark in the case of biblical literature. The Bible is really a collection of books and not the product of an individual author. Moreover, what a hypothetical author intended to say often is difficult (if not impossible) to recover for an ancient text like the Bible. More accessible (and perhaps more important) is understanding what the text meant to its ancient readers, which does not necessarily resemble an author's intent. For example, what the U.S. Constitution means is usually more a reflection of its readers than its authors. Consequently, the meaning of the Constitution keeps changing along with the changing generations of its readers. Although the framers' intent is certainly important, from a practical standpoint it has been the historical moment when our society read the Constitution that has shaped the history of its interpretation. In the same way, biblical meaning has reflected its readers more than its writers. More than this, the community's role in the reading is even justified because the Constitution (as well as the Bible) is the product and property of the community more than of an individual.

When a text is central to a people or a nation, like the Declaration of Independence or the Constitution is, the history of its interpretation can serve as a window into the history of that people. One socially charged analogy in American history can illustrate. The landmark Supreme Court decision *Brown v. Board of Education* (1954) overturned "separate, but equal" (*Plessy v. Ferguson*, 1896) educational facilities for races as a violation of the Fourteenth Amendment to the U.S. Constitution that guarantees all citizens "equal protection of the laws." This corresponded to a changing American social landscape more than it did the intent of the authors.[8] The different interpretations of the Constitution in 1896 and 1954 reflected the changing social context of the interpreters. The text had not changed, but the readers and their social context had. Similarly, the meaning of the Bible will be imbedded in the history of the people who wrote it, read it, passed it on, rewrote it, and read it again. It is closely tied to when the traditions were collected, written down, edited, rewritten, and finally coalesced into the book we call the Bible.

In an earlier book, I took one example, the Promise to David in 2 Samuel 7, and showed how it functioned as a constitutional text in ancient Israel.[9] This text promised King David and his sons that they would forever reign on the throne of Israel. I illustrated how the interpretation of this text over the course of a millennium was closely associated with the social, religious, and political events and contexts of the Jewish people. The text had its origins in the tenth century B.C.E., during the transition of semi-nomadic pastoralists toward an urban state. The Promise to David served as a common ideology giving divine sanction to the politics of a new monarchic state. Later, under changes brought about by the emergence of the Assyrian Empire in the eighth century B.C.E., the Promise to David would give rise to rather unrealistic religious rhetoric that deluded itself into thinking that God "had promised a lamp for David forever" (1 Kgs 11:36, 15:4; 2 Kgs 8:19). In the religious reforms of the seventh century B.C.E., the Promise was applied both to the king and to the Temple, which was supposed to last forever as God's dwelling place on earth. The Babylonian exile in the sixth century B.C.E. thrust the Promise into crisis. The Promise had failed; David's sons were no longer on the throne, and the Temple had been destroyed. By reinterpreting the Promise, new readers were able to relocate the God of Israel as the God of the whole earth and to apply the Promise even to foreign kings (not from the line of David). The connection between the social setting of the readers and the interpretation was especially clear in the readings given to the Promise to David by different Jewish communities in the late Second Temple period. Early Christianity, of course, read in the Promise a final fulfillment in the person of Jesus of Nazareth. The interpretation of the Promise to David began within the Bible itself, but it would continue after the Bible became Scripture – that is, after the text became sacred writ.

The question about who wrote the Bible is also misguided because it emphasizes the individuality of the author. The emphasis on individual expression is not a universal cultural value, even if it is a god of modern American culture. In some cultures, the group takes precedence over the individual. In folk literature, for instance, the literature belongs to the group that shares the tradition. The meaning of the text is not tied to the singer of the tale. The concept of communal authorship is also reflected in the transmission of texts of oral tradition like the Talmud among certain Jewish communities.[10] Early Israel and its literature certainly reflect this emphasis on the group rather than the individual. So, for example, when we read a story like the sin of Achan recounted in Joshua 7, our modern sensibilities may be jarred by the fact that all Israel is punished for the individual Achan's stealing of booty dedicated to God. God says, "Israel [not Achan] has sinned" (Josh 7:11–12). Moreover, not only Achan is stoned for this sin but also his sons and daughters and "his whole tent" (as the Bible suggests in Josh 7:24). This is a strikingly different cultural system than our Western cultures. The individual is submerged into the group. On the whole, Israel's literature is not merely the expression of an individual, it is also a collective tradition.

The Authority of the Author?

Why are we so concerned with *who* wrote the Bible? That question did not become important until after the rise of Greek civilization in the fourth century B.C.E. – well after most of the books of the Bible had been written. In contrast, the importance of authorship was largely an unknown concept in the ancient Semitic world.[11] The famous Mesopotamian *Epic of Gilgamesh*, the Babylonian creation myth known as *The Enuma Elish*, the Egyptian tale *The Shipwrecked Sailor*, and the Canaanite epic literary account of the battle between the gods, *Baal and Mot*, have no authors. They have scribes who pass along the tradition. The scribes were first of all administrators or bureaucrats; they were not authors. The Classical Hebrew language does not even have a word that means "author." The nearest term would be *sofer*, "scribe," who was a transmitter of tradition and text rather than an author. Authorship is a concept that derives from a predominantly *written* culture, whereas ancient Israelite society was largely an *oral* culture. Traditions and stories were passed on orally from one generation to the next. They had their authority from the *community* that passed on the tradition rather than from an *author* who wrote a text. These stories and traditions were the things that fathers and mothers were obliged to teach their children, as Deuteronomy 6:6-7 commands, "Keep these words that I am commanding you today in your heart. Recite them to your children and talk about them when you are at home and when you are away."

The fall of the Persian Empire to Alexander the Great ushered in profound changes in the Near East. The age of Hellenism – that is, the spread of Greek language, culture, and values – brought with it the concept of authorship. The authority of a text came to be associated with its author. Jewish tradition naturally felt compelled to find authors for its literature in this age, although there was little explicit evidence about authorship in the Bible. The earliest Jewish text that identifies its author is the Wisdom of Ben-Sira, dating from the early second century B.C.E. In some places, the Bible indirectly would contradict later ascription of authorship. This is clear, for example, in the Book of Deuteronomy, which is framed as a third-person report of a speech by Moses and not as something that Moses himself wrote, "These are the things Moses *said* to all Israel . . ." (Deut 1:1). In the books of Exodus, Leviticus, and Numbers, Moses is a character, not an author. Genesis does not mention Moses in any capacity. In spite of this, Deuteronomy, along with the other four books of the Torah, has usually been ascribed to the pen of Moses rather than being understood as traditions passed down from Moses or more generally as traditions of the Israelite people.

A most remarkable attempt to address the authority of the Torah is found among the Dead Sea Scrolls, which were discovered in 1947. The Temple Scroll, one of the longest and most complete of the scrolls belonging to an Essene sect of Jews living on the shore of the Dead Sea, rewrites the Torah and particularly the Book of Deuteronomy. Although the first columns of the scroll are missing and hence it is difficult to say precisely how it begins, it fundamentally addresses the problem of authorship and authority by changing the voice from Moses to God. The scroll exchanges the third-person voice of Moses for the first-person voice of God. The change can be seen throughout the scroll, but one example will suffice:

> Deuteronomy 17:14. When you have come into the land that *YHWH your God* is giving you,[12] and have taken possession of it and settled in it, and you say, "I will set a king over me, like all the nations that are around me," 15 you may indeed appoint a king whom *YHWH your God* will choose. From one of your brethren you shall set a king over you. . . .

> Temple Scroll (11QT[a]) 56:12. When you have come into the land that *I* am giving you, and have taken possession and settled in it, 13 and you say, "I will set a king over me, like all the nations that are around me," 14 you may indeed set a king over yourselves – one whom *I* will choose. From one of your brethren you shall set a king over you. . . .

The change in voice makes a rather startling claim for authority. God is the author of the Temple Scroll. The issue of the authority of a text comes to the fore in this striking transformation of Deuteronomy. To be sure, the claim that God was the actual author becomes an increasingly prevalent view through history among certain religious groups. Here, however, this claim for the text's authority is imbedded within the text itself. It addresses the need of this new and important cultural artifact – the written text – to stake its claim as the bearer of orthodoxy.

The Hellenistic age produced a myriad of literary works that claimed to date back to the "golden age" of ancient Israel. These works, known as the pseudepigrapha, included books such as *Enoch*, the *Apocalypse of Moses*, and the *Life of Adam and Eve*. Often they addressed the issues of authority and authorship in strikingly direct ways. The Book of Jubilees, for example, begins in its very first verse with the gift of "two tablets of stone of the law and of the commandment, which I [i.e., God] have written." Jubilees further addresses the need for a written text in its fifth verse, where God enjoins Moses: "Incline your heart to every word which I shall speak to you on this mount, and write them in a book." Later, an angel is employed to help Moses with the writing. Throughout, the Book of Jubilees is preoccupied with its own textuality and its attribution to the figure of Moses. The term for such works, *pseudepigrapha*, derives from the Greek *pseudonymous*, which means "under a false name." They attempted to derive authority from their attribution to figures of classical antiquity. More than this, these works are self-conscious about the whole process of writing. By the third century B.C.E., pseudepigraphy was a norm for writing in Jewish religious literature. Whereas a few literary works were anonymous, many others were pseudonymous or incorrectly attributed to someone.

The Bible, in contrast, shows a distressing disinterest in who wrote it. It was distressing, that is, to Jewish readers living in a Hellenistic society where the authority of literature was closely tied to its author. It continues to be distressing to many pious modern readers who have inherited the Hellenistic emphasis that associates authority with authors. To these ancient and modern readers, the Book of Deuteronomy derives much of its sacred power from the presumption that Moses penned it. Or, the authority of the Book of Isaiah depends on the prophet actually having shaped the final text of the entire canonical book known under his name.

Dogmas have arisen concerning the authorship of all biblical literature. It was assumed that such prophets as Samuel, Isaiah, and Jeremiah sat down and composed their books. Ezra, the priest, then collected and edited these books into the shape we now know as the Bible. Very rarely, however, does the Bible itself ever point to *authors*, although it often attributes traditions to biblical characters. So, for example, the Book of Isaiah begins with the pronouncement that "These are the prophecies of Isaiah son of Amoz, who prophesied concerning Judah and Jerusalem" (Isa 1:1). Although this ascribes the traditions to Isaiah, it does not explicitly make him the author of the book itself. And, in fact, the Book of Isaiah suggests that Isaiah's disciples collected his teachings (Isa 8:16). The prophets are generally commanded to *speak* the words of God, not to *write* them. The example of Jeremiah may serve to highlight this. Writing comes to play a more central role in the Book of Jeremiah. Prophecies, for example, are for the first time explicitly written from a prophet to the king. Yet, Jeremiah himself does not write; rather, the scribe Baruch serves as Jeremiah's secretary (Jer 36:32). Indeed, until the later periods there was little reason to write things down. Few could read, and writing materials and the production of scrolls were expensive. There was no social infrastructure for book learning. The traditions of Israel were largely oral unless they dealt with the royal court or the temple, which had the economic resources and social infrastructures to have the traditions written down.

The Enlightenment period in the eighteenth century C.E. brought some questions to the conventional religious traditions concerning authorship. A French physician, Jean Astruc (1684–1766), accepted Mosaic authorship but argued that Moses had originally composed Genesis and Exodus in four columns and that two distinct documents were characterized by the use of the names of God (*Jahweh* and *Elohim*); it was only later scribes who carelessly combined the parts to make the canonical books. Several German scholars developed Astruc's observations. Johann Gottfried Eichhorn (1752–1827), for example, proposed that the Pentateuch was compiled from literary sources long after Moses' death. Wilhelm M. L. de Wette (1780–1849) connected the writing of Deuteronomy with Josiah's reform in the late seventh century B.C.E. These ideas received their crowning articulation by Julius Wellhausen (1844–1918). Simply put, Wellhausen argued that two original sources, J(ahwist) and E(lohist), were combined to make one document, which he labeled JE. D(euteronomy) was later attached; and, finally, the P(riestly Document) was added in the post-exilic period to JE + D to create our Pentateuch.[13] Such documentary theories begin with the worldview of a textual culture; that is, they begin with the worldview of modern critics, not ancient cultures.

Such documentary theories have dominated biblical scholarship over the past century even though they have never been without their critics. Many pious readers have rejected any attempt to even discuss the composite authorship of books, fearing that it somehow undermined the authority of the Bible. Some scholars have pointed out that the oral world of early Israel hardly suits a complex documentary approach to the literature of Israel.[14] Israel's traditions, they argue, were largely transmitted orally like the epics of Homer. The very fact that the Bible itself eschews discussion of authorship certainly lends little help to the search for the authors of the Bible. Ironically, for the *authors* of the Bible, *authorship* seems unimportant. The author apparently was not critical to the authority of the message or the meaning of the text.

Even if we could figure out who the authors were, would we be any closer to the meaning of the Bible? Probably not. But if we knew when the Bible was written, we would know something more about what it meant to its ancient readers. For good or bad, the interpretation of the Bible is tied more closely to the text's readers than to its scribes. The meaning of the Bible depends more on when the Bible was written than on who wrote it. Our question, then, should be not "Who wrote the Bible?" but "When was the Bible written?"

Why Is the Bible a Written Text?

The second topic of this book, namely, just why was the Bible *written* at all may be a more intriguing issue than who wrote the Bible. Widespread literacy is a relatively modern phenomenon. Ancient Israel was primarily an oral culture. Although an eloquent defense might be made for the literacy of a figure like Moses, it is difficult to imagine the hordes of slaves Moses led out of Egypt as *reading books*. Moses could have been trained in the Egyptian courts, but his followers were not. This raises the question, why is the Bible a book? Why was it written if nobody could read it? Why was it written if scrolls were expensive and had limited circulation?

Biblical traditions point to the orality of Israelite culture. James Crenshaw, in his book *Education in Ancient Israel*, shows that, according to biblical literature, wisdom was fundamentally transmitted orally in ancient Israel.[15] The Book of Proverbs admonishes, "*Hear*, my child, your father's *instruction*, and do not reject your mother's *teaching*" (Prov 1:8). This implies the oral teaching passed down through the family. The Psalms also stress the oral transmission of tradition. So, for example, we read in Psalm 105:1–2:

O give thanks to YHWH, call on his name,
make known his deeds among the peoples.
Sing to him, sing praises to him;
tell of all his wonderful works.

This psalm then proceeds to recount the story of Israel in song. Through such songs, stories, and proverbial sayings the traditions of the mothers and fathers were passed along to their sons and daughters. Even the Torah itself was primarily given orally to Israel – although it would come to be the *written* text above all others. The earliest account of the giving of the Ten Commandments, in Exodus 19–20, actually never even mentions writing the Commandments down. This glaring omission points to the antiquity of this account of the Sinai tradition, because it reflects a time *before books were central to Jewish culture*. The second telling of the giving of the law, in the Book of Deuteronomy (for this is what *deuteronomy* literally means, "second law"), as we shall see (Chapter 7), makes the writing of the revelation central and thus reflects the later movement from an oral culture toward a literate culture and "the people of the book."

The idea of literacy cannot be discussed without qualification. What is meant by "widespread literacy"? There are many types of literacy, from the quite mundane literacy involved in the reading and writing of short economic texts or administrative lists to the high levels of literacy required to read and write literary texts like the Pentateuch or the Book of Isaiah. Linguists have emphasized the fluidity between orality and literacy. The well-known sociolinguist Deborah Tannen, for example, pulls back from the sharp dichotomy, "let us not think of orality and literacy as an absolute split."[16] Biblical scholars have followed suit, stressing the orality of ancient Israel and showing how orality lingers even in the written texts of Israel. In an important survey of this topic entitled *Oral World and Written Word* Susan Niditch emphasizes the continuum between orality and literacy. Niditch's work rejects the simple diachronic approach, or a sharp dichotomy between oral and written, as misguided because it can devalue the power of oral cultures and overlooks the impact of orality upon written texts.[17] Orally composed literature should not be caricatured as rustic or unsophisticated. Works such as Homer's *Illiad* and *Odyssey* serve as prime examples of the power, complexity, and sophistication that oral literature can possess. Oral compositions can be complex, and written texts can be simple. Moreover, even when we begin to have written texts, the oral world leaves its mark on them.

The fundamental orality of early Israel is reflected in the genre of many of the society's primary texts. At the beginning of the twentieth century, Hermann Gunkel showed how the Book of Genesis was deeply dependent on folk literature.[18] More recently, scholars like Robert Culley and especially Susan Niditch have emphasized how deeply biblical literature depends on the oral culture of ancient Israelite society.[19] One example in biblical literature is the prophetic messenger formula, "Thus says YHWH." In the Bible, this phrase becomes a set written formula, but it has its setting in the oral delivery of messages.[20] In his book *Stories in Scripture and Inscriptions*, Simon Parker highlights the oral dimensions of ancient inscriptions as well as those of biblical texts.[21] Thus, even when we have written texts, the oral world often pervades their written expression.

Perhaps more importantly, oral tradition and written texts also represented competing centers of authority. While orality and *literacy* may exist on a continuum, orality and *textuality* compete with each other as different modes of authority. When a culture moves from oral tradition to written texts as a basis of authority, this is a radical shift in the social center of education. We need only to look to modern debates among educators about different approaches to education – for example, how much should the computer replace the teacher or professor – to realize how sensitive and often heated even minor changes in the traditional modes of education can be. Ultimately, written texts would supplant oral tradition – a transformation not taken lightly by those with an invested interest in the oral tradition. In studying the formation of biblical literature, both the diachronic movement from orality to literacy and the competition between oral tradition and written texts must be considered.

The transition from oral to written is also a profound cultural change. Jack Goody, the Cambridge anthropologist, stressed the enormous cultural impact that writing and literacy has had in the development of Western civilization.[22] There has been some critique of Goody, arguing, for instance, that he overstated the dichotomy between orality and literacy.[23] There is some truth to this, but neither does the critique fully account for the dichotomy between orality and textuality as competing loci of authority. The rise of writing and the spread of literacy would challenge oral tradition and the oral community with a new and independent basis of authority – the written text. Such an educational innovation was not made without resistance. And it was not made in one moment. The resistance to writing as a replacement for oral tradition is a well-known anthropological phenomenon. In ancient Greece, for example, Plato's Socrates complains to Phaedrus, "Written words seem to talk to you as though they were intelligent, but if you ask them anything about what they say, from a desire to be instructed, they go on telling you just the same thing forever. And once a thing is put in writing, the composition, whatever it may be, drifts all over the place" (*Phaedrus*, §275d). Of course, it is not the text that drifts so much as it is the readers who interpret the text without the guide of a teacher. Although Socrates complains bitterly about the written word, his complaint is preserved, ironically, only in a written account. In Plato's *Seventh Letter*, he wrote that "every serious man in dealing with really serious subjects carefully avoids writing, lest thereby he may possibly cast them as prey to the envy and stupidity of the public."

In the Greco-Roman world, there was a natural resistance to books and writing among all classes of society but especially among craftsmen artisans who observed that their skills were kept within a trade community and best learned from that oral context.[24] Galen, a Roman physician and philosopher (second century C.E.), belittled "those who – according to the proverb – try to navigate out of books."[25] Similarly, Pliny the Elder emphasized the importance of the oral transmission as opposed to books: "the living voice (*viva vox*), as the common saying has it, is much more effective" (*Ep.* II, 3). An important element in these (and other) popular critiques of the written word was the proverbial wisdom of the critic. It was just this proverbial wisdom – held within the community and passed on by tradition – that was most threatened by books and writing. Thus, while there was a continuum between orality and literacy, there is also tension and competition between a written text and a living voice. This tension tightens when the two compete as the basis of cultural or religious authority.

An ambivalence in formative Christian literature about writing reflects a critique of the entrenched religious and political establishments. Paul of Tarsus, for example, tells the Corinthians that "you are a letter of Christ, prepared by us, written not with ink but with the Spirit of the living God, not on tablets of stone but on tablets of human hearts" and furthermore that "the letter kills, but the Spirit gives life" (2 Cor 3:3, 6). This statement, using the analogy of the written word as opposed to the living voice, is not coincidental or isolated. Paul's assessment borrows a metaphor from an underlying cultural critique of writing and books that threatened to displace the spirit and the witness of the community. Early Christian writers were often apologetic about their own writing as, for example, in the second century C.E. Clement of Alexandria paradoxically begins his work *Stromateis*: "This treatise is . . . a remedy for forgetfulness, a rough image, a shadow of those clear and living words which I was thought worthy to hear."[26] Here, Clement's critique recalls the Platonic critique of writing. That is to say, the critique of writing was part of a larger cultural debate.

Orality was also an ideology of Rabbinic Judaism. In the first centuries of the Common Era, the Rabbis were strident in emphasizing that oral tradition (i.e., the oral Torah) served as a final authority greater than the written Torah. Again, however, this oral tradition was ultimately preserved in written texts (e.g., Mishnah, Talmud). Yet, the written tradition couched itself as vernacular Hebrew, reflecting the oral ideology. Oral ideology also worked itself out in other spheres of Rabbinic Judaism; so, for example, liturgy could not have a fixed form but had to be fluid. Prayers could not be written in one set form. Although oral tradition lay alongside written texts,[27] they existed in an uneasy relationship. On the one hand, the Rabbinic emphasis on oral Torah – sometimes at the expense of the written Torah – reflected a strong ideology that favored the oral over the written as authority. On the other hand, the references by the Qumran sectarians to "those who move the boundaries," "those who follow easy interpretations," or those who say the law "is not fixed" reflected a critique of oral tradition in favor of the written tradition. The Qumran sectarians were a priestly elite group that functioned in opposition to the Jerusalem priesthood. Likewise, the tension between the Sadducees and Pharisees over the authority of the oral tradition should be understood, as least in part, as tension between the literate social elites who controlled the written texts and the more lay population who were largely illiterate. Oral Torah was egalitarian, whereas Scripture was elitist. Both the early Christian church and Rabbinic Judaism initially distanced themselves from the sole authority of written texts, but the institutionalization of both Christianity and Judaism ultimately resulted in the resurgence of authoritative written texts (like the New

Testament and the Mishnah). The textualization of culture could not be stopped, even if it was temporarily stayed by the religious aristocracy and by the destruction of the Second Temple.

The shift in religious authority – from oral tradition to written texts – had far-reaching implications. As Haym Soloveitchik pointed out in his study of modern Jewish religious movements,[28] the shift portends a tendency toward religious stridency. It has the capacity to alter religious performance. It transforms the nature and purpose of education. It redistributes political power.

The reading of the authoritative (and innovative) religious text also often results in a sense of guilt and a subsequent need for radical reform. Two prominent biblical examples immediately leap to mind. First is the Josianic Reforms, which begin with the discovery of the Book of the Covenant: "When the king heard the words of the book of the law, he tore his clothes" (2 Kgs 22:11). After this, the king "*read in all the words of the book of the covenant* that had been found in the house of YHWH. The king stood by the pillar and made a covenant before YHWH, to follow YHWH, keeping his commandments, his decrees, and his statutes, with all his heart and all his soul, to perform the words of this covenant that were written in this book. All the people joined in the covenant" (2 Kgs 23:2-3). Guilt is immediately felt, and this dictates a change in religious performance. The people then participate in wide-ranging reforms that wipe out non-orthodox (according to the book) religious activities. Likewise, the story of the reforms under Ezra begins with an elaborate description of gathering the people together to read "the book of the law of Moses." Ezra gets up on a special podium, the people watch as he opens the book, and then he reads (Neh 8:1-8). The reaction is immediate: "all the people wept when they heard the words of the law" (v. 9). The people are then moved to celebrate the Feast of Tabernacles (*Sukkot*). Responding to the written text, the people enter into a binding written agreement to separate themselves from foreigners – even their own wives and children – in accordance with the written word (Neh 10:28-38). The violation of the written regulations has to be punished, or at least explained away. For example, David's many wives violated the injunction "not to multiply wives" (Deut 17:17). The Qumran sectarians explain that "David had not read the sealed book of the Law in the Ark; for the Ark was not opened in Israel from the day of the death of Eleazar and Joshua and the elders who served the goddess Ashtoret. It lay buried <and was not> revealed until the appearance of Zadok" (CD 5:2–5). The book has to be accounted for in religious praxis.

Just as the Protestant Reformation was enabled by the changing technologies of writing, the textualization of Judaism was enabled by social and technological changes.[29] As McLuhan showed in *The Gutenberg Galaxy*, technological innovations in writing could profoundly shape civilization. Martin Luther's cry *sola scriptura* would not have resonated without the invention of the printing press. But the technological change that first enabled the spread of literacy was the invention of the alphabet, which made literacy more accessible. Even though widespread literacy is possible in modern societies without alphabetic writing, like Japan, the spread of literacy in ancient societies without the alphabet would have been impossible. The alphabet, coupled with the rise of the first world empire (the Assyrian) in the eighth century B.C.E., became the catalyst for social changes that made the written word authoritative in ancient Israel. Later, the codex, invented in the first century of the Common Era, would bring scrolls together in a more functional way. Early Christians first adopted the codex for their sacred literature.[30] The codex was better suited than scrolls for use in preaching, teaching, and liturgical reading. When the writings of early religious communities were gathered into a defined canon, a single large codex offered physical representation to the concept of a scriptural canon. In this way, the codex sealed a final stage in our understanding of how the Bible became a book.

Exactly When Was the Bible Written?

A hot topic in recent biblical scholarship and the third major issue of this book is exactly *when* was the Bible written? I shall argue that biblical literature was written down largely in the eighth through the sixth century B.C.E., or, between the days of the prophets Isaiah and Jeremiah. The writing of biblical literature was closely tied to the urbanization of Jerusalem, to a growing government bureaucracy, to the development of a more complex global economy, and then to the spread of literacy. The two critical figures in the flourishing of biblical literature were the kings Hezekiah (r. 715–687 B.C.E.) and Josiah (r. 640–609 B.C.E.). I shall pursue this topic at length in Chapters 5 and 6.

My thesis will directly challenge what has become a fashionable trend among a minority of scholars who argue that the biblical texts were not composed until late into the Persian and Hellenistic periods, that is, between the fourth and second centuries B.C.E.[31] This trend crystallized in a book written by the British scholar Philip Davies, which was published in 1992 with the provocative title *In Search of "Ancient Israel."* Davies argued essentially that biblical Israel was a fiction of Jewish nationalists writing in the fourth century B.C.E. (i.e., during the latter days of the Persian Empire). Davies considered King David to be no more historical than King Arthur. By answering the question of *when* in a much different manner than had traditionally been done, Davies gave the Bible a dramatically different meaning. After all, if the Bible was invented by Jews in the late Persian period, or even in the Hellenistic and Roman periods (i.e., in the fourth through second centuries B.C.E.), as some others have now also claimed,[32] then it would be a fraud propagated by clever charlatans. Or, it would be propaganda purveyed by nationalists or religious ideologues. As I shall detail in Chapter 9, this extremely late dating of the Bible has serious problems, but Davies's argument does illustrate how powerful the question of "when" is.

To be fair, the Bible – that is, the collection of canonized books of the Bible as we have come to know them – was produced between the fifth century B.C.E. and the fourth century C.E. This does not mean, however, that biblical literature was first composed or written down during this period; rather, it means that the editorial processes – decisions about which literature would become canonical, the order of the books, the relationships among the books, the editorial frameworks of the books – largely took place during these nine hundred years. My book is primarily concerned with the writing down of the scrolls of biblical literature and not the compilation of these scrolls into one book.

To ask how the Bible became a book is to ask something about the history of the Jewish people because the writing of the Bible is central to that history. This book then tells something of the early history of the Jewish people and of their book, the Bible, or the *Tanak* (an acronym for the *Torah*, the *Nebi'im* [= prophets], and the *Ketuvim* [= writings], which are three divisions of the Jewish Bible). The focus of this book then is the Jewish Bible or the Christian Old Testament, hereafter referred to simply as "the Bible." Although the fragmentary beginnings of the Bible as written literature may date back to the days of kings David and Solomon (in the tenth century B.C.E.), the majority of the Bible was written a few centuries later, from the time of Isaiah the prophet (late eighth century B.C.E.) until the waning days of the monarchy and the time of the prophet Jeremiah (early sixth century B.C.E.).

The Complexity of Biblical Literature

In this book, I will not pretend that the Bible is a simple book. The Bible reflects a diachronic richness and complexity that must be accounted for in any discussion of its composition. What do we mean by this? The Bible was not written at one time or in one place. Part of the richness of biblical literature is the complexity that results from its composition over a long period of time. Perhaps this may best be illustrated by the Dead Sea Scrolls – the earliest extant biblical manuscripts. Although the oldest biblical manuscripts among the Dead Sea Scrolls date to the third century B.C.E., this cannot be taken as the date of their composition. Indeed, before the discovery of the Dead Sea Scrolls a little more than fifty years ago, the earliest manuscripts were medieval, but no one would have argued that the Bible was therefore a medieval composition. (Well, actually, you can always find someone who will argue anything.) But it is simply an absurd reduction to argue that biblical literature was composed at whichever date we give to the first manuscript evidence we find. Moreover, it needs to be recognized that the Dead Sea Scrolls also include a great number of commentaries, paraphrases, and other reworkings of biblical literature. This active process of interpretation and even revision of Scripture points to a much earlier period for the Bible's composition. This is also seen in the language. The language of the biblical commentaries that are among the Dead Sea Scrolls reflects a much later stage of Hebrew than do the biblical manuscripts themselves, just as the English language in a modern commentary on Shakespeare differs from the language of Shakespeare himself. The linguistic evidence precludes a very late dating of the composition of the Bible.[33]

Let me give just one example of the long and complex literary history of the Bible from within the Bible. The example is the story of Pharaoh Shishak's campaign against Jerusalem that occurred about 925 B.C.E. This story illustrates some of the diachronic aspects of biblical literature that need to be addressed when we ask how the Bible became a book. In the First Book of Kings (14:25–28), we read:

> In the fifth year of King Rehoboam, King Shishak of Egypt came up against Jerusalem; he took away the treasures of the house of YHWH and the treasures of the king's

house; he took everything. He also took away all the shields of gold that Solomon had made; so King Rehoboam made shields of bronze instead, and committed them to the hands of the officers of the guard, who kept the door of the king's house.

Although by most scholars' assessments the Book of Kings was first written down in the late eighth century at the very earliest, the text accurately recalls a campaign of Pharaoh Shishak from at least two centuries earlier. The accurate historical placement of the story is attested to by an Egyptian account of this campaign that was recorded by Pharaoh Shishak (or, Sheshonk) on a wall of the Temple at Karnak in Egypt.[34] We have to account for the early scribal activity that preserved such an accurate chronological synchronism. Such written texts would serve as sources for the skeletal framework of the historical narratives in the Book of Kings, which was written down in the late monarchy (eighth–seventh century B.C.E.)

The Book of Chronicles, which was written in the Persian period (in the fifth or fourth century B.C.E.), used the Book of Kings in its retelling of the history of Israel. As a result, we have the opportunity to see inside the process of the composition of Scripture. Second Chronicles (12:2–9) elaborates on the Book of Kings:

In the fifth year of King Rehoboam King Shishak of Egypt came up against Jerusalem, because they had been unfaithful to YHWH. Twelve hundred chariots, sixty thousand cavalry, and a countless army came with him from Egypt – Libyans, Sukkiim, and Ethiopians. He took the fortified cities of Judah and came as far as Jerusalem. Then the prophet Shemaiah came to Rehoboam and to the officers of Judah, who had gathered at Jerusalem because of Shishak, and said to them, "Thus says YHWH: You abandoned me, so I have abandoned you to the hand of Shishak." Then the officers of Israel and the king humbled themselves and said, "YHWH is in the right." When YHWH saw that they humbled themselves, the word of YHWH came to Shemaiah, saying: "They have humbled themselves; I will not destroy them, but I will grant them some deliverance, and my wrath shall not be poured out on Jerusalem by the hand of Shishak. Nevertheless they shall be his servants, so that they may know the difference between serving me and serving the kingdoms of other lands." *So King Shishak of Egypt came up against Jerusalem; he took away the treasures of the house of YHWH and the treasures of the king's house; he took everything. He also took away the shields of gold that Solomon had made.*

The first thing one notices is that Chronicles has greatly expanded its primary source. The expansion, first of all, serves to explain why Shishak attacked Jerusalem – because they were unfaithful to YHWH. This is typical of Chronicles. The later historian wants to add an explanation. Why did God allow Shishak to ransack the Temple? It should also be observed that the author formally marks the expansion.

Notice that the statement, "King Shishak of Egypt came up against Jerusalem," is repeated exactly at the beginning and end of the expansion. This is a common editorial technique in the Bible (known as a "repetitive resumption," or *Wiederaufnahme*) when a later author or editor makes an addition.[35] It shows that the later writer is aware of drawing on an earlier text or tradition.

The next question is where does Chronicles' expansion come from? Is it entirely the original interpretation of an author or does it have sources too? When the text says that this happened "because they were unfaithful to YHWH," is this an author's interpretation or is this the religious community's traditional understanding? Part of this question revolves around whether we believe the writing is covert or intentional. Does the biblical text hide its dependence on an earlier text or is it referenced in some way? The notion of self-conscious textual dependence here is rather a modern idea. It implies a cultural assumption about the integrity of a text as text. It is no longer a story being retold, but a text being adapted. This self-consciousness about the integrity of a text and consequently its use and adaptation is a critical change reflected in the perspective of the Book of Chronicles. The first clue to the answer of this question must lie in the very editorial nature of this addition. It is formally marked. We would know where it began and ended without the Book of Kings before us. Remember that in antiquity, the readers of the Book of Chronicles probably would not have had easy access to the Book of Kings. The *scrolls* certainly were not bound together the way they are in our modern Bibles. The text does us the favor of marking the addition by a repetition. The text concludes the account of King Rehoboam by stating, "The deeds of Rehoboam, early and late, are recorded in the chronicles of the prophet Shemaiah and Iddo the seer, in the manner of genealogy" (1 Chr 12:15). Here again, the text gives us a clue to the compositional process. Is this an invention of fictional authorities, or does the text have some written tradition in mind? Although we do not know the exact nature of these sources, we should presume that the writer had recourse to these sources in some form. The alternative is to believe that the writer intentionally tries to deceive the audience – a rather jaundiced position especially given that the writer has already marked the expansion using repetition. Naturally, the use of traditions does not necessarily mean that the account is completely accurate historically, but it does give some insight into the compositional process. In sum, we must suppose a written text, perhaps royal or temple annals, that goes back to the tenth century B.C.E., which then is incorporated into the Book of Kings in the eighth–seventh century B.C.E. A later writer in the Book of Chronicles apparently interpreted and revised the Book of Kings by using other sources (e.g., the chronicles of the prophets) in the fifth–fourth century B.C.E.

This example illustrates one fragment of a long, rich, and complex process for the writing of the Bible. The question of when the Bible was written is often exceedingly complicated. In most cases, we have few explicit sources, markers, and references for the composition of biblical literature. Still, we can envision the process by moving from the clear examples to the less clear. And we can reconstruct the social settings in which traditions were passed on orally, then written down, and finally edited into what we now know as the Bible. Indeed, part of the power of biblical literature lies in this long involved process. It was the vitality of biblical tradition and its centrality to ancient Israel and early Judaism that led to its taking a written form that was read, interpreted and sometimes revised, and reread.

Where shall we begin the journey in this book? Before we can understand how the Bible became a book, we have to explore the nature of writing itself in early societies and then writing in early Israel. Writing had a numinous power in the ancient world. Its secrets were guarded by scribal guilds within the closed circles of palaces and temples. Early Israel reflects these pre-literate attitudes toward writing. Chapter 2 will explore the numinous power of writing and its role in early Israel. The development and use of writing, however, is closely associated with the rise of the state and urbanization. Chapter 3 will examine the central role of writing within the state. Chapter 4 will turn to the early Israelites and examine the limited role of writing in the early Israelite kingdoms. It would take a major social upheaval in ancient Israel for writing to spread into the popular culture. The flourishing of writing and then the spread of literacy took place in the eighth and seventh centuries B.C.E. Chapters 5 and 6 will sketch out some of the social changes in Israel that resulted in the writing down of early Hebrew traditions and then will focus on the spread of writing and literacy that made a textual religion possible. Chapter 7 illustrates this transition from an oral world to a written text through an examination of the way that the Torah is treated in biblical literature. Once writing had made a place for itself in the religious culture, the concept of Scripture naturally followed. The Babylonian exile was a crisis for both text and oral tradition. Chapter 8 shows how biblical literature is essentially completed with the end of the royal house and its sponsorship. Chapter 9 describes the darkest hour for biblical literature in the poverty of Persian Yehud, where there is a retrenchment and preservation of biblical literature. But biblical literature has its renaissance beginning in the third century B.C.E. in the wake of Hellenism and its interest in the written word and in the creation of libraries. Oral tradition and written texts had an uneasy relationship in antiquity. An epilogue sketches the tension between oral and written in formative Judaism and early Christianity as a canon of Scripture – the Bible – emerges in these traditions.

2

The Numinous Power of Writing

Writing had a numinous power, especially in pre-literate societies. Writing was not used, at first, to canonize religious praxis, but to engender religious awe. Writing was a gift of the gods. It had supernatural powers to bless and to curse. It had a special place in the divine creation and maintenance of the universe. According to one ancient Jewish tradition, the letters of the Hebrew alphabet as well as the art of writing were created on the sixth day (M. Avot 5:6). The idea that writing was given to humankind as part of the very creation of the world was known also in ancient Egypt and Mesopotamia. Writing was not mundane; rather, writing was used to communicate with the divine realm by ritual actions or formulaic recitations in order to affect the course of present or future events. According to Jewish tradition, the stone tablets given on Mount Sinai also were created on the sixth day. God himself writes on these two tablets with his very finger. Ancient Mesopotamia also described heavenly tablets (known as the Tablets of Destiny) in its creation myth, *The Enuma Elish*. According to biblical literature, God actually keeps a heavenly book, inscribed with people's names, which God adds to and erases thereby inscribing the eternal fate of those named. The books of Moses reflect this early notion of writing as supernatural. Such mysterious and numinous understandings of writing are typical of largely oral societies like early Israel.

In this chapter I wish to stress the uncommonness of writing, especially in antiquity. In modern society, writing is common. It is a mundane part of our existence. We sometimes forget that writing is an invention. It is a relatively recent development in human history. Moreover, the concept that writing or a text is authoritative, or even important, is certainly not innate. The value of literacy is something that we teach. In contrast, speaking is something we learn naturally in the course of our social interactions. The social structures for learning to speak are intrinsic to our very normal human development. However, we build schools in order to teach people to read and write. No child learns to read without being taught in an artificially created social context. The social institutions for learning to read and write are creations of a complex society. The authority and centrality of texts is also an acquired value. We teach our children that texts are important. We also teach our children which texts are important, even canonical. To be sure, literacy has been a core value in Western cultures, but the ascendancy of writing has a long and varied history. The transition from the oral state into our written world has been a monumental one. We need to be conscious of this as we witness the process in the very textualization of the Bible.

We usually discuss writing from the viewpoint of the literate.[1] Yet, early writing was controlled by the king and the priests. Very few people were literate. Estimates are that as few as one percent of people in ancient Egypt and Mesopotamia were literate. It will also be important to understand how the illiterate view writing since early Israelite society was largely non-literate. Here I distinguish between *non-literate* and *illiterate*. *Non-literate* denotes people who belong to societies where writing is either unknown or restricted, as in the ancient Near East. *Illiterate*, in contrast, is a pejorative term used in societies that have widespread literacy. As I discuss later (Chapter 6), widespread literacy does not develop in ancient Israel until the seventh century B.C.E. Consequently, early Israelite texts should (and do) reflect aspects of how the non-literate think of writing. Non-literates had magical notions about writing that were a reflection of the belief that writing was the domain of the divine.

The Divine Character of Early Writing

In early societies writing was a guarded knowledge of political and religious elites. At first, writing in ancient Israel reflected this typical restricted role within the palace and temple. In ancient Mesopotamia, writing proper was the domain of the goddess Nisaba (sometimes spelled Nidaba), the personal deity of scribes and the scribal academy. By the first millennium, this role had been transferred to the god Nabû, whose emblems were the scribe's stylus and tablet. Nabû was almost unknown before 1000 B.C.E. Beginning sometime late in the second millennium B.C.E, Nabû is described as the eldest son of the god

Marduk, who was the patron deity of the city of Babylon and the high god of the Babylonians. Nabû was held in great esteem by the Babylonians and Assyrians and later by the Persians. Marduk was the great king, and Nabû was his ready scribe, the servant of the great king, record keeper of the heavenly council, and custodian of the Tablets of Destiny, which were known from the great Mesopotamian creation epic, *The Enuma Elish*. According to the story, Marduk defeated the wicked Tiamat and her consort Kingu and became king of the gods. By virtue of this victory, Marduk controlled the Tablets of Destiny upon which were written the functions of moral, social, and political order.[2] These tablets were given over to Nabû, the secretary-general of the divine council. The rising status of Nabû in the Assyrian and Babylonian court undoubtedly mirrored the rising importance of scribes in the royal court.

The god Nabû (or, as he is called in Hebrew, Nebo) was undoubtedly known to the writers of the Bible. He had become quite prominent in the neo-Babylonian period and continued to be revered in the Persian period. He would have been well known to Jews living in Babylonia after the exile. Nabû is actually mentioned in Isaiah 46:1, but it is the geographical Nebo, a locale in the region of Moab, that appears more frequently in biblical literature. Biblical Nebo is best known as the place where Moses ascended to heaven at the end of his life (Deut 32:49). It is perhaps not a coincidence that Moses ascends to heaven from the top of Mount Nebo, a mountain apparently dedicated to a god of scribes. But no matter how tantalizing this association of Moses, Mount Nebo, and the god Nabû might appear, there is no elaboration upon this highly provocative connection in either biblical literature or later tradition. To add further mystery to the story of Moses and Mount Nebo, other biblical texts call this mountain Pisgah (Deut 3:27; 34:1). Perhaps this name reflected later sensibilities by trying to avoid just such an association between Moses and the Mesopotamian god of the scribes.

As early as the tenth century B.C.E., Israelite scribes show a knowledge of Egyptian scribal practice. Reflecting Egyptian influence, the Israelites borrowed, for instance, Egyptian hieratic numerals for their administrative texts. Consequently, these Hebrew scribes probably were aware of Egyptian religious concepts about writing. The Egyptian god of writing was Thoth,[3] and one of Thoth's titles is "Lord of the hieroglyphs" (the word *hieroglyph* means "sacred writing"). In Egyptian, the sacredness of writing is its very essence.

Thoth was not only the god of writing and scribes but also the god of magic. He is described as "excellent in magic." It was the god Thoth who revealed the secrets of the scribal arts to human beings.

The prominent role of writing in Egyptian magic can be seen in a variety of texts. For example, one spell in the Coffin Texts instructs the reader as follows:

> Write the name in myrrh ink on two male eggs. Regarding one, you are to cleanse yourself thoroughly; then lick off the name, break it, and throw it away. Hold the other in your partially open right hand and show it to the sun at dawn . . . Then speak the formula 7 times, crack the egg open, and swallow its contents.[4]

A critical part of this spell is the magical power of writing itself. The Old Egyptian Pyramid Texts from the third millennium B.C.E. reflect the belief that writing could actually spring to life. These spells and magic rituals use "multilated writing," that is, incompletely written hieroglyphic signs. Using this defective writing prevented the writing itself from becoming animated and thereby posing a danger to both the dead and the living.[5] A vestige of the notion of the magical power of hieroglyphic writing is seen in the modern folk custom of using powder scraped from the writing on ancient temple walls in concocting healing potions.

Ritual Writing

Egyptian Execration texts are among the earliest examples of the numinous power of writing.[6] Execration texts were curses directed at people or cities. The power of the curse is ritualized by the writing down of the words or of the name of the cursed person, often on a figurine depicting the one accursed (see Figure 2.1). These lists of names could also be written on pots or bowls. The magical effect is not in the writing itself, but in the ritual breaking of the figurine or bowl that contains the written text. The figurine pictured in Figure 2.1, for example, was broken as part of the ritual (and not because of the vagaries of time). These Execration texts are essentially the Egyptian counterpart of a "voodoo" doll. The Egyptian was destroyed in a ritual as the curses were recited over it.

The Egyptian ritual use of writing has a good parallel in the law of the jealous husband in the Bible. In the ritual described in Numbers 5:16–30, a priest brings the accused woman before YHWH and then

Figure 2.1. Egyptian Execration Text

concocts a potion in which the key ingredient is writing:

Then the priest shall put these curses in writing, and wash them off into the water of bitterness. He shall make the woman drink the water of bitterness that brings the curse, and the water that brings the curse shall enter her and cause bitter pain . . . and afterward he shall make the woman drink the water.

The critical moment in this ritual of the jealous husband is when the priest *writes* the curse down, probably on a broken potsherd (known as an ostracon), and then washes the writing off into the water of bitterness. The writing in the water gives the water a magical property. The magic water now can discern whether the jealous husband is right in his accusation. The ritual testifies to the power and magic of *written* words. The similarities between this ritual and Egyptian rituals suggest that the ancient Israelites had notions of writing that they shared with their southern neighbors.

The Written Name

A person's name was thought to contain something of the very essence of that person. The patriarch Abram's name (which meant "exalted father") was changed by God to Abraham ("father of multitudes") to mark the birth of the child that would make Abraham the father of many peoples (Gen 17:5). By changing someone's name one could actually manipulate that person's fate (e.g., Gen 35:18). The etymology of a name also contained something of the person bearing that name. Etymologies of personal names are basic features of folkloristic biblical literature. The stories of the biblical patriarch Jacob (whose name means "deceiver") show Jacob tricking his brother Esau and his own father. The turning point in Jacob's life is told in a strange tale in which he wrestles with an unidentified man – perhaps an apparition of the divine – and receives a new name:

> Jacob was left alone; and a man wrestled with him until daybreak. When the man saw that he did not prevail against Jacob, he struck him on the hip socket; and Jacob's hip was put out of joint as he wrestled with him. Then he said, "Let me go, for the day is breaking." But Jacob said, "I will not let you go, unless you bless me." So he said to him, "What is your name?" And he said, "Jacob." Then the man said, "You shall no longer be called Jacob, but Israel, for you have striven with God and with humans, and have prevailed." (Gen 32:24–28)

Jacob's new name, "Israel," captures his essence as a patriarch of the people Israel. His new name is explained by a pseudo-etymology that concludes this folk tale. That is, the biblical etymology suggests that "Israel" means "to strive or fight" (from the Hebrew word, *sarâh*) against God ("El"). More likely, it means "God fights" or perhaps "God rules."

The importance of the name is underscored by another folk etymology: the story of the naming of Moses. The biblical account of Moses' birth in Exodus 2 suggests that Moses (or *Moshe* in Hebrew) is so named because the daughter of Pharaoh *moshed* (i.e., "drew") him out of the water: "When the child grew up, she brought him to Pharaoh's daughter, and she took him as her son. She named him Moses because, she said, 'I drew him out of the water.'" However, the name Moses is from a well-known Egyptian word usually transcribed into English as – *masses*, or – *moses*. The Egyptian word means "born, begotten"; hence, the name of the famous Egyptian Pharaoh Ramasses means "begotten of the god Ra" and the name of Pharaoh Thutmoses means "begotten of the god Thoth." "Moses" was a quite common Egyptian name, or part of a name, in the late second millennium B.C.E. Moses' name thus would have meant "begotten of *X*" – the "*X*" being the name of a god, perhaps YHWH or El, or maybe originally an Egyptian god. However, the biblical narrative gives *Moshe* a new Hebrew etymology that captures some of the essence of the life of Moses.

Writing down a name could capture this human essence. This was part of the idea behind the Egyptian Execration texts. Writing could have a ritual power even when humans wrote names down in a list. Just as in some cultures making an image or a picture could capture the subject's essence (and then be magically manipulated), so in the ancient Near East (including Israel) writing down a name could be a ritual act used to manipulate a person's fate. As a result, taking a census – that is, the registering of names in a list – dabbled in the divine. Making a list of names could be a dangerous act because it could have disastrous consequences for those named in the list. In Exodus 30:11–16, God describes the delicate procedure for taking a census:

> YHWH spoke to Moses: When you take a census of the Israelites to register them, at registration all of them shall give a ransom for their lives to YHWH, so that no plague may come upon them for being registered. This is what each one who is registered shall give: half a shekel according to the shekel of the sanctuary (the shekel is twenty gerahs), half a shekel as an offering to YHWH. Each one who is registered, from twenty years old and upward, shall give the YHWH's offering. The rich shall not give more, and the poor shall not give less, than the half shekel, when you bring this offering to YHWH to make atonement for your lives. You shall take the atonement money from the Israelites and shall designate it for the service of the tent of meeting; before YHWH it will be a reminder to the Israelites of the ransom given for your lives.

The writing of names in a list must be countered by an offering to ward off a plague. The atonement offering serves as a reminder of the ransom that is given for the very lives of those named.

The biblical Book of Numbers begins with a census. God commands Moses, "Take a census of all the congregation of Israel, ... every male twenty and older" (Num 1:2). There are several strange aspects to this census. The most obvious is the vast numbers of people that were recorded. According to Numbers 1:46, there were 603,550 males twenty and older, which would imply that there were well over two million people wandering in the wilderness. Obviously, something is wrong with these numbers. It may have been corruption in the editorial process, but it also could have had something to do with ancient taboos about the whole process of enrolling names in a list. The descendants of the tribe of Levi (i.e., those of the same tribe as Moses) were excluded from the census here. The explanation given was that the Levites are appointed to serve the tabernacle and therefore they should not be enrolled (Num 1:47–51). This is hardly an explanation, however. Unless, of course, we also recognize some of the inherent dangers of writing down names in a census list. Finally, the Levites are commanded "camp around the tabernacle of the covenant, *that there may be no wrath on the congregation of the Israelites*" (Num 1:53). Why would there be *wrath* upon the Israelites at this time? Perhaps because a census was being taken. The role of the Levites was to serve at the tabernacle, making offerings to ward off wrath against those being registered in the census.

Once we understand the gravity of enrolling names in a list, we can begin to understand the story of King David's census as told in 2 Samuel 24. It begins, "the anger of YHWH was kindled against Israel, and he incited David against them, saying, 'Go, take a census of the people of Israel and Judah.'" When David asks his army commander Joab to take the census, Joab strongly protests, "Why does my lord the king want to do this thing?" Joab understands the gravity of such a request, yet David prevails upon him. The story continues, "Afterward, David was stricken to the heart because he had taken a census of the people. David said to YHWH, 'I have sinned greatly in what I have done. But now, O YHWH, I pray you, take away the guilt of your servant; for I have done very foolishly.'" What was David's sin? Traditional interpretation would have it that David simply did not trust God, but as we have seen, the writing down of names in a list treads in the realm of the divine. As a result, David *and Israel* must endure a pestilence, and seventy thousand Israelites die because their names were written down in a census list. The plague strikes not only David, who took the census, but also those whose names were written down in the list.

This sense of the numinous power of writing down names certainly continues in Judaism until this day. Already in biblical texts from the

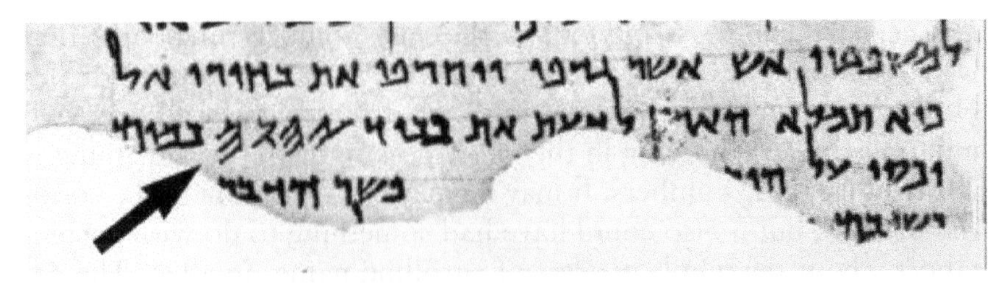

Figure 2.2. Special Writing of God's Name in a Dead Sea Scroll

Persian and Hellenistic periods we witness the increasing reverence for the name of God. The Book of Chronicles, for example, often replaces the sacred four letter name of God in its sources (known from the books of Samuel and Kings) with the more generic *Elohim* (which translates simply as "God"). In the Dead Sea Scrolls, several scribal devices indicate the reluctance to write down the name of God. Sometimes four dots replace the four letters of the name of God. In other places, an archaic paleo-Hebrew script is employed to represent the name of God (see Figure 2.2). This is an extension of the sense of the numinous power of a written name.

Yet, the concept of the numinous power of the written name would have to give way as writing became more important to the economy of the palace. The government administration would need to write names in lists for basic economic activities. This primitive and sacred concept of writing that is especially associated with the priests and the temple is in fundamental tension with the need of the state to record basic operations of a complex economy. Lists need to be made of provisions. Receipts need to be given for taxation and goods.

God's Writing

The numinous nature of writing reaches its height with the two tablets given to Moses on Mount Sinai. The Bible describes stone tablets written by the very finger of God that were received by Moses on Mount Sinai (Exod 24:12; 31:18). Although the contents of these tablets are a mystery (which we shall attempt to unravel later), the magical properties of these tablets are clear. After the tablets are placed into the Ark of the Covenant, the ark becomes a dangerous object. For example, to inadvertently touch the ark results in instant death (2 Sam 6:6–7). After the tablets are placed into the ark, the ark is put in its spot in the tabernacle (and later in the Jerusalem Temple).

When the ark comes into the tabernacle or the temple, the presence of God descends upon that place (Exod 40:20–21, 34–35; 1 Kgs 8:6–11). What does that presence of God have to do with the ark containing the tablets? Is there something about the ark's special writing that summons the very presence of God?

The story that surrounds the announcement of the divinely written tablets is one of the most remarkable in the Bible. It begins after the conclusion of the initial revelation of the Law on Mount Sinai told in Exodus 19:3–24:4. After the initial revelation, Moses apparently makes another trip up the Holy Mountain; the story begins in Exodus 24:9:

> Then Moses and Aaron, Nadab, and Abihu, and seventy of the elders of Israel went up, and they saw the God of Israel. Under his feet there was something like a pavement of sapphire stone, like the very heaven for clearness. God did not lay his hand on the chief men of the people of Israel; also they beheld God, and they ate and drank. YHWH said to Moses, "Come up to me on the mountain, and wait there; and I will give you the tablets of stone, with the law and the commandment, which I have written for their instruction."

The magic of these stone tablets may be related to the unusual nature of their production. This is one of the few places in the Bible where it is explicitly stated that people actually see the God of Israel. The people have a divine picnic on Mount Sinai. Then Moses goes up (further?), and God himself writes the tablets of stone.

The tablets function as a symbol, not as a literary text to be read and consulted. After the tablets are placed into the ark (Exod 25:21–22; 40:20), the ark gains its numinous power. Is this due – at least in part – to the divine writing? The ark is placed in the sanctuary, and God's presence (Hebrew, *kavod*) now hovers above the ark from where he speaks to Moses and the high priests. A veil is made to screen the divine presence from sight. One must carry the ark by poles to avoid inadvertently touching it (as in 2 Samuel 6). Thus the powerfully dangerous writing is sealed in the ark and curtained away.

The heavenly "book of life" is another example of the divine writing. There are several references in biblical literature to a divine book in which are written the names of all humanity. Erasing names from the book extinguishes life. When God threatens to wipe out Israel after they sinned with the Golden Calf, Moses pleads for his people, "But now, if you will only forgive their sin – but if not, blot me out of the scroll that you have written" (Exod 32:32). The "book of life" apparently finds its power in the writing down of names or, in the case of Exodus 32:32, the erasing of a name. This concept of a heavenly book persists into a much later period. According to the Book of Daniel, a heavenly figure called the "Ancient of Days" will judge the world by looking through a scroll: "The court sat in judgment, and the scrolls were opened" (Dan 7:10). This special scroll marks out the people of God, according to Daniel 12:1:

> At that time Michael, the great (angelic) prince, the protector of your people, shall arise. There shall be a time of anguish, such as has never occurred since nations first came into existence. But at that time your people shall be delivered, everyone who is found written in the scroll.

This book is undoubtedly related to the "book of life" featured in the Book of Revelation. In the Last Judgment, "anyone whose name was not found written in the book of life was thrown into the lake of fire." Yet, "those who are written in the Lamb's book of life" are allowed entrance into paradise (Rev 20:15; 21:27). The ultimate fate of every person depends on whether his or her name is written in or erased from the divine book.

Vestiges of early notions about writing persist into modern times. There remains a sense that names are meaningful, that they can communicate something of who a person is or who we wish a person to be. We like to write our names in places. We leave a memory of ourselves by carving our name in a tree or on a rock. There are vestiges of the importance of names in religious rituals too. Hence, we have special names to mark our initiation into religious groups. We have Hebrew names or Christian names. Some people change their names to reflect a transition in their lives. To this day, synagogues place a Torah scroll in an "ark" and celebrate the scroll's appearance in the service, thereby recalling a powerful image from Exodus. The Bible is placed on a pedestal and read from in an elevated pulpit. We revere the written word.

3

Writing and the State

Who wrote in antiquity? Why did people write? The origins and spread of writing follow upon the rise of nations and empires in antiquity. Nowhere did writing flourish in the ancient Near East without the auspices of the state. Writing became a part of the self-definition of early civilizations in Egypt and Mesopotamia. It became pivotal to administration and high culture, even though it was essentially restricted to the emergent scribal class. It was a central element of public monuments, even though the public was essentially non-literate. Writing projected royal power in public forums. Public written monuments were not for reading, but were displays of royal power and authority. Even the pettiest would-be kings of the ancient Near East desired their own royal scribes. The flourishing of writing and literature in the ancient Near East cannot be understood without the context of the state.

This chapter sketches out some of the important aspects of the development of writing both in the Near East more generally and in Israel specifically. In antiquity, writing was both complex and expensive. Writing was not a mundane activity. It required institutional support. Writing was primarily an activity of the state. The invention of the alphabet was one of the critical developments leading to the spread of writing outside state-supported institutions. Yet, the alphabet had already been invented at the beginning of the second millennium B.C.E., and this did not immediately result in a surge in literacy throughout the ancient world. The flourishing of writing, even alphabetic writing, would require state support and favorable political and economic conditions in antiquity.

The Early Use of Writing

Not only the origins but also the spread of writing is tied to the development of complex states.[1] Writing facilitated a sophisticated, urban

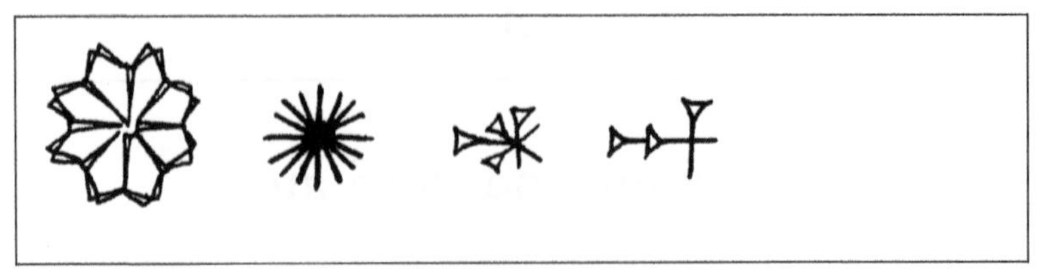

Figure 3.1. The Development of the Cuneiform AN Sign

economy in which merchandise could be identified, types and quantities of goods recorded, and knowledge accumulated. Writing seems to have first developed in Mesopotamia, during the fourth millennium, in connection with accounting practices of the city-states, probably to meet the administrative and economic needs of Mesopotamian cities.[2] Scribes incised ciphers and pictograms in tablets of soft clay to keep a record of transactions. These marks developed into more efficient methods of writing that indicated not only the objects or animals exchanged in a transaction but also entire words from the language in which the transaction took place. Eventually, these words also became symbols for syllables in the languages and thus the power and flexibility of written language grew. For example, the Sumerian cuneiform sign for "heaven" (AN) was originally shaped like a star and over time became increasingly stylized (see Figure 3.1). When the system was taken over in Akkadian, the sign was used to represent the god of heaven, Anu. Eventually, the sign became so stylized that it is only barely recognizable as a pictograph. To make the system more flexible, these signs also began to serve as syllables. In the case of this "star," it could serve as the syllable *il* or *el*. The use of signs for syllables allowed the cuneiform writing system to communicate abstract words and much more complex ideas.

Early systems of writing such as cuneiform and hieroglyphic were quite intricate. At any given time, cuneiform scribes employed about six hundred or more signs, many of which could represent words, grammatical (e.g., plural) or semantic (e.g., "man," "city") concepts, and syllables. Egyptian hieroglyphic writing also had several hundred signs, most of which were used to transcribe either full words (ideograms) or groups of only two or three consonants (Egyptian writing generally did not indicate the vowels). Egyptian also used signs, called determinatives, to classify the words and to distinguish between homographs. In addition to these, Egyptian employed about twenty "alphabetic" signs to represent single consonants; these signs were used initially to transcribe foreign names. These writing systems, complex as they were, largely confined literacy to professional scribes. Although writing played a significant role in artistic display in Egypt, literacy was nevertheless restricted to the inner elite and kings. Scribal training was quite formidable, as is reflected in one early Mesopotamian hymn: "Since I was a child, (I was in) the scribe school."[3] In both Egypt and Mesopotamia, literacy held few benefits for those outside administration and barriers to acquiring literacy were considerable. Moreover, there was no social stigma in illiteracy.

By its very nature, writing in Egypt and Mesopotamia was quite restrictive. The writing systems were so cumbersome and complicated that only the professional scribes who trained in special schools controlled by the palace or the temple could learn to read and write. The expense involved in ancient literacy was considerable and could be borne only by elites sponsored by the ruling groups. The scribes were not independent, but served at the discretion of the ruling groups who brought them into existence, provided for their sustenance, and controlled their access to the public. Thus, the role of writing was quite limited in antiquity. Although vast amounts of cuneiform and hieroglyphic texts have been recovered from Mesopotamia and Egypt, most of these texts deal with bureaucratic, economic, administrative, or religious matters.[4] Earlier texts are most often record keeping, with few literary pieces. Although the literature may have originated much earlier, it was only in the Old Babylonian period (between 2000 and 1600 B.C.E.) that many of these texts were copied down in scribal schools. The major collections of literary works actually date to the Assyrian libraries of the first millennium. The famous library of Assurbanipal (ca. 650 B.C.E.), in particular, collected a variety of Mesopotamian literary traditions, including texts dealing with rituals, myth, math, astronomy, and other subjects.[5] For the most part, however, writing served an administrative and bureaucratic role. Writing preserved the records of the court and the temple; its primary role was not to preserve the cultural heritage of antiquity.

Writing was also a display of royal power. Writing adorned major public monuments, even though no one could read the writing. For this reason, public monuments displaying cuneiform also included symbolic art that communicated the content of the writing to the masses. For example, the famous Code of Hammurabi (one of the first legal codes in human history, dating to the early second millennium B.C.E.) prominently included a visual image of the divine gift of the law to the king as well as the written text of the law code. In Egyptian hieroglyphs, the artistic and visual aspects were actually central to the written symbol.

The Invention of the Alphabet

A defining moment in the history of writing was the invention of the alphabet. Writing is usually analyzed in relation to speech, but writing and speaking are not necessarily related. In the case of early hieroglyphs and cuneiform, writing was only a mnemonic aid. Early writing systems were independent semiotic systems. They had only a loose relationship to speech. But the invention of the alphabet aligned the semiotic system of writing with speech and thereby made literacy more accessible.[6] The alphabet had the power to democratize writing and made it possible for literacy to spread beyond the scribal classes. This innovation also took the mystery out of writing. It is perhaps no surprise that the first alphabetic inscriptions are essentially graffiti.[7] Although alphabetic writing made it much easier to learn to read and write, more than a millennium passed after its invention before we have evidence that literacy actually spread significantly beyond the scribal classes. Contrary to what has been suggested by the anthropologist Jack Goody and the classical scholar Eric Havelock, the invention of the alphabet did not automatically result in the spread of literacy, the rise of democracy, or the emergence of critical thought. This was not because of the imperfections of the early alphabets, but because these social developments are much more complex than can be accounted for simply by the invention of the alphabet. This said, we should also not understate the potential of the alphabet as a technology that could transform society.

Early alphabetic texts were quite limited and suggest that writing still had a restricted role in society. The discoveries at Wadi el-Hol in the eastern Egyptian desert have enabled scholars to date the first alphabetic texts at the beginning of the second millennium B.C.E. (see Figure 3.2). However, the origins of alphabetic writing go back even further than this; consonantal signs had been used in Egypt for centuries to transcribe foreign names. Although the Wadi el-Hol inscriptions have yet to be completely deciphered, they nevertheless confirm that the invention of the alphabet emerged based on the system of Egyptian consonants. Although in Egyptian writing these consonants were not used systematically as they would be in alphabetic writing,

Figure 3.2. First Known Alphabetic Writing from Wadi el-Hol, Egypt (photograph by Bruce Zuckerman and Marilyn Lundberg, West Semitic Research. Courtesy of Department of Antiquities, Egypt)

they still provided a system that could be adapted into alphabetic writing. Additional evidence of early alphabetic writing comes from peoples speaking an early West Semitic language in Canaan and Sinai during the sixteenth through fifteenth centuries B.C.E. At a place known today as Serabit el-Khadem, forty-five "Proto-Sinaitic" inscriptions carved in stone were discovered. They have yet to be completely deciphered, but the signs are a simplified alphabetic system related to the Wadi el-Hol alphabet. The most well-known inscription is on a basalt statue and reads, *lb'lt,* "to the Lady." Alphabetic inscriptions dating to the late second millennium B.C.E. also have been found at Gezer, Lachish, and Shechem. As far as we understand, the letters are drawn according to an acrophonic principle; so, for example, the consonant *m* is a jagged line representing waves of water and corresponding to the word that begins with the sound /m/ in West Semitic languages (*mayim*, "water"). The early alphabet appears to be conceived by an attempt to represent every consonantal sound (phoneme) with one corresponding letter (grapheme), although this system would later be simplified and adapted.

The first extensive use of the alphabet known so far was at the ancient city of Ugarit during the late second millennium B.C.E. The texts were written in an alphabetic cuneiform with thirty letters, and the language has been labeled Ugaritic after the city where most of the texts were discovered. The excavated archive includes letters sent to Ugarit from other cities in Canaan, implying that these cities also used this writing system. In fact, tablets written in an alphabetic cuneiform have been discovered in excavations at a few Canaanite cities. Thus this alphabetic writing was apparently used quite broadly in Syria-Palestine during the late second millennium B.C.E., even though the vast majority of evidence comes from Ugarit. Moreover, Ugaritic writing introduces in a limited way the use of three vowels – *a*, *i*, and *u*. The texts discovered at Ugarit are almost universally related to scribal enterprises: religious, economic, diplomatic, or administrative texts from the palace and temple scribes.[8] Writing was still largely confined to scribal circles sponsored by the temple or the state. Despite dramatic finds of early alphabetic graffiti, writing was primarily an institutionally sponsored tool of government, religion, and commerce.

Royal Scribes

The scribe was among the most necessary figures in ancient Near Eastern governments. [One could not even pretend to be a king if he did not have a scribe.] Even small and unimportant city-states had scribes. This can be illustrated with two examples. In the late second millennium B.C.E. (in the Late Bronze Age), the political structures of Canaan were made up of small and petty city-states. The Amarna Letters, a cache of cuneiform documents written mostly in Canaan and sent to the Pharaoh in Egypt, bear witness to the Egyptian control of this region. Local rule was given to mayors who controlled small regions and looked to Egypt for support. Despite the small and petty nature of these rulers, all of them had royal scribes. These royal scribes wrote letters and kept administrative records. The Amarna Letters were written in a common "pidgin" dialect of the Akkadian language used by government scribes throughout the region of Syria-Palestine in the late second millennium.[9] Temple scribes must likewise have kept records of payments and might have preserved certain temple liturgies. The scribal infrastructure of both palace and temple was, however, quite limited. There is little reason to expect that extensive documents were kept beyond the needs of mundane record keeping and diplomatic correspondence. The literature of these small states was essentially the traditional literature used in scribal training. The purpose of writing was not for literary creativity, but for government administration.

Another example of a small kingdom with a royal scribe comes from the early ninth century B.C.E. in Moab (which was located on the plateau above the eastern shore of the Dead Sea). Moab was by its own account a small kingdom that had been under the domination of Israel. From an archaeological perspective, the early Iron Age kingdom of Moab was largely a pastoral-agrarian society. The first thing that Mesha, the king of Moab, does when he throws off Israelite domination is have a long inscription (over thirty lines) written to commemorate the victory. The inscription begins as follows:[10]

> I am Mesha, son of Chemosh-{yat}, king of Moab, the Dibonite. My father reigned over Moab thirty years, and I reigned after my father. I made this high place for Chemosh [the Moabite national deity] in Qarhoh because he delivered me from all the kings and caused me to triumph over all my adversaries. As for Omri, king of Israel, he humbled Moab many days because Chemosh was angry at his land. And his son [the Israelite king Ahab] succeeded him and he also said, "I will humble Moab." In my days he spoke thus, but I have triumphed over him and over his house, while Israel has perished for ever! Now Omri had occupied the land Medeba, and (Israel) had dwelt there in his time, and half the time of his son, forty years; Chemosh dwelt there in my time. And I built Baal-meon, making a reservoir in it, and I built Kiriathaim...

Several things become apparent in this inscription. First, notwithstanding the small size of this new kingdom – smaller than either Israel or Judah – the new "king" employs a royal scribe to make this long royal inscription. The fact that the tiny kingdom of Moab actually had a scribe has been a source of some consternation. Why did the king need to set up this large memorial stele? How could such a small kingdom have a scribe? To explain how the small Moabite kingdom could produce such an impressive written monument and why the writing was similar to Israelite Hebrew in its orthography and paleography, one scholar has even suggested that the Moabite king must have employed a captured Israelite scribe.[11] But this explanation is unnecessary. Almost no one could read this monument, which was intended to project royal stature for the new upstart king who had his scribe monumentalize (exaggerated) victories in writing. It is also clear from the inscription's content that the Moabite royal scribe was keeping administrative records describing building projects and borders as well as recording tribute and booty.

Figure 3.3. Tel Dan ("House of David") Inscription (photograph by Bruce Zuckerman and Marilyn Lundberg, West Semitic Research. Courtesy of Israel Antiquities Authority and Professor Abraham Biram)

A now-famous inscription dating to the late ninth century is the so-called House of David stele. Its fragments were excavated by archaeologists at the ancient city of Dan in northern Israel in 1993 and 1995. The stele was erected by an Aramean king of Damascus named Hazael after his conquest of the city. Apparently, he placed the monument in the city gate so that it could be on display to all who entered the city. City gates in the ancient Near East were central meeting areas. There the king would sit judging cases. The elders would conduct political, economic, and social business. A religious shrine would represent the patron deity. And, monumental inscriptions like the one found at the city of Dan would serve as a symbol of royal authority and power to those entering the city. The Tel Dan inscription is fragmentary (see Figure 3.3), but the remaining pieces read as follows:[12]

[...consp]ire against[...]and cut/made (a treaty) ?[...Baraq]el my father, went up [against him when] he was fighting at A[bel ?] and my father lay down; he went to [his ancestors.] Now the king of Israel entered formerly in the land in my father's land; [but] Hadad made me myself king, and Hadad went in front of me; [and] I departed from [the] seven[...] of my kingdom; and I slew seve[nty ki]ngs, who harnessed thou[sands of cha]riots and thousands of horsemen. [And I killed Jo]ram, son of [Ahab,] king of Israel, and [I] killed [Ahazi]yahu, son of [Joram, ki]ng of the House of David; and I set [their towns into ruins...the ci]ties of their land into de[solation...] other and to over[turn all their cities...and Jehu ru]led over Is[rael...] siege upon [...]

The inscription apparently commemorates a victory of this Aramean king over the two kingdoms of ancient Israel: the northern kingdom, which was known as Israel, and the southern kingdom of Judah, which was known as the "House of David." The conquest must have taken place about 841 B.C.E. and must have been coordinated with a coup in the northern kingdom of Israel led by the Israelite general Jehu (r. 841–814 B.C.E.). According to biblical tradition, Jehu was involved in the murder of these two kings. The biblical apologetic for Jehu's revolt indicates that Jehu had the support of the prophets Elijah and Elisha and that his revolt was coordinated with the Aramean king Hazael (see 1 Kgs 19:15–18).[13] At this time, the city of Dan passed from Israelite control over to the Arameans. King Hazael then erected this inscription in the city gate as a display of the new Aramean royal authority for all who entered. When the city reverted to Israelite control a few decades later, the Israelites smashed the inscription and used its pieces in the foundation for a new city gate.

Even though the Dan inscription is written in an Aramaic dialect, its language and literary register are actually quite similar to those of the Moabite Stone, as well as to those of contemporary Phoenician inscriptions. This should not be surprising.[14] Written language did not have a strong local orientation in antiquity. Rather, scribal schools created an artificial uniformity, even across different languages and dialects. Writing was a demonstration of power, but it was also a means of international communication. This meant that scribes received broad training in a pan-Canaanite tradition.[15] The rise of linguistic nationalism would only later, in the eighth century B.C.E., begin to result in the emergence of separate languages and alphabets. The ninth century inscriptions from Moab, Phoenicia, and Aram have similarities because scribes were trained in a common Canaanite tradition.

The prestige of a king was partly expressed through the collecting of the accoutrements of kingship. Regardless of the size of the early Israelite kingdom, the emerging monarchy and the newly founded

Figure 3.4. Royal Scribe before Bar-Rakib on Throne (photograph by author)

national shrine would have employed scribes. Near Eastern kings collected exotic animals like apes and peacocks. King Solomon is supposed to have raised a naval fleet for the purpose of trading "gold and silver, ivory, apes, and peacocks" (1 Kgs 10:22).[16] What was the purpose of apes and peacocks? Exotic animals were accessories of a real king, and one could not be a king without the accoutrements of kingship. Similarly, those individuals who aspired to be kings employed court scribes and kept records. These aspirants undoubtedly included the early Israelite leaders.

The importance of the royal scribe is illustrated in the royal relief of the Aramean king Bar-Rakib (Figure 3.4). Bar-Rakib was the "king" – if we can call him that – of a small kingdom in northern Syria. Bar-Rakib produced an impressive stele with a small inscription naming himself as the king. This statue was a display of his royal pretense. The relief is filled with the trappings of kingship: the king seated on the throne with his feet on a footstool, the lotus flower (or tree of life?) in his left hand, his right hand raised. The throne is at an elevated height as the scribe approaches. The inscription on the top identifies the royal patron: "My lord, Baal of Haran • I am Bar-Rakib, son of Panamuwa."[17] The inscription is dedicated to the local deity of the city-state of Haran in north Syria. The relief borrows Assyrian artistic motifs such as the lotus flower (in the left hand), the headdress, and the stylized beard, as Bar-Rakib adorns himself with the accoutrements of an Assyrian monarch. But the most important element of the relief is the scribe, who presents himself before his royal patron. The scribe has in his hand a scroll and carries another document under his arm. He writes for the king.

Writing as a Projection of State Power

The Assyrian Empire would eventually adopt a foreign writing system, the alphabet, and a foreign language, Aramaic, to advance its political and administrative aims.[18] Assyrian imperial ideology tried to unify peoples of "divergent speech" into a people of "one language." In the Dûr-Sharrukîn cylinder inscription, the task of linguistic unification is given to the Assyrian monarch Sargon (r. 722–705 B.C.E.):

> Peoples of the four regions of the world, *of foreign tongue and divergent speech*, dwellers of mountain and lowland, all that were ruled by the light of the gods, lord of all, I carried off at Assur, my lord's command, by the might of my scepter. *I made them of one mouth* and settled them therein. Assyrians, fully competent to teach them how to fear god and the king, I dispatched as scribes and overseers. The gods who dwell in heaven and earth, and in that city, listened with favor to my word, and granted me the eternal boon of building that city and growing old in its midst. (Luckenbill, *ARAB* 2.65–66)

The Assyrians pursued an activist linguistic policy rooted in political ideology. They were well aware of the relationship between language and nationalism. The Assyrian program would use a foreign writing system to help break the relationship between people, land, and language. The brilliance of this policy was that the Assyrians chose not to use their own language – Akkadian – to unify their empire. They chose instead an alphabetically written language – Aramaic – that was easier for scribes to master, in order to facilitate the administration of their growing empire. The imperial use of the alphabet alongside the growth of an urban and global economy would help spread writing in the West.

Writing at the Ancient City of Ugarit

The ancient city of Ugarit, located under a mound now known in Arabic as *Ras (esh-) Shamra*, serves as an instructive analogy for the early Israelite monarchy. Ugarit flourished in the middle of the second millennium until its destruction about 1200 B.C.E. The city controlled a small kingdom on the north coast of the eastern Mediterranean Sea. This kingdom was surrounded to the north, east, and south by mountains. A valley to the northeast of the city was the gateway to the larger kingdoms in Mesopotamia. The plain immediately around Ugarit was fertile, producing abundant wheat and barley; foothills that surrounded Ugarit were cultivated for vineyards and olives. The mountains provided a ready source of the famed "cedars of Lebanon" for construction and trade. As an international harbor, Ugarit had an economy that was naturally engaged in export and import.

The cosmopolitan character of Ugarit is reflected in the many languages and scripts discovered in the excavations at Ras Shamra. Clay tablets were found inscribed in a variety of scripts (cuneiform, alphabetic cuneiform, hieroglyphic) and languages (Ugaritic, Akkadian, Sumerian, Hurrian, Hittite, Egyptian, Cypro-Minonan), although the primary languages were Ugaritic and Akkadian. The use of cuneiform and hieroglyphic scripts highlighted Ugarit's relations with Mesopotamia and Egypt. Alphabetic cuneiform script was particular to Ugarit and may have been invented by the scribes there. The thirty letters of alphabetic cuneiform combined the graphic principles of syllabic cuneiform (wedge-shaped marks inscribed on clay) with the principle of the consonantal alphabet developed in Egypt. Nearly all the remains of the Ugaritic language have been discovered in excavations at the site, although a few short texts using the Ugaritic alphabet have been found elsewhere in the western Mediterranean area in Cyprus, Syria, Lebanon, and Israel (at Mount Tabor, Taanach, Beth-Shemesh). The corpus at Ugarit includes literary texts (myths), administrative documents, economic texts, letters, and school texts (e.g., exercises, lexicons, syllabaries).

The vast majority of texts from Ugarit are economic and administrative texts. These texts were found in palace areas and show the work of royal scribes. In addition to these texts, long mythic tales, such as the Legend of King Keret (or, Kirtu), the Legend of Aqhat, and the monumental Baal Cycle, were copied down by temple scribes. The main religious and mythological texts come from two priestly libraries, with the high priest's house probably functioning as a scribal school. Many of the most important mythological texts were written down or collated by a scribe named Ilimilku during the mid-fourteenth century B.C.E. These texts became part of the cultural heritage of Ugarit (as well as the entire Levant). Scribes were evidently persons of broad education and great standing in Ugaritic society. However, scribes were not authors in the conventional sense. They were the caretakers, not the inventors, of tradition and literature.

The Ugaritic language shows important affinities to Biblical Hebrew language and literature. In the area of lexicography, Ugaritic words frequently shed light on the meaning of otherwise obscure Hebrew words. For the study of biblical poetry, Ugaritic literature has been especially productive (as a glance at commentaries on the Book of Psalms would illustrate). Aspects of biblical poetry like the use of parallelism are richly played out in Ugaritic epic.[19] Umberto Cassuto, one of the early pioneers in the study of Canaanite literature, has observed that epic poetry of the Bible bears witness "to a well-established artistic tradition, as though they had been preceded by a centuries old process."[20] Cassuto suggests that biblical literature is the continuation of Canaanite antecedents. This implies that early Israelite scribes were, like their Late Bronze counterparts, part of a larger Syro-Palestinian scribal tradition and is seen not only in literary influences but also in linguistic and paleographic affinities. The eminent paleographer Joseph Naveh has pointed out, for example, that the West Semitic alphabets (Phoenician, Aramaic, and Hebrew) are almost indistinguishable in the tenth century B.C.E.[21] Scribes throughout the region learned the scribal arts in loosely connected pan-Levantine scribal schools. The affinities between Ugaritic and biblical poetry – especially early biblical poetry – thus point to Canaanite tradition as the heritage of early Israelite scribes.

The case of ancient Ugarit illustrates two important aspects of writing that will be instructive as we consider the development of writing in ancient Israel. First, the state and its development of a complex economy were important to the flourishing of writing. Second, the affinities between Ugaritic poetry and Israelite poetry indicate that ancient Israel was part of a larger cultural context that continued even after the destruction of the great Late Bronze Age city-states at the end of the second millennium B.C.E. Both Israel's oral tradition and its scribal tradition drew upon the rich legacy of ancient Canaan.

4

Writing in Early Israel

Early Israel was an oral society. Biblical literature depicts the early Israelites as semi-nomadic wanderers who finally settled in Canaan and followed a pastoral and later, an increasingly agrarian lifestyle. This was not a setting in which we should expect writing to flourish. Rather, the "literature" of the early Israelites was an oral literature – the songs and stories, proverbs and folktales of a traditional society. The orality of the early Israelite tribes is reflected in biblical literature. According to Deuteronomy, every Israelite *confessed* about his ancestors: "my father was a wandering Aramean" (Deut 26:5). Archaeological research also has suggested that the early Israelites in Canaan were pastoralists who eventually settled into an agrarian lifestyle.[1] This suggests that the roots of early Israel were semi-nomadic shepherds who lived on the desert fringes of the Near East until around 1300 B.C.E. Consequently, the origins of these wanderers in the archaeological record are obscure. When the early Israelites do begin to show up in the archaeological record, they are shepherds and farmers. But did these shepherds and farmers write books? Who would have read such books anyway? Few, if any, could read. The social infrastructure necessary for the widespread use of writing in Israel would not begin to emerge until the late monarchy. Rather, the beginnings of the Bible are to be found in oral literature – in the stories and songs passed on from one generation to the next.

It is significant that the Hebrew language originally did not even have a separate word meaning "to read." Rather, the Biblical Hebrew verb *qara'* means "to call out, proclaim" and was only rarely used in the sense of "to read out loud" as an extension of its primary meaning. In later biblical literature, however, we have the public *reading* of Scripture. The verb *qara'* in its sense of calling out or proclaiming had come to denote reading, as in Nehemiah 8:3, where Ezra reads the *Torah* to the people in the public square: "He *read* (*qara'*) from it facing the square before the Water Gate from early morning until midday, in the presence of the men and the women and those who could understand; and the ears of all the people were attentive to the book of the *Torah*." Later stages of the Hebrew language transform this word, and its primary meaning becomes "to read," thereby reflecting the increasing importance of texts and reading in Jewish society.

There were scribes in the major Canaanite cities during the second millennium B.C.E., even though the vast majority of people were non-literate. The use of writing and the early formation of written literature in ancient Israel depended upon the needs of the early Israelite state. Even petty Canaanite kings had royal scribes during the Late Bronze and early Iron Ages (between the fifteenth and ninth centuries B.C.E.). Writing was not unknown in early Israel, but the level and sophistication of early Israelite literature was necessarily tied to the development of the state.

The Early Israelites

Where did the Israelites come from? More importantly, how did their own stories about their origins take shape? The first appearance of the Israelite people in Canaan has been a matter of considerable scholarly debate.[2] The problem is simple. Outside of the Bible, we have no mention or record of "Israelites" until the late thirteenth century B.C.E. Not that we should expect to hear of them. After all, the biblical accounts of Abraham and his sons point to a patriarchal chieftain whose family is forced into slavery in Egypt by a famine in Canaan. Archaeological evidence suggests that the early Israelites emerged out of a society that was largely pastoral and agrarian. The biblical narratives depicting the emergence of Israel in Canaan, which were likely written down centuries later, also point to shepherds and farmers. There is little reason to believe that we would have explicit written evidence of such an early agrarian and pastoral people.

The first mention of the Israelites in a non-biblical text is a typical example of historical serendipity. The Israelites appear in a victory stele of Pharaoh Merneptah that dates to about 1207 B.C.E. Although the stele's main text actually addresses Pharaoh's campaigns against the Libyans, the very bottom of the stele contains a few lines recalling a campaign to the north by Merneptah. The relevant section begins with a short poem, and the stele concludes with this general statement of the Pharaoh's military prowess:[3]

The princes are prostrate, saying: "Mercy!"
Not one raises his head among the Nine Bows.
Desolation is for Tehenu; Hatti is pacified;
Plundered is the Canaan with every evil;
Carried off is Ashkelon; seized upon is Gezer;
Yanoam is made as that which does not exist;
Israel is laid waste, his seed is not;
Hurru is become a widow for Egypt!
All lands together, they are pacified;
Everyone who was restless, he has been bound by the King of Upper and Lower Egypt:
Ba-en-Re meri-Amon; the Son of Re: Mer-ne-Ptah Hotep-hir-Maat, given life like Re everyday.

Israel seems like an afterthought to Pharaoh's victory stele, and that Israel's seed "is laid waste" is only one of several statements mentioned in this little poem about the Pharaoh's northern campaign. The campaign evidently went as far north as Hatti (i.e., the Hittite Empire) in northern Syria. The coastal and lowland Canaanite cities of Ashkelon, Gezer, and Yanoam were conquered and plundered. None of these cities would have been Israelite during the late thirteenth century when the Israelites seem to have been confined to the hill country. The *people* of Israel are explicitly pointed to by the determinative marker in the Egyptian language of the stele. The Egyptian language used such determinative markers to classify nouns, including people, city, person, land, and nation.[4] An attempt at a literal translation reflecting these determinative markers might be as follows: "Yanoam$^{(city)}$ is made as that which does not exist; / Israel$^{(people)}$ is laid waste. . . ." Apparently, the Israelite people were to be distinguished from the Canaanite city-states like Ashkelon, Gezer, and Yanoam, which have the determinative marker for cities. Scholars have usually inferred from this that the people of Israel were not organized in city-states like the Canaanites were; the scholars have located the Israelites in the hill country, as the Bible itself suggests. All in all, the Merneptah stele is valuable but meager external evidence for the early history of Israel. At least it places them somewhere in Canaan by the end of the thirteenth century B.C.E. It is from here that we will take up the story of how the Bible became a book.

The early Israelites settled in Canaan in the thirteenth century amid widespread disorder throughout the eastern Mediterranean that flowed from a combination of economic, climatic, and military events.

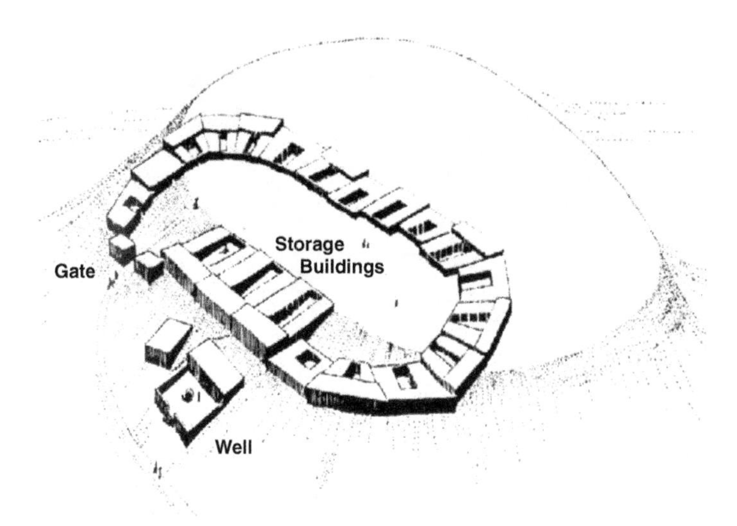

Figure 4.1. Early Israelite Village at Beersheba (adapted from Z. Herzog, ed., *Beer-sheba II* [Tel Aviv, 1984], p. 80)

They were pastoralists and became farmers. Their early settlements bear witness to their pastoral heritage. These settlements were usually shaped much like Bedouin encampments are until this day. The site of Beersheba illustrates the style of early Israelite settlements (Figure 4.1). A circular row of houses provided a central enclosed area where animals could be kept when not out grazing. Larger buildings at Beersheba (and other sites), which served as storage areas for agricultural products, became increasingly important in these settlements as the society moved slowly from a pastoral to an agrarian economy. Such villages might accommodate fifty to two hundred fifty people. There is no evidence that the early Israelites lived in larger urban cities as their predecessors had.

Village culture was hardly conducive to the development of writing. Writing flourishes in urban cultures, where it first of all must meet the administrative needs of government. Early Israel had a largely subsistence economy based on pastoralism and agriculture. But even people in such small villages had the capacity for writing that was afforded by the invention of the alphabet. In Mesopotamia and Egypt, the complexity of the writing systems restricted access to writing. This was not so in early Israel. One of the earliest examples of writing in ancient Israel comes from a small Israelite village called Ebenezer (now known as the ruins of Izbet Sartah),[5] where archaeologists discovered

Figure 4.2. The Hebrew Alphabet from Izbet Sartah (photograph courtesy of Israel Finkelstein)

a clay shard that while it was still wet had been inscribed with the Hebrew alphabet (see Figure 4.2). However, even though the alphabet made writing (and ultimately literacy) more accessible, writing still had only limited utility in an agrarian and pastoral society like early Israel.

Early Israelite villages contrast sharply with the urban palace-temple societies that characterized the Late Bronze Age (1550–1200 B.C.E.). These small Canaanite city-states developed scribal schools that have left ample evidence of writing, albeit largely in the form of administrative texts. Even a tiny city-state like Jerusalem, which numbered no more than two thousand people in the Late Bronze Age, had royal scribes. The two largest caches of writing in the region from this period are the Amarna Letters (from about 1350 B.C.E.) and the archives from ancient Ugarit (from 1300 through 1200 B.C.E.). The el-Amarna letters actually include six letters (EA 286–290) from the ruler of Jerusalem to the Egyptian Pharaoh.

The Songs of the People

The earliest biblical literature included songs of the people. These songs belong to what is usually called *oral literature*. The Israelite people passed on their early traditions through the singing of songs and the telling of tales. Songs undoubtedly were sung when people gathered at great festivals, and some of these songs are sung even to this day. So, for example, Exodus 15 (or, "the Song of Moses") continues to be recited daily as part of the morning service in the synagogue and read as part of the lectionary on the seventh day of Passover. These songs are sung even though their words are no longer completely understood. Much like the Homeric epic, which was preserved by bards who sang the tales of the Greeks, the early traditions of Israel were memorialized in song. According to the Bible, after Moses and the Israelites crossed the Red Sea, "Moses sang a song" (Exod 15:1). Likewise, after Deborah and Barak defeated the Canaanites, "On that day Deborah and Barak son of Abinoam sang" (Judg 5:1). By such statements, oral songs were integrated into written prose.

One collection of archaic Israelite songs has come to be known, infelicitously, as "the Book of Jashar." Of course, the translation of the word "book" here, from the Hebrew *sefer*, is an anachronism if by "book" we mean the modern codex. In Classical Hebrew, *sefer* meant generically a "text, document, letter, or scroll." Although most English translations understand *Jashar* as a personal name, the use of a definite article in Hebrew (that is, *sefer ha-Jashar*) normally indicates a common noun. Thus, *sefer ha-Jashar* might be translated as, literally, "the book of the upright." The two quotations found in the Bible from the Book of Jashar are archaic poetry. The first mention of this book follows the little poem in Joshua 10:12–13 recounting the day the sun stood still:

> On the day when YHWH gave the Amorites over to the Israelites,
> Joshua spoke to YHWH; and he said in the sight of Israel,
> "Sun, stand still at Gibeon,
> and Moon, in the valley of Aijalon."
> And the sun stood still, and the moon stopped,
> until the nation took vengeance on their enemies.
> Is this not written in the Book of Jashar? The sun stopped in mid-heaven, and did not hurry to set for about a whole day.

The other reference to "the Book of Jashar" appears with the Song of the Bow in 2 Samuel 1:19–27. A parenthetical note about this songbook precedes the psalm itself in verses 17–18:

> David intoned this lamentation over Saul and his son Jonathan. (He ordered that The Song of the Bow be taught to the people of Judah; it is written in the Book of Jashar.)

A third probable reference to the Book of Jashar is known from the Old Greek translation of 1 Kings 8:12–13 [= LXX 3Kgdms 8:53a], where an archaic poetic fragment is ascribed to "the Book of the Song" (βιβλίῳ τῆς ᾠδῆς).

The ancient Greek translation of *sefer Jashar* as "the Book of the Song" holds an important clue to its meaning.[6] The Greek translation gives us some insight into the association of several semantically related Hebrew words. The word "Jashar" (Hebrew *yashar*), though it appears at first to be a personal name, is actually a form of the Hebrew verb "to sing" (*yashir*). Alternatively, the word could reflect a metathesis of letters, which would yield the Hebrew word *shîr*, "song." The name of this text, the Book of Jashar, is actually an allusion to its contents, *the scroll of the songs*. This was evidently a collection of ancient national songs. Its antiquity is suggested by the archaic features in the language of the songs, which is not something that can be forged successfully.[7] Later writings from the Dead Sea, for example, try to imitate Classical Hebrew, but their authors are unable to avoid using later aspects of their own language and therefore betray the texts' later date. The reference to the Book of Jashar might be to an oral repertoire for temple singers who performed Israel's epic myths at festivals and other cultic occasions. The collection was probably much more extensive than these three citations. This becomes clear when we look at the introductions to other songs in the Bible:

Then Moses and the Israelites sang this song to the LORD (Exod 15:1)...

Then Moses recited the words of this song to the very end, in the hearing of the whole congregation of Israel (Deut 31:30)...

Then Israel *sang* this song: "Spring up, O well – sing to it" (Num 21:17)...

Such songs might have been included in an ancient Book of Jashar. It is important to note the clash of orality and textuality implicit here. Presumably, these oral songs carried the traditions of Israel, yet they could be written down and taught to the Israelites.

The Song of Moses in Exodus 15, or "the Song of the Sea" as it is also known, is regarded as one of the earliest examples of biblical literature, perhaps dating back as early as the thirteenth century B.C.E. The Song of the Sea finds its closest stylistic and literary parallels with Ugaritic literature, a group of texts that date to the fourteenth and thirteen centuries B.C.E. Linguistic features of the song certainly support an early date, even if it is difficult to precisely date a text using such a methodology.[8] The use of case endings, the enclitic mem, the relative use of *zû* are among those features that point to the early date.[9] The archaic features of the song were preserved despite the song's continual use in Israelite liturgy, particularly in the liturgy of the feast of Passover. The content of the song suggests that it also could have been used during the New Year's festival as well as in royal enthronement ceremonies. The Song of the Sea was part of the sacred liturgy of ancient Israel.

The songs of Israel changed little over the centuries. They were circumscribed by their meter. Certainly, they could change, but the meter dictated rigidity in their form. But the Song of Moses (Exod 15) does come to be a written text, becoming part of the Book of Exodus, a literary work. In this process, the song is framed by a literary narrative. Exodus 14, which immediately precedes the song, essentially gives an account of the crossing of the Red Sea in narrative prose. The song that follows is then introduced as "the Song Moses and the Israelites sang" after the Israelites crossed the Red Sea (Exod 15:1). Thus, the text simultaneously preserves the oral tradition of ancient Israel and introduces an entirely different type of account – the written prose narrative. Other early Israelite songs receive similar treatment. The Song of Deborah is also prefaced by a prose account of Barak and Deborah's battle against Sisera in the preceding chapter (Judg 4–5). In this way, the historical narrative gives a literary framework to the oral poetry of ancient Israel.

The Israelites' inclusion of oral liturgy in their written prose was critical to the formation of this literature as sacred Scripture.[10] Indeed, oral liturgies are not literature in its strictest sense; that is, the self-described genre of the text, namely, an oral song, is not pure literature because it was not *originally* a written text. The forms and devices of oral literature differ considerably from written literature. The characteristic repetition of biblical poetry, for example, is a typical rhetorical device used by bards and storytellers. When such a song is integrated into the prose narrative of biblical literature, it results in a poetic repetition of the prose. Thus, the song in Exodus 15 about the crossing of the Red Sea is preceded, in the biblical narrative, by a prose account in Exodus 14. Likewise, the Song of Deborah in Judges 5 is preceded by a narrative counterpart. Although it is objectively clear from analyzing the language that the songs predate their written narrative frameworks, the narratives are only loosely related to the earlier hymnic accounts. References and allusions to the Book of Jashar in biblical literature suggest that the writing down of a collection of ancient Israelite songs had already occured by the tenth century B.C.E. Again, a good analogy for this process is ancient Ugarit, where several oral epic texts were written down by the scribe Ilimilku. Though the preponderance of texts at Ugarit was administrative, economic, or diplomatic, scribal training made it possible for the scribes to write down oral literature as well. This would have been as true for ancient Israel as it was for ancient Ugarit.

From Canaanite to Israelite Scribes

What is the relationship between the old Canaanite scribal systems and the early Israelite scribes? If there were continuity in the scribal infrastructure, it would certainly suggest that writing continued much the same way as it had in the second millennium B.C.E. before the Israelites settled in Canaan. Although there was a rather limited scribal culture in Syria-Palestine in the late second millennium, this culture does seem to have continued into the first millennium and influenced the scribal institutions of the early Israelite state.

Some scholars have suggested that the scribal institutions of Canaanite society ended with the Israelite conquest. And, even though archaeologists have now recognized that the early Israelite tribes settled a mostly depopulated Canaan, notions about a catastrophic end to scribal institutions have persisted in the scholarly literature. In a widely influential book, David Jamieson-Drake argued that scribal institutions were not passed from one society to another like the family silver.[11] Depending on the theories of George Mendenhall and Norman Gottwald concerning the Late Bronze–Iron Age transition, Jamieson-Drake wrote, "Israel's settlement represents a non-urban culture's rejection of the administrative control characteristic of the Canaanite urban system."[12] This "rejection," however, is actually a very late idealization of what religious reformers during the time of Josiah believed *should have happened*. In other words, the rejection of Canaanite culture is a feature of the Josianic religious reform and its literature. Accordingly, there is increasing evidence of continuity between the Late Bronze and Iron Ages, and this would imply continuity also in the scribal institutions. Even biblical literature portrays David as employing Hittites in his administration and Solomon as utilizing Phoenician craftsmen. Moreover, David's personal militia were foreign mercenaries, according to the Bible. In fact, we have already pointed out the similarity between

Ugaritic epic and early biblical poetry that suggests a common literary culture across Syria-Palestine at the end of the Bronze Age and into the Iron Age.

Arguments suggesting an Israelite rejection of the Canaanite urban system feed on a simplistic reading of the biblical settlement narrative from Joshua. It was the later Josianic reform narrative (in the late seventh century B.C.E.) that emphasized the need for cultural distinction. The Josianic reading of the "conquest" reflects a quite typical human longing for the past – "the good old days" when life was simple and pure. The Josianic reform (see Chapter 6) was an attempt to purge the country of foreign influences and return it to the idealized times when Israel first entered the land. In contrast, continuity is evident in the archaeological record that demonstrates continued Egyptian presence in Canaan from the Late Bronze Age (1550–1200 B.C.E.) through the early Iron Age I period (1200–1000 B.C.E.).[13] Moreover, the stories in the Book of Judges (see particularly Judg 1; also see Josh 13) also testify to substantial continuity between the urban culture of the Late Bronze Age and that of the early Iron Age. These stories are folktales – oral literature about the heroes (or "judges") of pre-monarchic times, and from a critical perspective their historicity must be measured by the realization that they are folktales. Nevertheless, they demonstrate aspects of the real continuity that existed between the Canaanite and the Israelite cultures.

In the archaeological record, cultural continuity was particularly strong at coastal and lowland sites (e.g., Megiddo, Beth-Shan). In fact, some scholars suggest renaming the Iron I period (i.e., the period of the emergence of the Israelites) as the Late Bronze III (which was the last period of the great Canaanite city-states) to reflect the continuity between the Late Bronze and Iron Ages. In short, no archaeological evidence attests to an Israelite rejection of Canaanite cultural institutions, even though there is some breakdown in the Late Bronze Age palace-temple infrastructure, especially in the central highlands where the Israelite tribes settled down. Although some later biblical narratives advocate a cultural break, the stories of Judges and the accounts of the early monarchy from Samuel and Kings suggest that the early Israelite kings drew heavily upon a Canaanite administrative infrastructure. It was only the Deuteronomic ideology stemming from the late seventh century Josianic religious reforms that advanced the notion of a complete cultural break with Canaanite social institutions.

The Emergence of the Early Israelite Monarchy

The size and complexity of the early Israelite state have been the subject of some rancorous debate among scholars.[14] Essentially, the debate boils down to splitting scholarly hairs over exactly when the period of monarchy began (tenth or ninth century B.C.E.) and exactly what the size and complexity of the state were. I believe I can sidestep the scholarly acrimony here.

As I pointed out in the last chapter, even though flourishing literary activity requires a complex state, writing itself does not. I also pointed out that scribes had been employed by small, petty kingdoms like Iron Age Moab or Late Bronze Jerusalem. In the case of early Israel, whatever the size of the state (or kingdom), writing was merely an extension of kingship, a tool for mundane record keeping, and a means of diplomatic communication. There is little evidence that writing was much more than a projection of royal power (real or desired). Even in the great kingdoms of Egypt and Mesopotamia, writing was largely an administrative tool. Literary texts were primarily used for the training of scribes; they were certainly not written for the general public, which was essentially non-literate. Working for the king or temple, scribes kept lists and records and were responsible for diplomatic correspondence. Although scribes were also required to create inscriptions for public display, these inscriptions were meant to have visual impact and not to be read.

The Gezer Calendar, an ancient poetic calendar of agricultural activities, is the most pristine example of writing in Israel during the days of David and Solomon (see Figure 4.3). The calendar dates to the tenth century B.C.E. and was discovered at the ancient biblical city of Gezer (situated between Jerusalem and modern-day Tel Aviv). It reads,

two months of ingathering [olives],
two months of sowing (grain),
two months of late sowing,
a month of hoeing flax,
a month of harvesting barley,
a month of harvesting (wheat) and measuring,
two months of grape harvesting,
a month of ingathering summer fruit.

Although the Gezer Calendar is early evidence for writing in Israel, its language is not Classical Biblical Hebrew. A number of linguistic

Figure 4.3. The Gezer Calendar (tenth century B.C.E.)

peculiarities would suggest a more generic classification for it as Canaanite.[15] Of course, it is *a priori* unlikely that the classical language of the Bible would reflect the early Israelite monarchy. Rather, the Classical Hebrew language of the Bible indicates the emergence of the urban culture of the late Judean monarchy.[16] Just as the Amarna Letters and Ugaritic writings demonstrate a broader writing tradition in Syria-Palestine, so also there is little evidence to suggest that the early Israelite monarchy developed an independent writing tradition and scribal schools. This development would await Israel's transition to a more urban state in the eighth century (see Chapter 5).

To be sure, David and Solomon employed court and temple scribes. An early text from the Book of Samuel lists some of David's officials:

> Joab was commander of the whole army of Israel; Benaiah son of Jehoiada was commander of the Cherethites and the Pelethites; Adoram was in charge of forced labor; Jehoshaphat son of Ahilud was herald; Sheba was the scribe; and Zadok and Abiathar were priests. Ira the Jairite also served David as priest. (2 Sam 20:23–26)

In addition to military and temple functionaries, the list includes an official in charge of the conscripted labor force, a royal herald, and a scribe. A list of officials for King Solomon also includes a court scribe:

King Solomon was now king over all Israel. These were his officials: Azariah son of Zadok – the priest; Elihoreph and Ahijah sons of Shisha – scribes; Jehoshaphat son of Ahilud – herald; Benaiah son of Jehoiada – over the army; Zadok and Abiathar – priests; Azariah son of Nathan – in charge of the officials; Zabud son of Nathan the priest – companion of the king; Ahishar – in charge of the palace; and Adoniram son of Abda – in charge of the forced labor. (1Kgs 4:1–6)

Solomon's list is more elaborate than David's, suggesting that the administration had grown. There were now two court scribes in addition to the royal herald, the official in charge of the conscripted labor force, and the official overseeing the palace. Moreover, an official, Azariah, son of Nathan, was placed in charge of the officials over the twelve regional governors (cf. 1 Kgs 4:7–19). One indication of the antiquity of the list is the names on it. By this, we simply note that the theophoric element (i.e., the suffix or prefix indicating a deity that is added to the name) does not use the divine name of the God of Israel.[17] Pre-Yahwistic names in these lists include Adoram, Ahilud, Sheba, Abiathar, Ira, Shisha, and Ahishar. A name like Adoram means "may Hadad be exalted." The Yahwistic theophoric element is easily identified in the English endings (*-iah*) to names like Hezek*iah*, Isa*iah*, or Jerem*iah*. It can also be easily identified in beginnings (*Jeho-*) of names like *Jeho*shaphat. It is noticeably absent from such names as Abraham, Jacob, Moses, David, and Solomon. From research in personal names used in ancient Israel, the addition of the Yahwistic theophoric element develops slowly and predominates only from the ninth century B.C.E. onward. Thus, these lists of David's and Solomon's officials give every indication of being authentic and ancient lists from the early Israelite monarchy because they include many non-Yahwistic names. The general drift of scribal transmission tended to replace these non-Yahwistic names with Yahwistic names. So, for example, the name Shisha comes from an Egyptian word for scribe. In 2 Samuel 8:17, this name is "YHWHized" as Seraiah. The personal name Adoram, meaning "Hadad is exalted," in David's list of administrators becomes the more neutral Adoniram, "my lord is exalted," in Solomon's list. These changes are often subtle and probably also often unconscious scribal variations. Such shifts probably mask the entire extent of the Canaanite administrative infrastructure of the kingdoms of David and Solomon.

The exact role of one official, the "herald" from the Hebrew term *Mazkîr*, has been the subject of some discussion. Although it is sometimes translated as "recorder," suggesting a scribal function, the etymology of the term points instead to a royal herald.[18] The word is formed from the root *ZKR*, which relates to "remembrance, memory." This verb almost invariably refers to speaking, often with the sense of a proclamation or an official speaking, although sometimes with the weaker sense of mentioning; it never refers to writing.[19] In later post-exilic texts, there is a definite shift in the meaning of the term. Translations of the Biblical Hebrew term *Mazkîr* into Greek and Aramaic reflect an understanding of the function as a "recorder";[20] however, these translations demonstrate the substantially different social and political context of the Roman Empire, where writing had become more central to government and society. In fact, the semantic development of this word from "herald" to "recorder" corresponds to the development of other terminology dealing with writing (like the Hebrew word *qara'*, whose meaning shifts from "to call out" to "to read") and mirrors the process of textualization of Jewish culture.

Nevertheless, there were scribes in the employ of the early Israelite monarchs. The main task of these royal scribes would have been administrative record keeping. Writing would not have been a tool primarily used for either the preservation or the dissemination of culture. It is probably not a coincidence that we have little written inscriptional evidence from the tenth century in Israel. To be sure, inscriptions like the Gezer Calendar or the earlier Izbet Sartah Ostracon prove that scribes were active even in the formative stages of the Israelite state.[21] It is pure luck that we happened upon reasonably well-preserved monumental inscriptions from the ninth century in Transjordan (the Moabite Stone discussed earlier) and in Galilee (the Tel Dan inscription[22]). There are also two very fragmentary monumental inscriptions (one from Jerusalem and one from Samaria) that date to the ninth century B.C.E.[23] Whereas the discovery of monumental inscriptions is a matter of pure chance, the relative paucity of mundane writing from early Israel is telling of the limited role that writing played during the twelfth through ninth centuries B.C.E.

Let us look at an example from the limited inscriptional evidence of this early period. The most mundane type of administrative writing is seal impressions and ostraca. Seals would have been used to stamp jars and to seal documents (usually made from papyrus); the resulting seal impressions, found in great abundance, date from the eighth to sixth centuries B.C.E. in Israel. The most substantial texts of extra-biblical writing come from ostraca. The term "ostraca" is the plural form of a Greek word, *ostrakon*, meaning "shell, shard." It refers to inscriptions written on broken pottery shards. Most ostraca were written on the shards with ink, but sometimes they were inscribed in the wet clay or scratched on the hardened baked clay. The broken pot shards come in all shapes and sizes and contain texts of varying lengths. Ostraca were a practical and inexpensive writing material as compared to leather or papyrus and were used primarily for ordinary administrative and economics texts, including receipts, letters, and other ephemeral documents. Sometimes they were washed to remove the ink, covered with a yellow slip, and then used over again. The major collections of ostraca come from excavations in the ancient cities of Samaria, Arad, and Lachish. Ostraca have been found in relatively large numbers for the eighth through sixth centuries B.C.E. A few of these types of writing have been discovered dating to the twelfth through ninth centuries B.C.E.

At Tel Arad (which is located about 30 miles south of Jerusalem on the fringe of the desert), four ostraca were found that give evidence of early administrative activities of Judean scribes. These four very fragmentary ostraca were found in excavations and date to the tenth century B.C.E. Arad was a fort built in the late eleventh or early tenth century on the southern desert border as an administrative and military outpost. The fort is mentioned as having been destroyed in the military campaign of Pharaoh Shishak in 925 B.C.E., so there is little doubt that the fort had been built in the days of the first Hebrew monarchs. The most complete ostracon reads,

Son of B[...]M [...]
Son of H[...] *hekat* (barley) 10
Son of MN[...] 100 *hekat* (barley)
[... *hekat* (barley)] 2[0]

Although this inscription is exceedingly fragmentary, it is clearly some type of accounting text. The term *hekat* is an Egyptian term for measuring barley. The four Arad texts use hieratic numerals and signs borrowed from Egyptian accounting systems known from the tenth century B.C.E. Thus, not only were scribes doing government accounting at this remote outpost, but they had also borrowed a concept of numerals and accounting abbreviations from their contemporary

Egyptian scribes.[24] This Egyptian system of hieratic numerals continued to be used until the end of the Judean monarchy.

As surely as Abdi-Kheba (the fourteenth century B.C.E. mayor of the city of Jerusalem) or Mesha (the early ninth century B.C.E. ruler of the kingdom of Moab) had scribes, so also did the early kings of Judah and Israel. Such scribes would have done accounting, written letters, and overseen the writing on public monuments. Royal scribes apparently kept some kind of abbreviated annals where they recorded important events like the Egyptian campaign of Shishak against Jerusalem (e.g., 1 Kgs 14:25–30). There is evidence for these types of activities even among the most petty rulers and officials. However, shaped by its use in the affairs of the king, writing had a limited role in society. It is difficult to assume that royal or temple scribes would have engaged in the composition of large literary works.

It is often argued that David and Solomon commissioned great literary works. Since the nineteenth century, some scholars have suggested that one of the main sources of the Pentateuch, a tenth-century writer known as the Jahwist (reflecting the writer's preference for the divine name), composed the first great prose work on earth.[25] Others have pointed to parts of the Book of Samuel that might have been an apologia written for David.[26] Certainly, there are elements of the stories in Genesis and Exodus or of the tales in Judges or of the account of King David that seem to be historically accurate, and, as already noted, there were royal scribes who kept royal annals as well as administrative and economic texts. However, it is difficult to prove that extended prose narratives were being written down in the days of David and Solomon. The social and historical contexts suggest the opposite. Writing had a limited role in Israel during this early period. The literature of Israel was primarily oral. There is no reason to insist that the supposed "J" source of the Pentateuch had to be a document rather than an oral tradition. Nor is there any reason to insist that the stories of Samson and Delilah or of Deborah and Barak in the Book of Judges had to have been written down in the days of David and Solomon. At some point, of course, these stories did take on a written garb, but that time had not yet come. Writing did not play an important enough role in early Israelite society to warrant writing down these songs and stories, proverbs and parables. That time, however, would come in the eighth century.

5

Hezekiah and the Beginning of Biblical Literature

The Bible as we know it began to take shape in Jerusalem in the late eighth century B.C.E., in the days of Isaiah, the prophet, and Hezekiah, the king of Judah. Powerful social and political forces converged at that time resulting in the collection of earlier, mostly oral, traditions and the writing of new texts. In addition, Jerusalem emerged then as a powerful political center. The small, isolated town of Jerusalem mushroomed into a large metropolis. Writing became part of the urban bureaucracy as well as a political extension of growing royal power. These changes would be the catalyst for the collecting and composing of biblical literature. It was the dawn of the literature of the Bible.

What were the local catalysts for such a dramatic transformation of Judean society? Why did biblical literature begin to flourish in the late eighth century? The answers to these questions begin with the rise of the Assyrian Empire and the social, economic, and political challenges that it would present. In particular, the exile of the northern kingdom by Assyria and the subsequent urbanization of the rural south were the catalysts for literary activity that resulted in the composition of extended portions of the Hebrew Bible. The exile of northern Israel also gave rise to the prophetic works of Amos, Hosea, Micah, and Isaiah of Jerusalem, to priestly liturgies and to ritual texts, as well as to a pre-Deuteronomic historical work. The idealization of a golden age of David and Solomon also inspired the collection of wisdom, traditions, and poetry ascribed to these venerable kings. Consequently, to best understand this critical phase in the Bible's history, we must first try to understand the last decades of the eighth century, under the shadow of the rising Assyrian Empire.

The Assyrian Empire

The impact of the rise of the Assyrian Empire on Judah, on Syria-Palestine, and, indeed, even on the course of Western civilization is difficult to overstate. Assyria was the first in a succession of great empires. With ruthless efficiency the Assyrian monarch, Tiglath-Pileser III (r. 745–727 B.C.E.), unified Assyria and Babylon, conquered the kingdom of Urartu to the north (in Asia Minor), and expanded the empire west to the Mediterranean Sea. Later Assyrian kings would conquer all of Syria-Palestine and even briefly conquer Egypt. When the sun set on the Assyrian Empire at the end of the seventh century B.C.E., the empire, rather than disappearing, passed to the Babylonians and later to the Persians and then to Alexander the Great. Thus, Assyria built the first in a series of expanding world empires.

Assyria moved the Near East toward globalization: one polity, one economy, one language. As the Assyrian king Sargon (r. 722–705 B.C.E.) expressed the imperial ideology:

> Peoples of the four regions of the world, *of foreign tongue and divergent speech*, dwellers of mountain and lowland, all that were ruled by the light of the gods, the lord of all, I carried off at Ashur, my lord's command, by the might of my scepter. *I made them of one mouth* and settled them therein. Assyrians, fully competent to teach them how to fear god and the king, I dispatched as scribes and overseers. (Dûr-Sharrukîn cylinder)

Not only did the Assyrians carve out a true empire that eventually stretched from India to Egypt, they also implemented an imperial administration for governing their vast empire. Writing became an increasingly important tool in administrating the empire. No doubt the Assyrians chose to use Aramaic (rather than their native Akkadian) as they dispatched "scribes and overseers" to administer their conquered lands in the west because Aramaic – with its alphabetic writing system – was easier to implement in training these bureaucrats than the exceedingly complex syllabic cuneiform system.

The spread of writing accompanies the rise of the empire. Here, I do not mean simply the spread of a lingua franca among scribes but the skill of writing, which begins to spread to different social classes. Writing is increasingly used in daily administrative and economic activities throughout the Near East. In Phoenicia, for example, a marked increase in epigraphic remains parallels the rise in epigraphic remains in Israel. Alan Millard, a professor of Oriental studies at the

University of Liverpool, has noted that from the eighth century onward there is a noticeable increase in graffiti on pots and in tombs in Phoenicia. He surmises, "Their distribution in Phoenicia, elsewhere in the Levant, and further afield is evidence that reading and writing was not confined to palace and temple."[1] The spread of writing that begins in the eighth century is thus not an isolated Judean phenomenon. It is part of a larger trend in the ancient Near East that is associated with the spread of the Assyrian Empire, yet the spread of writing in Judah would have unique and social consequences.

The Assyrian Empire swallowed up smaller states as it marched westward. The Galilee region fell to Tiglath-Pileser III in 734 B.C.E. The northern kingdom of Israel was reduced to a rump state, a direct vassal of the Assyrian Empire. The tiny state of Judah also began paying tribute to Assyria. Israel rebelled against the empire in 722 B.C.E., and the Assyrian armies rolled in and wiped the rebels out. Refugees flooded south into Judah in the wake of the Assyrian onslaught. The north now came under direct Assyrian rule. Israel was exiled. Judah stood alone.

Urbanization

The rise of Assyria in the mid-eighth century devastated smaller states and transformed the landscape of the entire Near East. One result was urbanization. The ferocity of the Assyrian Empire pressured rural populations to settle in the cities where they could find relative security.[2] Cities concentrated the economic resources and technical skills necessary to build fortifications and thereby afforded protection from the invading armies. Village settlements could not take full advantage of a society's military power, which was most effectively deployed around cities. Judah, like the rest of the Near East, experienced a marked transition during the late eighth century toward a more urban society.[3]

Many examples of urban-rural conflict in biblical literature can be adduced, but a particularly pointed one can suffice here. In the ninth century, Queen Athaliah laid claim to the throne of Judah through intrigue and murder, according to the biblical narrative (cf. 2 Kgs 11). Her reign was brought to an end in a revolution orchestrated by "the people of the land" (Hebrew, *'am ha-aretz*). The biblical narrator sums up this coup d'état by noting, "So all the people of the land rejoiced, but the city was quiet after Athaliah had been killed with the sword at the king's house" (2 Kgs 11:20). The narrator juxtaposes "the people of the land" – a rural politic – with the city that had apparently supported Athaliah's rise to power.[4] In short, biblical authors certainly do seem to have been aware of the dichotomy between urban and rural and the profound impact that the emergence of urbanization had in Judah during the late monarchy.

The specific character of the urbanization of Judean society between the eighth and seventh centuries B.C.E. can be seen in the changes in Judah's material culture. Pottery is generally the most plentiful remnant of the material culture uncovered in archaeological excavations. Archaeologists use it as one guide to the life of a people. There is an almost surprising uniformity in the pottery of the late eighth century, especially when compared with the variety of influences to be seen in pottery from the late seventh century.[5] The uniformity of the earlier pottery indicates the isolation of Judah until the eighth century B.C.E. Judah's material culture reflects few outside influences and little foreign trade. In contrast, the material culture of the seventh century gives evidence of diverse cultural influences. This reflected the integration of Judah into the world economy promulgated by Assyria.

Archaeologists have unearthed other aspects of the material culture that depict similar trends. In architecture, the classic four-room Israelite house, for example, became smaller, in keeping with an increasingly urban and mobile population. Domestically, even the size of cooking pots shrank as the society evolved toword smaller, nuclear, families.[6] Implicit in these differences is the momentous transformation of Judean society, from an isolated, rural nation to an urbanized, cosmopolitan one. Especially in the days of Hezekiah, Judah experienced significant growth not only in population but also in the size of its cities. There was also a marked increase in the numbers of inscriptions and public monuments as well as in the availability of luxury goods – all signs of urbanization.[7]

Urbanization would be the catalyst necessary for more widespread literary activity. Although scribal activity did take place in the less fertile ground of the early monarchy (eleventh–ninth centuries B.C.E.) and during the Babylonian and Persian periods (sixth–fourth centuries B.C.E.), social conditions favored the flourishing of Hebrew literature in the eighth through seventh centuries B.C.E. Such changes in the social life of the Jewish people were especially noticeable in the city of Jerusalem.

The Urbanization of Jerusalem

We must assume that the political and religious capital, Jerusalem, was the center for the collection and composition of biblical literature. Indeed, the first moves to collect the literary traditions of Israel (and Judah) must have been sponsored by the institutions of the monarchy and the temple. So, it is to Jerusalem in particular that we must turn our attention in order to understand how the Bible came to be a book. Before the excavations in Jerusalem during the 1970s, there was considerable debate about the size of Jerusalem during the period of the Judean monarchy.[8] The debate has subsided since Nahman Avigad's discovery of an enormous city wall (dubbed the "broad wall"), measuring more than twenty feet wide, on the western hill of Jerusalem (see Figure 5.1). The wall dates to the late eighth century and is attributed to Hezekiah as part of the preparations that he made for an expected Assyrian onslaught. It is now clear that Jerusalem grew more than fourfold in the late eighth century B.C.E. and continued to expand until the last days of the Judean state.

Jerusalem's growth was a by-product of the rise of the Assyrian Empire. First of all, Assyria destroyed the northern kingdom of Israel resulting in the immigration of Israelites to Jerusalem and other cities in the south. A few years later, another influx of dispossessed refugees came into Jerusalem from the foothills of Judah following the campaign of Sennacherib against Judah in 701 B.C.E.[9] These two military events only intensified the predilection for urbanization that was manifested throughout the Assyrian Empire in response to political and economic realities. Thus, as we will see, these events can be placed within the larger context that shaped the city of Jerusalem and the writing of the Bible there.

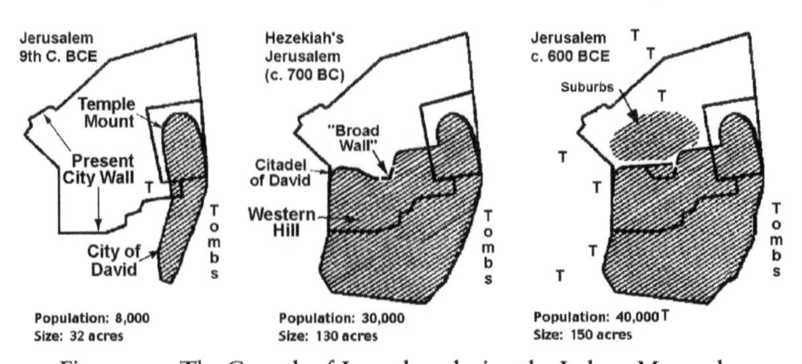

Figure 5.1. The Growth of Jerusalem during the Judean Monarchy

In 722 B.C.E., Hezekiah was faced with a flood of immigrants from the defeated northern kingdom. Rather than barricading his borders, Hezekiah tried to integrate these refugees into his realm, hoping thereby to restore Israel's idealized golden age, the kingdom of David and Solomon. Thus, the famous "messianic" prophecies of Isaiah of Jerusalem must have been understood by the citizens of Jerusalem as commentary and political policy. In Isaiah 9:1–7, for example, we read:

> But there will be no gloom for those who were in anguish. In the former time he brought into contempt the land of Zebulun and the land of Naphtali, but in the latter time he will make glorious the way of the sea, the land beyond the Jordan, Galilee of the nations. The people who walked in darkness have seen a great light; those who lived in a land of deep darkness – on them light has shined.
>
> ... For the yoke of their burden, and the bar across their shoulders, the rod of their oppressor, you have broken as on the day of Midian....
>
> For a child has been born for us, a son given to us; authority rests upon his shoulders; and he is named wonderful counselor, mighty God, everlasting father, prince of peace. His authority shall grow continually, and there shall be endless peace for the throne of David and his kingdom.

The Book of Isaiah itself places this prophecy between 730 and 715 B.C.E. – just a few years after the fall of Galilee to Tiglath-Pileser III and perhaps several years after the final defeat of the north. However, the prophecy offered hope to those "people who walked in darkness." That is, it extended the Davidic Promise to the northern kingdom. Israelites walked in darkness not only because of the gloom and despair ravished upon them by the "rod of their oppressor [the Assyrians]" but also because they had rejected the rightful king of the united north and south – the son of David. Who was this child that was born? Who was this son given to us? An earlier prophecy had already spoken of this Davidic son. In Isaiah 7:14, in the days of Ahaz, king of Judah (r. 735–715 B.C.E.), God gave a sign to the house of David: "Look, the young maiden is with child and shall bear a son, and shall name him Immanuel" (the Hebrew literally, "God is with us"). To Isaiah's audience, this child could be none other than Hezekiah! Nostalgically, the people of Jerusalem looked to Hezekiah, the son of David, to restore the golden age of peace and prosperity.

Hezekiah tried to recreate the Camelot of David and Solomon but his attempts ended in disaster. When the Assyrian king Sargon died in 705 B.C.E., Hezekiah led a (foolhardy) coalition against the Assyrian Empire. The new Assyrian monarch, Sennacherib (r. 705–681 B.C.E.), was on the throne for four years before he was able to address Hezekiah's rebellion in the remote western part of the empire. When the Assyrian finally did come down, in 701 B.C.E., the consequences were devastating. In his annals, Sennacherib recorded:

> As to Hezekiah, the Jew, he did not submit to my yoke, I laid siege to 46 of his strong cities, walled forts and to the countless small villages in their vicinity, and conquered them by means of well-stamped earth-ramps and battering-rams brought thus near to the walls combined with the attack by foot soldiers, using mines, breeches as well as sapper work. I drove out 200,150 people, young and old, male and female, horses, mules, donkeys, camels, big and small cattle beyond counting, and considered them booty. Himself I made a prisoner in Jerusalem, his royal residence, like a bird in a cage. I surrounded him with earthwork in order to molest those who were leaving his city's gate. His towns which I had plundered, I took away from his country and gave them over to Mitinti, king of Ashdod, Padi, king of Ekron, and Sillibel, king of Gaza. Thus I reduced his country, but I still increased the tribute and the katrû-presents due to me as his overlord which I imposed upon him beyond the former tribute, to be delivered annually.[10]

A second cascade of refugees followed Hezekiah's ill-advised attempt to assert his independence from Assyria. Sennacherib's invasion devastated the Judean foothills west of Jerusalem. According to archaeological calculations, there was an 85 percent decrease in the *number* of cities and towns in the foothills west of Jerusalem at the end of the eighth century as a result of Sennacherib's invasion. The population decreased by about 70 percent, suggesting that the depopulation affected the smaller agricultural towns and villages more than the cities.[11] Thus, Sennacherib's invasion resulted in both depopulation of rural areas and further urbanization.

The royal scribes of Hezekiah claimed a victory of sorts in the midst of the devastation: Hezekiah remained on the throne. God had saved him. The Assyrian army mysteriously withdrew. One biblical account attributed this reprieve to the angel of the Lord who slew the Assyrian army. The fifth-century Greek historian Herodotus apparently knew a legend about this deliverance of Jerusalem. He tells of how the Assyrian army was forced to withdraw because a legion of mice ate the bowstrings of the army while the soldiers were sleeping. The royal spin allowed Hezekiah to assert victory, but he could not fulfill his dream of a new golden age.

A government bureaucracy burgeoned along with the population of Jerusalem. Many public construction projects reflected the growing central government. These included fortifications (as in the famous "broad wall"), major water projects (like Hezekiah's Tunnel), and a

Figure 5.2. Royal Storage Jar and *Lemelek* Stamp (used with permission of David Ussishkin)

new government administrative center (known today as Ramat Rahel) about two miles south of Jerusalem. The government also instituted a new system of administration. Hezekiah created four administrative cities and a system of taxation and supply. The most visible archaeological remains of this administration are the royal storage jars and their seal impressions (see Figure 5.2).[12] The average royal storage jar could hold about 10.5 liters (or 2 baths – a biblical measurement). Hundreds of royal seal impressions have been found in excavations throughout Judah. They have even been found in excavations in northern Israel, reflecting Hezekiah's aspirations to incorporate the northern kingdom after it had fallen to the Assyrians. The seals were stamped on jar handles while the clay was still wet. The royal insignia, probably best understood as a flying sun disk, occupies the center of each seal. Above the insignia, the seal bears the Hebrew inscription *lemelek*, "belonging to the king," and the name of one of four cities – Hebron, Socoh, Ziph, or *MMŠT*. The last of these, the enigmatic *MMŠT*, probably referred to the new local government administrative center at Ramat Rahel, which was built in the late eighth century. In the seventh century, the royal *lmlk* stamps were replaced with rosette stamps.[13]

One of the more famous inscriptions from the late eighth century period is a monumental graffito discovered inside Hezekiah's Tunnel (sometimes called the "Siloam Tunnel"). The inscription celebrates the engineering feat of constructing a quarter-mile-long rock-hewn tunnel to direct Gihon Spring water under the city of David toward the western hill and into the reservoir called the Siloam Pool. Although this engineering project must have been sponsored by the Judean government, the inscription was evidently executed by tunnel workmen.[14] Two independent biblical texts – Isaiah 22:9–11 and 2 Kings 20:20 – allude to this project. The latter text is part of the source citation for the reign of King Hezekiah that reads, "The rest of the deeds of Hezekiah, all his power, how he made the pool and the conduit and brought water into the city, are they not written in the Book of the Annals of the Kings of Judah?" The complete text of the tunnel inscription is as follows:

> [...] Now this is the account of the breach. While [the masons were wielding] their pick-axes, each man towards his neighbors, and while there were still three cubits to be [tunneled through], a man's voice [was heard] calling to his neighbor because there was a fissure in the rock running from south [to nor]th. Now on the day the breach was made, the mason struck, one man towards his co-worker, pick against pick; and the water flowed from the spring to the pool, a distance of one thousand two hundred cubits. A hundred cubits was the height of the rock above the head of the masons.

Perhaps the spirit of celebration reflects the unlikely success of the tunnel. As described in the inscription and revealed in the archaeological investigation, the tunnel was dug from both ends at once. The meeting in the middle was an engineering feat that still has scholars amazed.[15] The inscription itself was written on a prepared panel, about .5 meters high and .66 meters wide, but the text occupies only the lower half of the panel. This curious fact has led to several theories. Clermont-Ganneau originally suggested that some sort of relief might have been intended for the panel's upper half.[16] Others have suggested that the arrival of the Assyrian troops interrupted the process of inscribing the panel leaving it incomplete. Such explanations assume that the inscription was carefully planned and is indeed unfinished. Taken as it is, however, the blank part of the panel might suggest poor planning and execution of the inscription. If this were the case, then we would take a different approach to the interpretation of the text itself. That the panel and text demonstrate rudimentary planning and execution is supported by the fact that the inscription does not mention either the king or the gods – a lapse unparalleled in royal building inscriptions. Moreover, the inscription was located 6 meters *inside* the tunnel from the outlet at the Siloam Pool. In other words, only those who worked on the tunnel and engraved the inscription would have known of the inscription's existence. At the same time, this inscription is not a simple graffito. Although not a royal inscription, the wall on which it appears was carefully prepared and its letters are elegantly carved into the hard limestone. Here, outside the royal palace and the temple, writing is being used by engineers, craftsmen, and laborers to memorialize their accomplishment. That this writing takes place away from the palace or the temple is most significant. It portends major shifts in the role of writing in Judean society.

The growth of Jerusalem also was reflected in urban sprawl. New farming villages cropped up as an agricultural hinterland for Jerusalem.[17] As already mentioned, a new royal administrative center at Ramat Rahel was established two miles south of Jerusalem as a secondary capital to that city and to help alleviate its overcrowding.[18] The city of Gibeon (5 miles north of Jerusalem) emerged as a major industrial center for agricultural products and wine.[19] Jerusalem's growing sprawl corresponded to (1) the demographic shift from the western foothills to the hill country, (2) the need for agricultural production to supply Jerusalem and Hezekiah's administration, and (3) the replacement of the devastated agricultural infrastructure of the Judean foothills.[20]

In sum, the late eighth century witnessed a process of rapid centralization and urbanization. Judah shifted from a large *rural* state to a smaller but more centralized and urbanized state. The centrality of Jerusalem was the de facto result of the exponential increase in the city's population and the depopulation of the foothills to its west. Jerusalem, which held about 6 percent of Judah's total population in the mid-eighth century B.C.E., would grow to about 30 percent in scarcely two generations.[21] These processes were coordinated with a political ideology that envisioned the restoration of a golden age to Judah and the reunification of the northern kingdom. This golden age would be textualized by the collection, composition, and editing of literature by the royal scribes of Hezekiah.

Hezekiah's Creation of a Golden Age

The pivotal figure in the early formation of biblical literature was King Hezekiah. His father, Ahaz (r. 735–715 B.C.E.), had survived the incursions by local enemies, the kings of Samaria and Damascus, by becoming a loyal surrogate of the Assyrian Empire. Hezekiah presided over the exponential growth of Jerusalem and put into place a strong central government to oversee the urbanization of Jerusalem and the organization of its military. A burgeoning government bureaucracy is evident in the sudden explosion of epigraphic remains, including royal and government seals. This government bureaucracy oversaw a new system of taxation, the revenues of which provided funds for vigorous building projects throughout Judah. All this led to Hezekiah's bold, if foolhardy, attempt to break free from his Assyrian overlord and create an independent kingdom of Judah. Although Hezekiah's dream of an expansive and independent kingdom was devastated by the Assyrians, the legacy of his vision lived on in biblical literature.

A central part of Hezekiah's political agenda seems to have been to recreate the golden age of Israel, namely, the age of David and Solomon. Even though archaeology has suggested that the Davidic-Solomonic "Empire" was a rather modest affair, the first kings of Israel had managed to create a unified kingdom from the diverse tribes and clans that characterized the second millennium.[22] The brevity of the Davidic-Solomonic kingdom probably contributed to its later idealization. Just as it took only a few years to immortalize the assassinated American president John F. Kennedy, the division of the kingdom of Israel into north and south probably led shortly thereafter to the idealization of David and Solomon. To be fair, this yearning for the golden age was likely not started by Hezekiah. Nostalgia for the past and for roots is part of the fabric of the human condition. Hezekiah, however, gave this nostalgia a political and literary form. He and his royal scribes codified the golden age of David and Solomon through literature.

Among the important accoutrements of a king was his scribe and the royal library. Even royal pretenders like Abdi-Kheba, the fourteenth-century mayor of Jerusalem, or Mesha, the ninth-century chief of Moab, had scribes. Not surprisingly, the flourishing of writing and of the scribal arts was not an exclusively Judean phenomenon. The contemporary neo-Assyrian kings were also creating archives and libraries.[23] The number of archives and libraries in the Near East rose sharply beginning in the eighth century and reached its apex in the seventh century. Almost every major city of the neo-Assyrian empire has given evidence of libraries and archives. Even Nabu, the Babylonian god of scribes, was adopted as an Assyrian god in the seventh century B.C.E.[24] The most famous of these libraries was the great library in

Nineveh. It was established in the days of the Assyrian monarch Sennacherib (Hezekiah's contemporary and nemesis), who made Nineveh the Assyrian capital. The building of libraries was particularly a passion of the Assyrian king Ashurbanipal (r. 668–627 B.C.E.). In one letter, he writes.

> ... every last tablet in their establishments and all the tablets that are in Ezida [the name of the scribe god Nabû's shrine in the city of Borsippa]. Gather together the entirety of ... (a long list of text types) and send them to me. ... If you see any tablet which I have not mentioned and it is appropriate for my palace ... send it to me!"

A similar phenomenon seems to have occurred in Egypt. For example, Pharaoh Shabaqa (r. 716–702 B.C.E.) recovers "books of the Temple."[25] This Egyptian contemporary of Hezekiah encouraged the re-establishment of the older, second millennium Memphite theology of the creator gods. Thus, Hezekiah's collecting and editing of texts had parallels among both the Assyrians and the Egyptians.

The Men of Hezekiah

Within biblical literature, the increased activity of Hezekiah's scribes is attested to by a seemingly offhand remark in Proverbs 25:1. There we read that "these too are proverbs of Solomon, which the men [i.e., scribes] of King Hezekiah of Judah copied." We may wonder whether this text correctly attributes these proverbs to Solomon. After all, most scholars agree that these texts were committed to writing much later than the days of Solomon. For the writer of Proverbs, however, the assertion that these proverbs were derived originally from the great King Solomon was an issue of primary importance. The point of the observation, in the very first verse of the chapter, that Hezekiah's men copied down some of the proverbs of Solomon is that the proverbs are Solomonic. That Hezekiah's men committed them to writing seems merely an aside. For our purposes, this offhand remark holds one key to understanding when the writing of the Bible began.

The statement that Hezekiah's men collected these proverbs certainly is not laden with the same ideological implications associated with the proverbs' attribution to Solomon. Their prestige was derived from their Solomonic attribution, not from Hezekiah's collecting them. Hezekiah lived nearly two centuries after Solomon's death. Indeed, Hezekiah plays no role in literary themes of the Book of Proverbs; although the venerable King Solomon has an implied role as the wise royal father and teacher (see Prov 1:1, 8; 2:1; 3:1, 21; 4:1–11; etc.). Hezekiah, in contrast, is an afterthought. It is just this type of *disinterested* statement that can be the key to historical research. We have no a priori reason to discount the remark that Hezekiah's scribes wrote down the proverbs.

Though these proverbs are traditionally attributed to Solomon, they found their written form in the days of Hezekiah. How much more of the Bible can we ascribe to the days of Hezekiah? The literary activities of Hezekiah's scribes, which tried to recover the literature of a golden age (and by doing so helped create the golden age), undoubtedly went further than merely collecting Solomon's proverbs. Indeed, we are fortunate to have this offhand remark, but it is only a portent alerting us to an important stage in the writing down of the Bible. The Song of Songs is attributed by implication to the acclaimed King Solomon as well. The Book of Kings tells tales of Solomon's wisdom (e.g., 1 Kgs 3:10). And although the dating of the Book of Ecclesiastes is a matter of some debate,[26] it also implies that it comes from the lips of King Solomon. The collection and attribution of this literature to a golden age coincide with other activities during Hezekiah's reign.

The time has come to briefly assess how this sociopolitical context might have shaped the composition of biblical texts. The literary activity of Hezekiah's reign was a projection of royal power and ideology, particularly as it related to the fall of the north and the survival of the house of David in Judah. Hezekiah's literary projects apparently included historical work, the collection of Mosaic and priestly traditions, and the writing down of the prophetic traditions, including Isaiah of Jerusalem, Amos, and Hosea.

Writing also became a vehicle for a critique of urban and royal power, as in the Book of Micah. The prophet Micah came from a small Judean village called Moresheth in the foothills west of Jerusalem. Not surprisingly, Micah is a supporter of the people and a critic of the urban elites. He decries those "who build Zion with crime, Jerusalem with iniquity!" (Micah 3:10). He condemns the social injustices that the people of the countryside saw as arising from urbanization. Micah gives a voice to the "people of the land," who still strongly support the Davidic monarchy. They will later rise up after the assassination of King Amon (640 B.C.E.) to put the young boy Josiah on the throne. Josiah's family also came from a small village (Bozkath), which was quite close to Micah's village. Micah himself supports the ideal of the shepherd king from the village of Bethlehem: "And you, O Bethlehem of Ephrath, least among the clans of Judah, From you one shall come forth To rule Israel for Me – One whose origin is from of old, From ancient times... He shall stand and shepherd by the might of YHWH" (Mic 5:2–3). Earlier, in the ninth century B.C.E., in the days of Queen Athaliah (r. 845–837 B.C.E.), the "people of the land" had rushed to support the re-establishment of the Davidic line when it was threatened by "the city." The people helped end Queen Athaliah's threat to the line, and the narrator notes that "the people of the land rejoiced, but the city was quiet" (2 Kgs 11:20).

A Historical Work

The dating of the Book of Kings has been a subject of intense scholarly debate over the past century. Recent attempts to date the Book of Kings take as their departure point the seminal work of Martin Noth on the so-called Deuteronomistic History.[27] Noth hypothesized that a single exilic historian composed the narrative from Deuteronomy to 2 Kings using earlier written sources. This narrative has been called the "Deuteronomistic History" to describe its dependence on the religious ideology of the Book Deuteronomy, which shaped its interpretation of Israel's history. In the wake of Noth's analysis, scholars have followed four basic lines.[28] Some adhere to the theory of a single exilic edition, written after the Babylonian exile in 586 B.C.E. and before the return from exile that began with the decree of the Persian king Cyrus in 539 B.C.E. Other scholars isolate an exilic history with two further redactional hands (prophetic and nomistic), although they differ on whether to characterize this process as editions or scribal additions, and, of course, they argue over exactly which verses to assign to which source. A third school follows the dual-redaction theory associated with Frank Moore Cross, who argued that the original edition of the Deuteronomistic History was written in the pre-exilic period to support the reforms of Josiah (r. 640–609 B.C.E.) and was later updated by an exilic editor (ca. 550 B.C.E.) who was concerned to explain the Babylonian exile. The fourth approach can be attributed to scholars like Helga Weippert, Andre Lemaire, and Baruch Halpern; these scholars identify two pre-exilic editions written under the royal sponsorship of the Judean kings Hezekiah and Josiah followed by an exilic redaction.[29] The idea that there was a pre-exilic Hezekian historical composition appears to be gaining momentum and is the one that interests me most because it attributes the first stage in the writing to the period of King Hezekiah.

Most of the arguments for the Hezekian redaction are based on the formal structure of the historical narrative. These include accession/succession formulas, judgment formulas, the David theme, and the attitude toward the various cultic shrines (or "high places"). These characteristics are consistent in the historical narrative up until the account of King Hezekiah, and then they abruptly change. Because of the formulaic nature of these arguments, they are quite objective and difficult to dismiss. What makes the evidence especially compelling is the historical situation, which I have discussed earlier, that prompted the Hezekian composition. It is difficult not to see that the first "conclusion" of the Book of Kings is with the fall of the northern kingdom of Israel and its capital Samaria (2 Kgs 17). Although this text has been reworked, it marks the end of the northern kingdom. Later authors adopted an almost entirely negative attitude toward the north, but remnants remain that point to a positive, almost nostalgic view of the northern kingdom. These include the Elijah-Elisha narratives (1 Kgs 17–2 Kgs 9), which are mixed in their attitude toward the northern kingdom, varying from unabashedly negative (e.g., 1 Kgs 18, 21) to rather supportive (e.g., 1 Kgs 22; 2 Kgs 6–7; 13:14–21). Additionally, the northern kings are generally praised for their military strength whereas the southern kings rarely are (cf. 1 Kgs. 16:5, 27; 22:45; 2 Kgs. 10:34; 13:8, 12; 14:28). This sometimes positive and nostalgic view of the north can easily be attributed to Hezekiah's scribes, who were working in the historical context of the incorporation of numerous northern refugees and in the ideological context of a new golden era.

How were these earlier sources transmitted? The Elijah-Elisha tales seem likely to have been a collection of oral prophetic stories. However, details about military campaigns, building projects, and the lengths of reigns were likely drawn from royal archives. To account for certain historical details in the biblical text, one must assume that the author was using royal archives from the north. For example, we have two ninth-century historical inscriptions from foreign kings: the Tel Dan Stele (ca. 825 B.C.E.; see Figure 3.3) and the Moabite Stone (ca. 840 B.C.E.). Although these inscriptions tell the story of Israel's foreign relations from a much different historical perspective, they relate *the same events* as the biblical narrative preserved in the Book of Kings relates. We may argue over whose account is more accurate, but there is no arguing that the foreign inscriptions and the biblical narrative are talking about the same people and historical events. In order for the biblical narrative even to be in conversation with ancient inscriptions, the Bible had to have had sources dating back to the earliest days of the monarchy. Given the nature of the correspondences, one major source for the biblical narrative must have been royal archives (from both Israel and Judah).

The use of a standard formula to praise the northern kings seems to stem from a Hezekian composition. There seems to have been a preexilic account written during the period of Hezekiah that probably reflected upon the fall of Samaria and the survival of Jerusalem. This historical work would also serve as a source for later authors/redactors. It may be that this composition has been so completely rewritten by Josianic and exilic authors that it is no longer entirely recoverable. For present purposes, however, it is enough to point out the existence of this Hezekian historical work and the literary activity that it implies.

The Book of Kings preserves two similar assessments that must have originated within the Hezekian period of the division of the Davidic-Solomonic kingdom. The first summarizes the narrative of the division in which Rehoboam foolishly follows his young counselors: "So Israel has been in rebellion against the house of David until this day" (1 Kgs 12:19). The expression "until this day" implies something about the continuing relevance of the divided kingdom at the time the author wrote this historical narrative.[30] It is also noteworthy that there is no prophetic justification in this summary statement (in contrast to 1 Kgs 11:9–13). The transgression implied by the verb "to transgress, rebel" (Hebrew, *pasha'*) is against the *house of David.* The highly edited narrative about the fall of Samaria in 2 Kings 17 also preserves a second fragment with this perspective. In 2 Kgs 17:20–21a we read,

> YHWH rejected all the seed of Israel; he punished them and gave them into the hand of plunderers until he had banished them from his presence *because Israel had torn away from the house of David.* Then they made Jeroboam, son of Nebat, king.

Here the exile of the northern kingdom results from Israel's breaking away from Judah. Although the Hebrew syntax is clear, translations sometimes miss this point, translating the action as passive. For example, the New Revised Standard Version has this as a clause dependent on its following statement, "When *he* had torn *Israel* from the house of David, they made Jeroboam son of Nebat king." But in the Hebrew text, the noun "Israel" is the subject, not the object.[31] It was Israel that tore away from Judah. It was Israel that had left the house of David. It was Israel that was now being punished for rending asunder the kingdom of David. The royal scribes in Jerusalem interpreted the fall of Samaria as a vindication of the Davidic dynasty, especially in the years immediately following the exile of the north. This perspective was fundamentally political, though there were obvious religious aspects as well.

These two passages (1 Kgs 12:19 and 2 Kgs 17:20) echo the perspective of a longer Hezekian historical work that vindicated the Davidic line as the legitimate heirs to a united kingdom. Both parts of the kingdom were important to this historical narrative because Hezekiah intended to reunite the divided kingdom. The early division of the kingdom, after Saul, was critical because David reunited the kingdom, and Hezekiah followed in his steps. Hezekiah re-established the Davidic kingdom. Here I agree with Ian Provan and others who have argued that Hezekiah is presented in the Book of Kings as the "new David."[32] Hezekiah is the only king described as follows: "And he did right in the eyes of YHWH *according to all that David*, his father, had done" (2 Kgs 18:3). The import of this singular comparison between Hezekiah and David appears to be primarily political, not religious. That is, Hezekiah began to rebuild the kingdom of David in the wake of Samaria's destruction just as the prophet Isaiah suggests (Isa 7:17; 9:1–6; 11:1–2). But this was more than a literary viewpoint, it reflected a political policy conditioned by the situation in the late eighth century.[33] Hezekiah's scribes sought to create a new golden age, but this golden age was a political vision.

The military vision of Hezekiah appears in the Book of Joshua. The narrative story of Joshua gives a utopian interpretation of the conquest of the entire land of Israel, both north and south. The inclusion of the north, and in fact, the emphasis on the north, is itself quite telling. In Joshua, the north is central to the historical narrative. The hero of the story is a northerner – Joshua, son of Nun, from the northern tribe of Ephraim. It is also noteworthy that the famous covenant ceremony in Joshua 24, at which Joshua gathers all the tribes together to pledge their fidelity to YHWH, takes places in Shechem, the first capital of the northern kingdom. That the Book of Joshua makes a point of recording this northern conquest indicates that the context of the book's composition was a time just like the days of Hezekiah, a time when Judah dreams of reclaiming the lost northern tribes of Israel and their territories.

The Judean and later Jewish view of the northern kingdom changes dramatically in subsequent generations. By the time of the Josianic Reforms, a century had passed since the north's exile. The world had been tramsformed. Assyria's power was quickly fading. Josianic themes were focused on religious rather than political issues. The north had become the scapegoat for Judah's religious infidelity to YHWH. Whereas Hezekiah had tried to *integrate* the north, Josiah only *castigates*. Positing substantive Hezekian collecting and composing of historical narratives answers a lingering question about the historical books of the Bible, that is, the Books of Joshua, Judges, Samuel, and Kings. How relevant was an extinct northern kingdom a century later? Two centuries later? In the Josianic period, the religious reforms are a violent reaction against the north. The Book of Chronicles informs us about the role of the north in later Persian period literature – it is omitted. The north either becomes the archenemy of the Jewish people or is forgotten. Only in the second century B.C.E., with the rise of the Jewish Hasmonean kingdom, do the Hasmoneans try to reclaim the north. But this attempt ultimately fails. The Jewish people revile the Samaritans, as the northerners are known in the New Testament. The Hezekian historical account, in contrast, preserves the stories from the kingdom of Israel as an integral part of the Judean (or, "Jewish") people. (Note that the Hebrew word *yehudi* is the etymological origin for both "Judean" and "Jewish.") The fate of the northern kingdom weighs most heavily on the life and literature of Judah in the years immediately following Samaria's destruction and exile, that is, during the reign of Hezekiah. This historical work is revised by later authors, but traces of the first Hezekian historical account remain and form the framework for the writing of the biblical books of Joshua, Judges, Samuel, and Kings.

Pentateuchal Literature

Scholars have dated Pentateuchal literature everywhere from the tenth century B.C.E. to the third century B.C.E. The reason for this is quite simple: there are few objective internal criteria by which to date the first five books of the Bible. One thing is clear. Writing and written texts do not play a significant role in Genesis, Exodus, Leviticus, or Numbers. As we shall see in Chapter 7, only in Deuteronomy will writing come to the fore. This observation about the role of writing in the Pentateuch is all the more striking if we compare biblical literature with the retelling of the Pentateuch stories in the Hellenistic Book of Jubilees. In Jubilees, writing becomes a main topic from the very first verse! This observation has significant implications. It suggests that the first four books of the Pentateuch were written when writing was not self-consciously important. Deuteronomy's emphasis on writing remedies this gap: Deuteronomy recognizes the need to address the writing down of the law and the stories of early Israel.

Before bypassing the dating of the Pentateuch, a few comments are in order. For two reasons, it is difficult to assume that the Pentateuch was essentially *composed* at a very late date (i.e., the Persian period, or fifth–fourth centuries B.C.E.). The first reason is simply that the language is Classical Hebrew, not late Hebrew. Although scholars have made this observation before,[34] it has not sufficiently taken root. Once we describe the social and political contexts of the Persian period as they have come to light in the last few decades of archaeological investigation (see Chapter 9), these linguistic observations should prove even more compelling. In a similar vein, recent linguistic investigations have noted distinct characteristics of an oral register in the language of patriarchal and origins narratives in the Pentateuch. In contrast, later Hebrew demonstrates a striking shift toward a more scribal chancellery style.[35] Of course, this shift from an oral style to a chancellery style would have been gradual. But the linguistic changes are perceptible. They provide objective criteria for dating most of the Pentateuchal literature in the pre-exilic period.

The second reason that the Pentateuch is unlikely to have been very late is the prominent role given in it to the northern tribes of Israel. The northern kingdom had disappeared in the eighth century B.C.E. and by the end of the seventh century B.C.E. was the pariah of the religious and political orthodoxy. This attitude did not change even when the Hasmonean kings tried to conquer the northern territories in the second century B.C.E. Examples of the prominence of the northern tribes abound in the Pentateuch. The stories of Genesis, for example, are the stories of the twelve tribes of Israel. Although Genesis privileges the tribe of Judah as the tribe from which the kings of Israel should emerge, the book is a story about all of the twelve brothers. Let me put an edge on this observation. Genesis tells a story of Israel's origins that is consistent with Hezekiah's political vision. The Book of Exodus also tells a story of all the tribes of Israel that will become the people of Israel. The story begins in Exodus 1:1–4 by naming the tribes:

> These are the names of the sons of Israel who came to Egypt with Jacob, each with his household: Reuben, Simeon, Levi, and Judah, Issachar, Zebulun, and Benjamin, Dan and Naphtali, Gad and Asher.

These twelve tribes are essentially a pre-exilic concept. The concept does not appear, for example, in the Persian books of Ezra and Nehemiah. Those were books written in the fifth or fourth century B.C.E. when the northern tribes were not only lost – as a result of the Assyrian exile – but also irrelevant. But in the days of Hezekiah, the northern tribes were still on the minds of the people in Judah. Indeed, many of them were refugees living in Jerusalem. Hezekiah dreamed of reincorporating their territory. The Book of Numbers begins with a census of *all Israel*, and so on. Yet, there are ways that a negative pall is cast upon the northern tribes. So, for example, the sin of the Golden Calf (Exod 32–33) reflects directly and poorly on the northern kingdom that repeats the sin (1 Kgs 12). Moreover, the story of the spies is critical of the northerners politically because the tribes do not trust God to give them the "promised land."

The Book of Deuteronomy, in particular, seems to incorporate aspects of the northern tradition. For example, Mount Sinai in Deuteronomy is called Mount Horeb. Thus, Mount Sinai, the very place where God is supposed to have come down and delivered the Ten Commandments to Moses, has a special name. When we search for where and how Mount Sinai is called Mount Horeb, we immediately notice that the name is also given to the mountain of God when the northern prophet Elijah goes to meet God. Scholars therefore have proposed that "Horeb" was the name of the mountain in northern traditions, whereas "Sinai" was the name of the mountain in southern traditions. Several scholars have proposed that the Book of Deuteronomy had its origins in the religious and political reforms of King Hezekiah.[36] These traditions do not originate in one place at one time. They reflect a long history of oral transmission before being collected. The critical moment for the Book of Deuteronomy will come in the Josianic Reforms (as I will discuss in the next two chapters).

Throughout this book, I have been thinking of three questions: who could write? when could they write? and why did they write? The stories in the Pentateuch tell of the origins of the people of

Israel – both north and south. These stories certainly served the purpose of the ideology of the royal court. The collection of these traditions also fits in with the general desire of kings to build a library as an accoutrement of royalty. The temple too had its scribes, but temple writing was still an internal affair. There was no temple library per se to be built. We must presume that the priests would have wished to retain for themselves the numinous and ritual aspects of writing. In addition, cogent arguments have been made suggesting that the priests were also busy composing some of the early priestly compositions. Most notably, several scholars have suggested that the Hezekian Temple priests composed a "Holiness Code," the core of which made up Leviticus 17–26.[37] As Israel Knohl, professor of biblical studies at Hebrew University, demonstrates in *The Sanctuary of Silence: The Priestly Torah and the Holiness School*, there were two distinct priestly schools in ancient Israel – a Holiness school and a Priestly school. The "Holiness" school engaged three basic issues in late-monarchic Judah: the incursion of northern idolatrous practices, the economic and social polarization of urban elites and rural farmers, and the detachment of morality from cult. Although these issues were certainly current in the late eighth century, they continued to be of concern until the end of the monarchy. Knohl contends that this "Holiness" school continues into the exilic and post-exilic periods and is eventually responsible for the final editing of the Pentateuch. Separation and dating of the layers of priestly literature are however, difficult. Any precise schema is unlikely to be compelling. So, I will retreat to generalities.

The Eighth-Century "Writing" Prophets

Ironically, the so-called early writing prophets – that is, Isaiah, Micah, Amos, and Hosea – were not writers at all. By calling them "writing" prophets, they are contrasted with figures like Nathan or Elijah, who do not have independent books. But in the books ascribed to them, the early writing prophets are rarely portrayed as having *written* anything. God commands them to speak, not to write. There are no books in their books! Writing is a marginal activity for the eighth-century prophets. So, who wrote their books? The prophetic books of Isaiah, Micah, Amos, and Hosea contain superscriptions that place them in the second half of the eighth century B.C.E. These superscriptions point to the editorial activity of collecting prophetic oracles.

Although the prophetic superscriptions are widely regarded as later additions to the prophetic literature, they do seem to accurately place the prophets historically. Indeed, it is probably no accident that none of the superscriptions to these prophetic books mentions any king after Hezekiah. As David Noel Freedman, professor of biblical studies at the University of California, San Diego, has suggested, "the collection of the books of the four prophets was assembled during the reign of Hezekiah, to celebrate and interpret the extraordinary sequence of events associated with the Assyrian invasion of Judah and investment of Jerusalem, along with the departure of the Assyrian army and the deliverance of the city."[38] Ultimately, all of these books support the Davidic monarchy, and Hezekiah's scribes would have had good reason to collect them.

As we would expect, writing was not an important part of the popular culture in the eighth century. Rather, writing was still closely tied to the palace. It was an activity of royal scribes. The temple would also have had scribes, but there is no reason to assume that temple scribes were suddenly interested in writing for public consumption. The state, however, was always interested in writing as a projection of royal power and authority to the general public. The role of writing would become much more central in the later prophets, like Jeremiah, Ezekiel, or Zechariah, reflecting the rising importance of writing in Israelite culture. The act of writing is rarely mentioned in the eighth-century prophets, and, certainly, reading and writing are not part of the prophetic call. There is scant mention of writing, texts, or scribes in the other prophetic works of Hosea, Amos, and Micah, and this is hardly coincidence.

The few references to "writing" (Hebrew, *katav*) in Isaiah 1–39 reflect early attitudes about writing. Writing is magical; or, writing is a tool of power and royal administration. In Isaiah 4:3, for example, the mechanics of writing in the Book of Life become a metaphor for the survivors of war "who are inscribed for life in Jerusalem." Isaiah 10 chastises government officials who use written documents to subvert justice and rob the poor, the widows, and the orphans. Writing in the Book of Isaiah can also be for public monuments (Isa 30:8). There is no hint that the prophecies of Isaiah himself needed to be written down. The most famous incident of writing in Isaiah is when God commands Isaiah to write out the strange name of the prophet's son, "Maher-shalal-hash-baz." The writing out of the name has ritual significance and magical effects. The written name seals the divinely ordained fate of the rival kingdoms of Samaria and Damascus that were threatening Jerusalem (Isa 8). This task did require that Isaiah, as a court prophet in the employ of the king, have at least a rudimentary knowledge of how to write. Overall, however, writing does not play a significant role in Isaiah's prophetic message. The prophet is a speaker and an actor, not a reader and writer.

Why do these prophetic texts come to be written down? In the late eighth century B.C.E., writing seems to still be restricted to the government and probably also the temple. Not surprisingly, these prophetic works all develop themes that justify the Davidic monarchy. In the late eighth century, the Davidic monarchy was threatened by a Syro-Ephraimite alliance that tried to replace the Davidic king. The monarchy also responded to the fall of Samaria, justifying itself in the wake of Israelite refugees. Naturally, the fall of Samaria was understood as vindicating David as God's only chosen and legitimate king. The interests of the Judean royal court can be seen in all the eighth-century prophets.

Hezekiah's contemporary, the prophet Isaiah, makes it clear that the restoration of the kingdom of David and Solomon was a central ideological goal in the late eighth century. Isaiah recounts, for example, the attack by a coalition from Aram and Israel, led by King Rezin and King Pekah, on Hezekiah's father, Ahaz. The "house of David," Isaiah notes, was threatened by this coalition, and "the heart of his people shook as the trees of the forest shake before the wind" (Isa 7:2). These pretenders threatened the *house of David*, an expression that recalls the eternal Promise to David and his sons in the oracle given by the prophet Nathan: "Your house and your kingdom shall be made sure forever before me" (2 Sam 7:16).[39] This concept, *the house of David*, became the focal point for a restored kingdom under Hezekiah precisely because it harkened back to the golden age of the united monarchy.

Isaiah's prophecies highlight that the disastrous end to Israel resulted from the division of the kingdom. Isaiah's famous prophecy of the child, born of a young maiden, to be called Immanuel (Isa 7:14) culminates with a vision for the end of the northern kingdom. Isaiah sees the destruction of Samaria as an appropriate consequence of the division of the north from the south after the death of Solomon: "YHWH will bring on you and on your people and on your father's house such days as have not come *since the day that Ephraim departed from Judah* – the king of Assyria" (Isa 7:17). The attempt by an Aramean and Israelite coalition to undermine the house of David recalls the first time that the north broke away or rebelled from the sons of David (2 Kgs 17:21; 1 Kgs 12:19). This time the punishment will be final; the Assyrians will destroy Samaria, exile much of the population, and resettle the territory.

The destruction of Samaria by Assyria becomes the opportunity for Hezekiah to rebuild the kingdom of David. Isaiah predicts the final destruction of Samaria (Isa 8:4) but then turns to a more hopeful message of the restored kingdom: "But there will be no gloom for those who were in anguish. In the former time he brought into contempt the land of Zebulun and the land of Naphtali, but in the latter time he will make glorious the way of the sea, the land beyond the Jordan, Galilee of the nations" (Isa 9:1 [Heb 8:23]). The prophet suggests that the gloom will disappear now in these latter days of Hezekiah. According to this interpretation of events, God despised the division of the kingdom and the rebellion against the rightly appointed Davidic kings. Isaiah envisions, however, the days when the son of David's "authority would grow continually and there will be peace without limit upon David's throne and kingdom" (Isa 9:7 [Heb 9:6]). Isaiah speaks of a remnant of the north returning (Isa 10:20–22). The shoot of David (Isa 11:1) will gather this remnant and return them (Isa 11:11). The prophet Hosea is more to the point: "Afterward the Israelites shall return and seek YHWH their God, and David their king; they shall come in awe to YHWH and to his goodness in the latter days" (Hos 3:5). The vision of these days was to reestablish the kingdom of David and Solomon, to revisit the golden age of Israel. It was this vision that would lead to Hezekiah's foolhardy and disastrous attempt to rebel against Assyria. It was undoubtedly also this vision that drove Hezekiah's scribes to collect and copy "the proverbs of Solomon" and other traditions that would be attributed to the golden age of Israel.

There is ample reason to believe the Book of Amos also received its final form in the Hezekian period. According to the biblical Book of Amos, its prophetic namesake prophesied in the northern kingdom during the mid-eighth century B.C.E. It might be somewhat surprising then that the book was preserved by scribes in the southern kingdom. The composition of the Book of Amos has been a matter of considerable debate. The most recent commentaries by David Noel Freedman and Shalom Paul argue that the book essentially dates to the days of the prophet (i.e., in the mid-eighth century B.C.E.) and had little subsequent editing.[40] To arrive at this conclusion, however, one must dance around rather unequivocal references pointing to the late eighth century. Certainly the clearest of these is the reference in Amos 6:2 to the disappearance of Philistine Gath, which was known to have been destroyed by Sargon's invasion in 712 B.C.E.[41] Undoubtedly, Amos was preserved in the south because (1) the prophet was understood to have correctly foreseen the exile of Samaria, and (2) this was interpreted as further legitimizing the Davidic dynasty. The verse in Amos 9:11, "On that day I will raise up the booth of David that is fallen, and repair its breaches, and raise up its ruins, and rebuild it as in the days of old," has been widely analyzed as a late addition to the book.[42] The ruins here are of the "booth of David" and not the city of Jerusalem; in other words, the ruins relate to the division of the "house of David," not to the destruction of Judah. Scholars have often thought that this language points to the destruction of Jerusalem, but actually the language is a metaphor for the division of the kingdom – "the booth of David." Given the socio-historical background described in this chapter, the royal court of Hezekiah is actually a quite favorable setting for the final editing of the Book of Amos. It was Hezekiah who was presented as restoring the house of David and "rebuilding it as in the days of old."

The superscription to the Book of Hosea also describes the prophet's activity as continuing into the Hezekian period. This northern prophet too was preserved in the south because he was characterized as a critic of the legitimacy of northern kingship. Many commentators have pointed out the largely negative portrait of monarchy in the Book of Hosea. Perhaps the most oft-quoted example is Hosea 8:4, "They made kings, but not through me; they set up princes, but without my knowledge." This statement is in accord with the critique that emerged from the Hezekian historical work, which blamed the division of the kingdom on the north's rejection of David's sons (cf. 2 Kgs 17:21; 1 Kgs 12:19). Ultimately, however, the meaning of this critique within the book as a whole must be read through the lens of Hosea 3:4–5:

> For the Israelites shall live many days without king or prince, without sacrifice or pillar, without ephod or teraphim. Afterward the Israelites shall return and seek YHWH their God, and David their king; they shall come in awe to YHWH and to his goodness in the latter days.

A temporal movement here is marked by "afterward": for a period, the northern kingdom did not have a king, but was then drawn into the fold of the Davidic dynasty. This must refer to the period following the fall of Samaria. The argument that David is "*their* king" implies that the former northern kingdom and its kings were illegitimate. The idea that the Israelites would be incorporated *again* into the kingdom fits when we realize that Hezekiah had to integrate thousands of northern refugees after the destruction of Samaria. Northern prophetic texts would have had to be compiled in Hezekiah's royal court – that is, if they were to be preserved at all. Naturally, they were preserved only if they served the interests of the royal library.

The Book of Hosea actually prophesies the miraculous deliverance of Jerusalem: "But I will have pity on the house of Judah, and I will save them by YHWH their God; I will not save them by bow, or by sword, or by war, or by horses, or by horsemen" (Hos 1:7).[43] This verse seems to be part of an editorial framework given to the prophecies of Hosea when they were written down and preserved in Jerusalem after the fall of Samaria in the eighth century B.C.E. In contrast, the late seventh century was characterized by a fierce polemic against the northern king Jeroboam's religious practices and hardly made an appropriate context for the integration of northern prophetic traditions. By the post-exilic period, the northern kingdom was a distant memory and was even ignored by the author of the Book of Chronicles. If there was an integration of northern literary traditions in Jerusalem, it makes more sense to place the process in the immediate aftermath of the fall of Samaria, with its concomitant influx of refugees to the south, than to place it a century later amid religious reforms aimed at eradicating northern cultural influences.

In sum, the exile of the northern kingdom and the urbanization of the rural south– particularly Jerusalem – set into motion the collecting and editing that resulted in the writing of extended portions of the Hebrew Bible. This began in the court of King Hezekiah in the late eighth century B.C.E. with the collecting and editing of prophetic works such as Amos, Hosea, Micah, and Isaiah of Jerusalem. In addition, Hezekiah's scribes gathered wisdom traditions that they attributed to old King Solomon. The royal scribes also produced a pre-Deuteronomic historical work that ended with the fall of the northern kingdom. Current events, the exile of the north, and the survival of the sons of David were the backdrop for this literature. The temple priests probably also collected and edited some priestly traditions like the Holiness Code (Lev 17–26). Traditional stories of early Israel, such as those found in Genesis and Exodus, were likely collected as well. The story of the Exodus already served as powerful symbol of exile, redemption, and royal power. Each of these writings ultimately pointed to the sons of David.

Urbanization, centralization of political power, and social change in Jerusalem naturally attracted social, political, and religious interpreters. Where these interpretations could be put down on parchment and papyrus was the royal court. The political situation invited, even necessitated, the collection of oral traditions and the writing of literature. The process began in earnest in the late eighth century under King Hezekiah, but it would spread and reach its apex in the latter days of the Judean monarchy. In the time of Hezekiah and Isaiah, writing was still closely associated with the king and the state. This, however, was about to change.

6

Josiah and the Text Revolution

With the emergence of literacy and the flourishing of literature a textual revolution arose in the days of King Josiah. This was one of the most profound cultural revolutions in human history: the assertion of the orthodoxy of texts. As writing spread throughout Judean society, literacy broke out of the confines of the closed scribal schools, the royal court, and the lofty temples. Beginning in the burgeoning government bureaucracy, the use of writing spread throughout society. Basic literacy became commonplace, so much so that the illiterate could be socially stigmatized. The spread of literacy enabled a central feature of the religious revolution of Josiah: the religious authority of the written text. This was the great and enduring legacy of the Josianic Reforms in the development of Western civilization.

It is ironic that the spread of literacy does not necessarily translate into a higher level of literature.[1] Quite the contrary, its democratization increasingly takes writing out of the hands of professionals and places it into the hands of the general public. Writing in the days of Hezekiah had largely been done by court or temple scribes. Writing in the days of Josiah spread throughout the government bureaucracy and the economy. This spread of literacy meant that writing was more broad, but also more shallow. The quantity of writing tended to diminish the quality of writing. The important innovation that emerged with the Josianic Reforms was not the spread of literacy, but the concept of textual authority.

Much of the scholarly debate has centered around the consequences of literacy. In 1982 the linguist Walter Ong published his seminal work in linguistic anthropology, *Orality and Literacy: The Technologizing of the Word*. The book helped touch off a controversy among classical scholars. Eric Havelock, a professor of classics at Yale University, built on the work of Ong as well as on that of the Cambridge University social anthropologist Jack Goody, arguing that a literate revolution first began in Greece in the fifth century B.C.E. Havelock begins his book *The Muse Learns to Write* by acknowledging that Ong had shaped his own thinking about the oral-literate problem in ancient Greece.[2] Although Havelock pushed the topic of orality and literacy to the front of scholarly discussion, his work has been criticized on several fronts.[3] Havelock argues for a special theory of Greek literacy, suggesting that it was only the Greeks' development of vowel letters that made widespread literacy possible. This is just plain wrong.[4] The importance of vowel letters for reading greatly depends on the morphological structure of a language. Certainly, the Semitic alphabet was difficult to use for Greek texts before the development of vowels; however, this had to do with the differences between the Greek and Semitic languages. Vowel letters never fully develop for ancient Hebrew simply because they are not as critical to reading that language as they are for Greek.[5] A simplified system of vowel letters that is useful for Hebrew reading did develop, and is used for Modern Hebrew.

The introduction and spread of vowel letters in Hebrew can be associated with the explosion of writing in the late Judean monarchy. A simplified system of vowel letters began to be used in Judah in the seventh century B.C.E., probably influenced by the spread of writing outside of scribal schools. It is the literati – even today – who doggedly insist on "proper" spelling and grammar. Do not split the infinitive, for example, is a rule that most "literate" people today do not even know. Some academics, however, are simply aghast when someone writes "to boldly go" instead of the grammatically correct "to go boldly." In Phoenicia during the seventh century B.C.E., for example, writing continued to be confined to scribal schools and not surprisingly spelling continued to be very conservative. In Judah, by contrast, spelling practices became quite inconsistent in the Hebrew ostraca, reflecting the lack of scribal training.

Widespread literacy, even if quite basic, began in Judah in the seventh century B.C.E. But, what I mean when I say *literacy* needs to be addressed. Technological, social, economic, and cultural factors that developed over the last centuries have fundamentally changed what it means to be "literate." The invention of the alphabet was the seed of literacy, and it has often been suggested that the alphabet democratized writing. But the alphabet was invented about 2000 B.C.E., and literacy did not spread until centuries later. It is true enough that the invention of the alphabet made it easier to learn to read and write, but literacy could not grow from the invention of an alphabet alone. It needed to be fertilized by changes in the social fabric of ancient societies. Writing had long been the property of either the state or the temple, which guarded the secrets of writing in closed scribal schools. The alphabet could break this monopoly, given the right circumstances. But it took the growth of centralized political power in Jerusalem, the development of an extensive bureaucracy, a shift toward an urban society, and the globalization of the economy to plow the fields for the spread of literacy. Finally, literacy needed to be watered by political revolution. Writing had been confined to the scribal classes and closely held within the palace and the temple. The Josianic revolution tried to return to the older, decentralized social structure of Judean society. It was this political revolution that also allowed knowledge of writing to spread outside the scribes and cultural elites. The written word would be a tool for the Josianic political, social, and religious revolution. In order to better understand the nature of this textual revolution, we need to step back and look at the broader social context.

The Social Context of Literacy

Writing flourishes in certain social, cultural, and political conditions. The ideal conditions reflect factors such as demographics (i.e., urban vs. rural), politics (centralized government vs. decentralized tribal leadership), economics (prosperity vs. poverty), and technological innovation (including the invention of the alphabet, the development of papyrus and parchment, the invention of the codex, and, most famously, the invention of the printing press). The spread of literacy is grounded in both social and technological changes.

Urbanization

Urbanization followed in the wake of Assyrian campaigns in the Near East. Villages were overrun. People fled to cities. The Assyrians encouraged economies of scale to maximize production and export from the periphery to the center. One of the best examples of the Assyrian policy was the city of Ekron. After destroying its regional neighbor, the city of Gath, the Assyrians established Ekron as a center for olive oil production. The city grew exponentially, and it had an enormous industrial area that was devoted to the production of olive oil for export to Assyria.[6] Ekron is an excellent example of the craft specialization that accompanied urbanization and made writing a practical tool. It could be used in record keeping, writing receipts, making lists. Just as writing developed because it was practical for everyday commerce and administration, so also did literacy begin because it was useful. Urbanization and the development of complex economies spurred on by globalization under the Assyrian Empire made writing a practical tool.

As previously noted, urbanization was particularly evident in Jerusalem. Two catalysts for Jerusalem's growth were the immigration of Israelites who came to Judah from the north after the fall of Samaria in 721 B.C.E. and the influx of refugees from the Assyrian king Sennacherib's invasion in 701 B.C.E. The first group was perhaps the more transformative. Hezekiah had tried to integrate the northern refugees politically into his kingdom. As was often the case in the ancient world, religion followed politics. According to biblical tradition, the Judean king Manasseh (r. 687–642 B.C.E.) accommodated the religious practices of the northern king Ahab. Indeed, it should hardly be surprising that the northern émigrés left their mark on religious practice in Jerusalem (2 Kgs 21:3; cf. Mic 3:9–10).[7] As it happens, the northern kingdom was always much more prosperous, populated, and cosmopolitan than Judah. Judah was isolated in the southern hills, whereas its northern neighbor had a more fertile ecosystem and easy access to ports and international trade routes.

The Judean royal family actually had ties to the north through marriage. But Judah always played second fiddle to Israel, its richer, more urbane neighbor. Once Israel was gone, however, refugees flooded into the south and into Jerusalem. Not everyone was happy with this invasion from the north. The rural prophet Micah, a contemporary of Isaiah and Hezekiah, criticized the social changes that these northern immigrants brought to Jerusalem (Mic 3:9–10):

> Hear this, you rulers of the house of Jacob and chiefs of the house of Israel, who abhor justice and pervert all equity, who build Zion with blood and Jerusalem with wrong!

King Hezekiah, however, seems to have been intent on incorporating the north. Perhaps most telling, Hezekiah gave his son the name Manasseh, well known as the name also of a leading tribe of the northern kingdom. The king also arranged a marriage between his son and the daughter of a family from Jotbah in Galilee. These actions would have found favor among northern refugees in his capital.[8] Hezekiah no doubt saw the destruction of the northern kingdom as both a confirmation of the legitimacy of the sons of David and an opportunity to restore the glorious kingdom of the past. A story in 2 Chronicles, which recounts that "Hezekiah sent word to all Israel and Judah, and wrote letters also to Ephraim and Manasseh, that they should come to the house of YHWH at Jerusalem, to keep the Passover to YHWH the God of Israel" (2 Chr 30:1), corresponds to the political situation.

Who were the refugees from the north? How did they impact the formation of biblical literature? These new immigrants were not the north's farmers or pastoralists, who would have stayed on their ancestral lands. A disproportionate number of the refugees would have been the social and cultural elites: nobles, government officials, scribes, craftsmen, temple priests. In other words, a significant number of the immigrants who fled south into Judah and Jerusalem would have been literate. One is reminded of a modern example: the refugees who poured into the modern state of Israel after the breakup of the Soviet Union. This huge flood of immigrants was largely composed of cultural elites, but there was no room immediately for all of their skills. As a result, concert pianists worked as street cleaners. In a similar way, ancient Jerusalem must have received a very large number of skilled and literate refugees. Many of these people, however, could be put to work in the burgeoning government bureaucracy. The demographics of literacy added a catalyst to the development of literature at the end of the eighth century B.C.E.

As I discussed in the last chapter, the second phase of Jerusalem's urbanization followed Sennacherib's invasion in 701 B.C.E. Sennacherib's invasion devastated the foothills west of Jerusalem. According to the calculations of the archaeologist Israel Finkelstein, "about 85 percent of the settlements of the Shephelah in the eighth century had not been reoccupied in the last phase of the Iron II. The total built-up area decreased by about 70 percent."[9] The devastation of the Judean foothills along with the growth of Jerusalem resulted in a corresponding *increase* in the number of smaller settlements around Jerusalem that were established in the late eighth or seventh century B.C.E. New agricultural villages, hamlets, and farmsteads formed an agricultural and industrial hinterland for Jerusalem. As noted earlier, a new royal administrative center two miles south of Jerusalem (known today as Ramat Rahel) served as a secondary capital and administrative center alleviating overcrowding in Jerusalem. This further growth may be accounted for as the aftermath of Sennacherib's campaign wherein he claims to have "laid siege to 46 of [Hezekiah's] strong cities, walled forts and to the countless small villages in their vicinity." Jerusalem's growing suburbs corresponded to (1) the demographic shift from the western foothills to the central hill country, (2) the need for agricultural production to supply Jerusalem and Hezekiah's administration, and (3) the need to replace the devastated agricultural infrastructure of the foothills.

Centralization

Urbanization, or demographic centralization, also facilitated political and religious centralization. Obviously, changes in demographics aided the centralization of political power in Jerusalem. They also led to a centralization of religious authority. This was expressed by the destruction of all cultic places outside of Jerusalem, an act that had political, economic, and religious implications. The temple and the palace are closely connected in the economies of the ancient world.[10] Although this religious centralization is usually associated with King Josiah in the late seventh century B.C.E., scholars have long recognized that it first began under Hezekiah in the eighth century B.C.E. (cf. 2 Kgs 18:4, 22).[11] Since the temple was a centerpiece of the economy and essentially under the control of the palace in ancient Judah, any religious centralization was likely an extension of political centralization.[12]

Centralization of state control tended to provoke harsh reactions from the countryside. Ancient Judah was a decentralized society with an agrarian and pastoral economy. The informal political structures of the rural Judean state were the tribal elders, "the house of the father," or "the people of the land." These groups were marginalized as power shifted to the urban center in Jerusalem. Along these lines, we should probably understand the negative portrait of Manasseh in the Book of Kings as resulting from the societal dynamics of centralization and urbanization. At the same time, the revolution that followed the assassination of King Amon and placed the eight-year-old Josiah on the throne was surely tied to the social tensions generated by urbanization and centralization. Although the changes in the demographics of the Judean state favored centralization, the reaction by the older traditional agrarian and pastoral elements of

Judean society against political centralization was ever present. This is evident in the Book of Deuteronomy's concern for social justice; it is also evident in the Book of Jeremiah's idealization of the wilderness (e.g., Jer 2:2–3). Thus, the movement toward political and religious centralization was neither simple nor linear.

The growth of a centralized state required the employment of a great many bureaucrats. The government took advantage of the simplicity of the alphabet for keeping records and receipts, sending military and government communiqués, and overseeing the distribution of resources. For example, most of the eighty-eight Hebrew ostraca excavated at the administrative fort at Arad (about 50 miles south of Jerusalem on the desert fringe) concern the administration of the late Judean monarchy.[13] One letter orders, "Send fifty men from Arad and from Qinah; and send them to Ramat-negeb under Malkiyahu, son of Qerbur." Another letter states, "And now, give to the Greeks [mercenaries?] two *bath*-measures of wine for four days, three hundred loaves of bread, and a full *homer*-measure of wine. Send them out tomorrow; do not wait. If there is any vinegar left, give it to them." Writing is used by government for rather mundane, everyday administration. The Jerusalem Temple's apparently close association with the government is suggested by another recently published ostracon: "According to that which <J>osiah, the king, commanded, to give through [Ze]kariyahu *Tarshish*-silver for the house of YHWH – 3 shekels."[14] Here the Temple is receiving some sort of tax required by the palace. In addition to this receipt, there are a variety of Hebrew seals and seal impressions from individuals holding various offices in the Judean administration, including "the one over the house," "servant of the king," "son of the king," "the one over the forced labor," "the scribe," "the steward," "servant of YHWH," and "the priest." There is also one woman mentioned, with the title "daughter of the king," which may have been a simple lineal reference but likely belonged to a woman with some administrative position.[15] A practical level of literacy, particularly the ability to read the name in a seal and perhaps some basic administrative documents, is suggested by this evidence. If this is the case, then writing is no longer something that can be deciphered only by highly trained scribes. Writing begins to lose its exclusivity as well as its mystery.

The rise of texts fits with the process of individualization and the breakdown of community values. Both the prophets Jeremiah and Ezekiel recall the traditional proverb, "parents have eaten sour grapes and the children's teeth are set on edge" (Jer 31:29; Ezek 18:2). The proverb reflects the kinship relationships of a traditional society, but the prophetic literature raises some question about whether these traditional values were still valid. Oral tradition was the commonly held tradition of a community. The stories and wisdom of the community were held socially by the group. The transmission of tradition depended on the groups. The assertion of the individual, however, undermined the community. The advantage of textual orthodoxy for political revolution is that textual orthodoxy does not rely on tradition.

Written texts had the power to emancipate the individual from the authority of the community-held tradition. In the case of the Protestant Reformation, the cry *sola scriptura* ("scripture alone") was a cry of freedom against the supposed tyranny of the community (or, the Roman Church). By another interpretation, however, the written text – Scripture – in the Protestant Reformation was a pretext authorizing social, political and religious revolution.[16] As we shall see, texts not only could emancipate religion, they also could restrict access to it to the social and religious elites who were literate and able to interpret texts. Texts and literacy had the power to both liberate and oppress.

Evidence for Writing in Judah

Hundreds of Hebrew inscriptions of a variety of types testify to the widespread use of writing during the late Judean monarchy. Already, there is a marked increase in epigraphic remains in the late eighth century. This epigraphic explosion continues until the invasions and exiles by the Babylonians in the early sixth century B.C.E. This spread of writing was a critical moment in the formation of biblical literature.[17]

The evidence for writing in the late Judean monarchy is so vast that we cannot rehearse it all here. To quote archaeologist Ephraim Stern's survey of ancient inscriptions, "Taking into consideration the size of the Judean kingdom during this period, this large body is truly astonishing."[18] The first thing to impress the observer is the volume and variety of the epigraphic remains. These include seals and seal impressions, ostraca, display inscriptions, and graffiti. With the exception of graffiti, epigraphic remains are mostly confined to administrative, economic, or bureaucratic texts. Normally a survey of this vast corpus of inscriptions would focus on large, impressive inscriptions or religiously and historically important inscriptions. For the present purposes, however, I want to take a different route. The rise of literacy is reflected as much in the mundane as in the monumental.

The most commonplace yet powerful evidence of writing is the mass of seals and seal impressions dating to the seventh century B.C.E. A recently published collection includes about seven hundred Hebrew seals, most of which date to the seventh century B.C.E.[19] This is only a fraction of the personal and private seals used during the late Judean monarchy. They point to a great quantity of papyrus and parchment documents that did not survive the vicissitudes of climate and military conflict. Only one papyrus letter has been discovered that pre-dates the Babylonian conquest of Jerusalem in 586 B.C.E. This is an extremely fragmentary letter (papMur 17), dating to the seventh century B.C.E., which was discovered in the arid region near the shores of the Dead Sea. The larger mass of papyrus documents has perished, but the seals and seal impressions suggest the large quantity of written documents dating to the late monarchy that have been lost (e.g., see Figure 6.1).

Seals were used in a variety of economic and administrative activities in ancient Israel. In the previous chapter, I cited an example of the royal seal impressions (see Figure 5.2). Royal seal impressions bear the insignia of the king along with the inscription "belonging to the king" (*lemelek*) and the name of one of four cities.[20] One illustrative archive was excavated in Jerusalem in the City of David in the summer of 1982.[21] This collection included forty-five bullae (or seal impressions) in a private residence that the archaeologists have hence dubbed "the House of the Bullae." One of the most interesting aspects of this archive is that it demonstrates that many of the seals were crudely made. In other words, they reflect the activity of both private citizens and skilled government artisans. A few of the seal

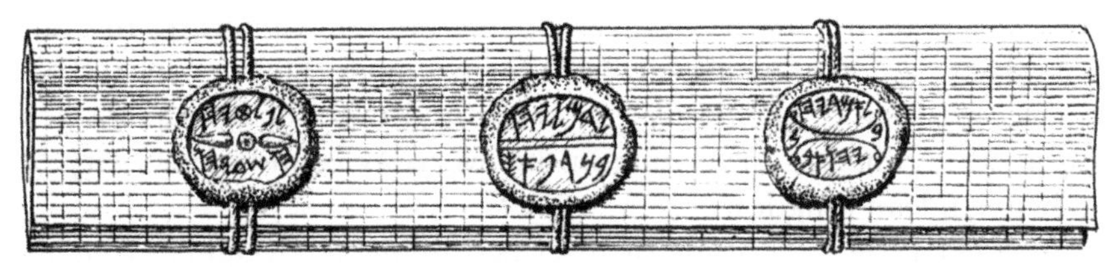

Figure 6.1. A Conjectured Reconstruction of a Sealed Deed with Seal Impressions (after Avigad)

impressions, like one of the government scribe Gemaryahu, son of Shaphan (whom we know from the Bible), are elegantly made. Many others, however, display irregular and imperfect forms of the letters of the alphabets. Yet, all these bullae come from the one archive, which was burned in 586 B.C.E. in the Babylonian destruction of Jerusalem.

The large number of seals and seal impressions that have been discovered reflect the entire scope of Judean society, including the lower classes. Nahman Avigad, who published a collection of seal impressions excavated in a residential section of Jerusalem, points to "a number of carelessly executed bullae and clumsy forms of many of the inscriptions."[22] He suggests that these seals were executed by their owners. One has the impression that seal ownership became something of a status symbol in these times. It is also noteworthy that Judah represents the first evidence for the widespread use of aniconic seals, that is, seals without pictures. In the ancient Near East, seals generally used graphic images to tell something about the owner. Alan Millard notes the contrast with contemporary Phoenician seals: "almost all published Phoenician seals bear a design of some sort, whether a simple divine emblem or an elaborate scene, and so that by itself could be sufficient to express identity. On those seals the letters of an owner's name are strictly superfluous."[23] This fact is especially important in a largely non-literate society. The widespread use of aniconic seals, in contrast, presumes that the seals could be readily identified by the writing. This may be rather mundane literacy, but it also implies that writing itself has become a common part of the culture. The widespread use of seals is also evidence for an increasingly complex economy that prompted the rise of literacy. The use of seals is representative of the spread of writing in Judean society.

The pervasive use of seals and weights minimally points to signature, or craft, literacy, that is, to the ability to read and write one's own name, to read and write receipts, and perhaps to read short letters. This beginning level of literacy is supported by a recently published ostracon that contains a list of seventeen different signatures of individuals apparently signing a receipt for payment (Figure 6.2).[24] This ostracon is one of the better preserved and more elaborate ostraca representing the use of writing in the everyday economic activity of the late Judean kingdom.

Another growing corpus of inscribed items are weights. Weights have abbreviations for the different words of measurement as well as hieratic numerals (borrowed from Egyptian).[25] Some of the terms

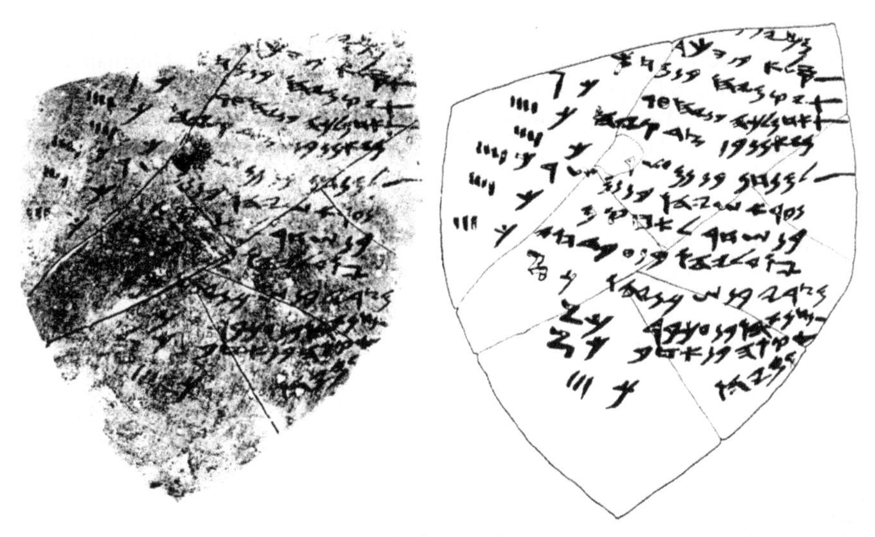

Figure 6.2. A Receipt for Payment of Silver with Seventeen Signatures (photograph and drawing by R. Deutsch and M. Heltzer)

inscribed on weights, like the word *shekel*, continued to be used until the Roman period and are even used today. Other terms, like *pîm*, which refers to "2/3 of a shekel," are known only from the Hebrew inscriptions of the Iron Age or from the Hebrew Bible. Such inscribed weights testify to the increasing administrative use of writing in the late monarchy. They are further evidence of the connection between the growth of writing and developing economic activity.

The Letter of a Literate Soldier

One important ostracon discovered at Lachish (the second major city of Judah; it was located in the foothills southwest of Jerusalem) provides rather remarkable testimony to the spread of literacy in the seventh century B.C.E. Lachish Letter 3, the so-called Letter of a Literate Soldier, captures a debate between a junior and a senior officer on the topic of the ability to read.[26] The ostracon is written on both sides, and the text reads as follows:

Your servant Hoshayahu sent to inform my lord Yaush: May YHWH cause my lord to hear a report of peace and a report of good things. And now, please explain to your servant the meaning of the letter which you sent to your servant yesterday evening because the heart of your servant has been sick since your sending to your servant and because my lord said, "you do not know (how) to read a letter." As YHWH lives, never has any man had to read a letter to me. And also every letter that comes to me, surely I read it and, moreover, I can repeat it completely! And concerning your servant, it was reported saying, "The commander of the army, Konyahu ben-Elnathan, came down to enter into Egypt. And he sent to take Hodavyahu ben-Ahiyahu and his men from this place." And as for the letter of Tobyahu, servant of the king, which came to Shallum ben-Yada through the prophet, saying, "Beware!" your servant sent it to my lord.

Almost the entire issue of the letter is simply the junior officer's assertion of his competence to read. His commanding officer, Yaush, had obviously questioned it. Hoshayahu, the junior officer, is offended by the suggestion that he cannot read! Even when the letter turns from the issue of Hoshayahu's literacy, it seems to be just reporting the contents of previous communiqués. In other words, the purpose of the last few lines is to demonstrate that the junior officer had accurately read the earlier letters! In sum, the whole letter addresses the issue of literacy in a non-scribal class of society. We may infer from the passion of the junior officer's protestations that illiteracy carried a social stigma, which would be a first.

The tone of the letter is most instructive because it indicates that literacy was the *expected* norm by both the senior and the junior officer. It is sometimes asserted – incorrectly – that this letter is part of a corpus of Lachish Letters that represent "Official Hebrew."[27] This assumes that the military commander had a professional scribe and, consequently, that the Lachish Letters would reflect the Official Hebrew from a trained scribe. Yet, these assertions fly in the face of the text itself. After all, Lachish Letter 3 is mostly devoted to protestations that the junior officer needed no professional scribe. The content of the letter undermines assertions that it is from the pen of a trained scribe. In a scholarly article, I have argued that the linguistic idiosyncrasies of the letter suggest that it was penned by a junior military officer with rudimentary linguistic skills.[28] These linguistic problems include spelling errors, grammatical errors, and the use of nonstandard formulas in the letter. We might even say then that the junior officer should have taken his superior's advice and gotten a scribe. The junior officer could read, but only on an elementary level. Given the importance of clear and accurate writing in military communiqués, it made sense for the senior commander to request that the junior officer get a scribe. What is most remarkable is that he had to ask at all, and then that the junior officer was so offended at his request!

Despite the debate over the level of the junior officer's literacy, the letter still represents movement along the continuum between orality and literacy. The letter is powerful evidence pointing to seminal changes in the social fabric of society during the late Judean monarchy – even if the level of this soldier's literacy was basic and he could have used a scribe to help him.

Mesad Hashavyahu Ostracon

Another ostracon, known as the Mesad Hashavyahu Letter, also speaks to the spread of writing and literacy in the late Judean monarchy.[29] The ostracon was found in a guardroom of the small military fortress, Mesad Hashavyahu, which apparently also served as an agricultural administrative center at the time. The letter comes from an agricultural worker who is complaining that his garment was unjustly confiscated:

> May the official, my lord, hear the plea of his servant. Your servant was working at the harvest. Your servant was in Ḥaṣar Asam. Your servant did his reaping, finished, and stored it a few days ago before the Sabbath. When your [se]rvant had finished reaping and had stored it a few days ago, Hoshayahu, son of Shobay came and took your servant's garment. When I had finished my reaping at that time, a few days ago, he took your servant's garment. All my companions will testify for me, all who were reaping with me in the heat of the sun; my brothers will testify for me. Truly, I am innocent from any gu[ilt]. [Please return] my garment. If the official does not consider it an obligation to retur[n your] ser[vant's garment, then please hav]e pi[ty] upon him [and ret]urn your [se]rvant's [garment]. You must not remain silent [when your servant is without his garment.]

In this rather redundant letter, a worker entreats the governor to intervene and see that the garment is returned to him. This letter is especially noteworthy because it recalls the biblical law of a garment taken in pledge. Exodus 22:26–27, for example, enjoins a creditor (also see Deut 24:10–15; Amos 2:8):

> If you take your neighbor's cloak in pawn, you shall restore it before the sun goes down; for it may be your neighbor's only clothing to use as cover; in what else shall that person sleep? And if your neighbor cries out to me, I will listen, for I am compassionate.

The issue of a garment taken in pledge was apparently a well-known legal issue. The worker need not have had any direct knowledge of the written legislation in order to file his complaint. It is usually assumed that this worker had a scribe write out the complaint for him. If so, it would have to have been dictated and written down with only minor editing; this is the only way to account for the redundant style of the letter. Of course, the assumption that a scribe was involved is just that – an assumption, which is predicated on the implausibility of an agricultural worker being able to write. This may or may not be well founded. The real question is, however, why did the complaint need to be written at all given the small size of this remote outpost? Does writing come to command such an important role in the Judean government bureaucracy that even the complaint of a poor worker at a remote and tiny agricultural outpost had to be written down?

Graffiti

Other telling evidence for literacy is graffiti. Whereas the Letter of a Literate Soldier addresses the ability to read, graffiti points to the ability to write among non-scribal classes.

The most famous corpus of graffiti was discovered in the burial caves at Khirbet el-Qôm. The inscriptions are notable for their lack of religious orthodoxy. One graffito, for example, asks for a blessing from "YHWH and his Asherah."[30] The workman may have known how to write, but he was apparently not well versed in monotheism! Another and less well-known graffito from Khirbet el-Qôm is a recently published inscription scrawled by the tomb cutter, who asks for a blessing upon himself. Graffiti are not uncommon in the ancient world, but what is of interest here is the social class of the person who inscribes the graffiti. Ancient graffiti can usually be attributed to scribes or bureaucrats doodling away under assorted circumstances. In the case of the Khirbet el-Qôm graffiti, the author identifies himself as the tomb cutter.

Another group of graffiti was discovered in the tombs at Khirbet Beit-Lei, about five miles east of Lachish. A number of the inscriptions and pictures carved on the walls of these tombs date to the end of the Judean monarchy.[31] The graffiti are badly preserved but clear enough to be read, and they give a lively description of a catastrophic situation. The graffiti probably describes either the invasion of Sennacherib (701 B.C.E.) or, perhaps, the first campaign of the Babylonians (597 B.C.E).

Ketef Hinnom Silver Amulets

A tomb within a tomb complex located on the western shoulder of the Hinnom valley, on the old road that would have led from Jerusalem

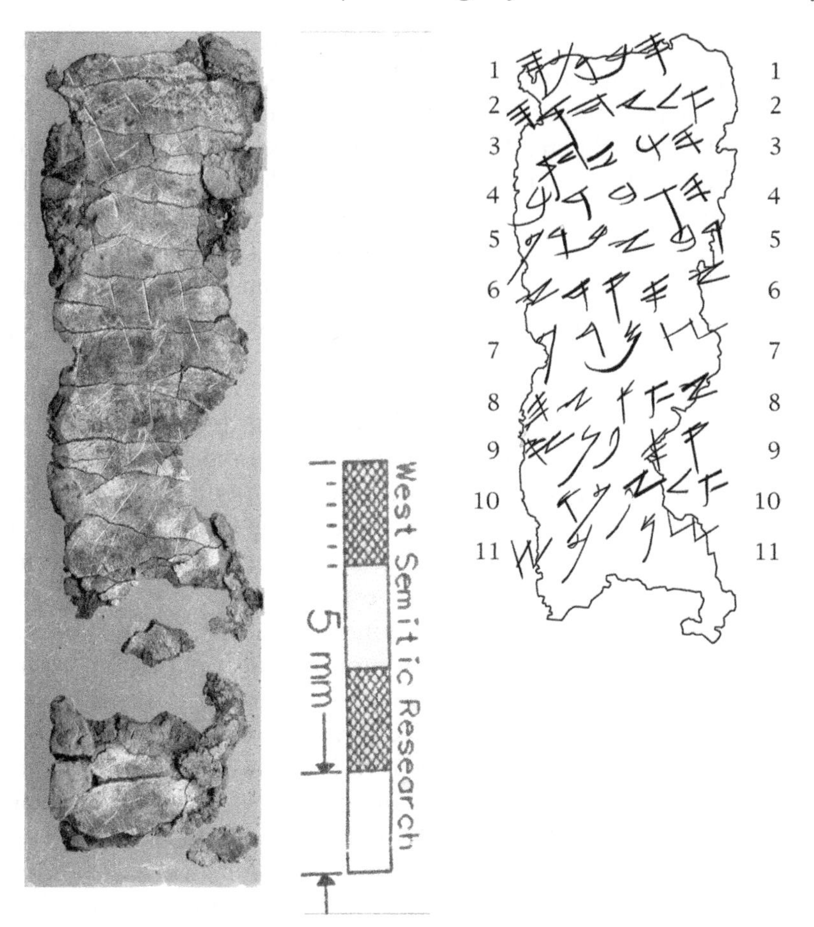

Figure 6.3. The Earliest Biblical Text: Silver Amulet II from Ketef Hinnom, Jerusalem, Dating to the Seventh Century B.C.E. (photograph by Bruce Zuckerman and Marilyn Lundberg, West Semitic Research. Drawing by Bruce Zuckerman. Courtesy of Israel Antiquities Authority and Gabriel Barkay)

toward Bethlehem, was the site of one of the most remarkable recently discovered inscriptions dating from the end of the monarchic period. The archaeologist Gabriel Barkay excavated two small silver amulets or charms, which were finely engraved with more than twenty lines (see Figure 6.3).[32] The archaeological context requires that these amulets be dated to the late seventh century B.C.E.[33] The text of the amulets paraphrases two well-known biblical passages. The first is the priestly blessing known from Numbers 6:24–26: "May YHWH bless you and keep you. May YHWH make his face to shine upon you and give you peace! May he be gracious to you. May YHWH lift up his face upon you." The second passage is the well-known text from Deuteronomy 7:9–10: "Know, therefore, that only YHWH your God is God, the steadfast God who keeps His covenant faithfully to the thousandth generation of those who love Him and keep His commandments." This latter passage continued to be an important text in the Second Temple period (cf. Dan 9:4; Neh 1:5).[34] The use of these biblical texts in amulets, furthermore, seems to be an attempt to carry out the injunction of the *Shema*, namely, "Bind them [the teaching] as a sign on your hand and let them serve as a symbol on your forehead; *inscribe* them on the doorposts of your house and on your gates" (Deut 6:8–9). Indeed, writing on the doorposts (the *mezuzot*) became a Jewish tradition practiced even today. The use of these amulets might be regarded as an early expression of the later practice of using phylacteries (or *tefillin*; cf. Matt 23:3; M. Shevuot 3.8, 11). Wisdom literature mentions the wearing of words of wisdom around the neck, on the fingers, or on the chest (cf. Prov 1:9; 3:3; 6:21; 7:3); however, usually this is understood metaphorically. What is notable about the development of this tradition is that it is the text from a particular book, the *Torah*, which is to be written on the doorposts, in the phylacteries, or – in the present case – on the amulet.

These two amulets would not have been unique. They were not one-of-a-kind objects. We must assume that these chance finds represent a much larger phenomenon in the late monarchic period. People would use traditional texts as amulets that were worn around the neck. Although these texts were not to be read, their use speaks to the religious power that *written* texts came to have in the late Judean monarchy.

Orthodoxy of a Book

The spread of literacy and with it the orthodoxy of the book would be watered by political revolution. Urbanization and political centralization had resulted in some resentment among the more rural towns and villages. Older political and social structures were discarded as the central government in Jerusalem grew more powerful and prosperous. This process is reflected, for example, in the rural prophet Micah, from the countryside town of Moresheth-Gath, as cited earlier:

Hear this, you heads of the houses of Jacob and chiefs of the house of Israel, who abhor justice and pervert all equity, who build Zion with blood and Jerusalem with wrong! Its rulers give judgment for a bribe, its priests teach for a price, its prophets give oracles for money; yet they lean upon YHWH and say, "Surely YHWH is with us! No harm shall come upon us." (Mic 3:9–11)

The "heads" and "chiefs" are related to the houses of "Jacob" and "Israel" – that is, the north – and these refugees from the Assyrian invasion of northern Israel are the ones who "build Jerusalem." In the context of the enormous growth in Jerusalem's size at this time, the use of the verb "to build" (√בנה) should be understood as having a concrete referent. The new inhabitants of Jerusalem – apparently, many of them from the north – are accused of introducing perverted social values. The northern kingdom had been more urban, economically prosperous, and culturally diverse than Judah. Undoubtedly, many of the refugees from the north were the elites, who most reflected the cultural diversity and economic prosperity of the region. They invaded the culturally isolated, rural south and brought with them the social values of the "city." The prophetic critique, as we saw earlier in Micah (and which can also be found in Amos and Hosea), reflects this social tension between the city and the countryside.

The critique of new cultural influences climaxed in the assassination of Hezekiah's grandson, Amon. Amon ruled for only two years (642–640 B.C.E.) before he was assassinated. At that point, a group, called in Hebrew *'Am Ha'aretz*, which can be translated as "the people of the land," moved in to insure a favorable succession. They placed the government in the hands of an eight-year-old king named Josiah (r. 640–609 B.C.E.); obviously, Josiah began his rule as the puppet king of the *'Am Ha'aretz*. The changed social location of power is perhaps indicated by the fact that the new king's family came from Bozkath, a small village in the Judean foothills.[35] Power had apparently shifted from the urban elites with ties to northern Israel back to the rural tribal leaders.

The role of the enigmatic *'Am Ha'aretz* in the Josianic coup suggests that they represented the old rural tribal leaders.[36] The tension between the *'Am Ha'aretz* and the urban elite is quite explicit in an earlier political coup, Joash's (r. 835–796 B.C.E.) overthrow of Queen Athaliah (r. 841–835 B.C.E.). Athaliah, the daughter of the northern king Omri, had been married to the Judean king, Ahaziah, in a political union intended to reunite the divided kingdom. When her husband was murdered in a palace intrigue in Samaria, Athaliah seized the throne. The account of Athaliah's reign concludes with the telling statement: "So all *'Am Ha'aretz* rejoiced, but the city was quiet after Athaliah had been killed with the sword at the king's house" (2 Kgs 11:20). Both coups demonstrate the tension that existed between urban and rural factions in ancient Judah.

The Josianic coup was a reaction to changes in Judean society – an attempt to recover the old values and social structure. But there was no going back. The bell could not be unrung. Although certain changes in the world brought on by globalization under Assyria were irreversible, they could be made to serve the revolution.

The story of the Josianic revolution is told at length by a Deuteronomic author in 2 Kings 22–23. Religious reform is sparked by the discovery of a scroll (or "book," as it is often erroneously translated). We can follow the story beginning in 2 Kings 22:8:

> 8 The high priest Hilkiah said to Shaphan the secretary, "*I have found the scroll of the law in the house of YHWH.*" When Hilkiah gave the scroll to Shaphan, he read it. 9 Then Shaphan the secretary came to the king, and reported to the king, "Your servants have emptied out the money that was found in the house, and have delivered it into the hand of the workers who have oversight of the house of YHWH." 10 Shaphan the secretary informed the king, "The priest Hilkiah has given me a scroll." Shaphan then read it aloud to the king. 11 *When the king heard the words of the scroll of the law*, he tore his clothes.... 23:1 Then the king directed that all the elders of Judah and Jerusalem should be gathered to him. 2 The king went up to the house of YHWH, and with him went all the people of Judah, all the inhabitants of Jerusalem, the priests, the prophets, and all the people, both small and great; *he read in their hearing all the words of the scroll of the covenant that had been found in the house of YHWH.* 3 The king stood by the pillar and made a covenant before YHWH, to follow YHWH, keeping his commandments, his decrees, and his statutes, with all his heart and all his soul, to perform the words of this covenant that were written in this scroll. All the people joined in the covenant.

Josiah uses the discovery of the scroll to justify purging Jerusalem and Judah of the corrupting influences of the northern kingdom.[37] The centrality of the "book" in the account of Josiah's reforms is critical. The written word becomes the litmus test of religious orthodoxy. In Jack Goody's classic work on the anthropology of writing, *The Domestication of the Savage Mind*, he notes, "literacy encouraged, at the very same time, criticism and commentary on the one hand and *the orthodoxy of the book* on the other."[38] Goody's observation recalls the discovery of the "scroll of the covenant" that became the basis of the Josianic Reforms. Josiah's reforms precipitate from the *discovery of a scroll*, and the execution of Josiah's reforms follow the *prescription of a scroll*. It is hardly coincidental that these textually inspired religious reforms are alleged to have happened precisely at a time when we see the social conditions necessary for writing emerge and the archaeological evidence tells us there was an explosion in writing.

The biblical book that forms the blueprint for the Josianic Reforms is the Book of Deuteronomy. When we look carefully at specific elements of the Josianic Reforms – for example, the centralization of the cult (cf. Deut 12), the covenant with YHWH (cf. Deut 26), or the destruction of foreign cults – they mirror the Deuteronomic legislation. The covenant ceremony that launches the reform, "The king stood by the pillar and made a covenant before YHWH, to follow YHWH, keeping his commandments, his decrees, and his statutes, with all his heart and all his soul, to perform the words of this covenant that were written in this scroll" (2 Kgs 23:3), echoes Deuteronomic language (e.g., Deut 4:40; 6:17; 7:11; 26:17). The relationship between Josiah's reforms and the Book of Deuteronomy is quite clear.

Writing is central to the revelation in Deuteronomy. This certainly distinguishes Deuteronomy from the rest of the Pentateuch (as we shall see further in Chapter 7). A few examples will highlight the centrality of writing in Deuteronomy. In contrast to Exodus, Deuteronomy makes a repeated point of the fact that the revelation on Sinai was written down (4:13; 5:19; 9:10; 10:4; 27:3, 8; 31:24). Not only was the Torah written, but Moses' teachings needed to be written again "when you have crossed over to enter the land, *you shall write down all the words of this teaching/Torah*" (27:3). Even the king needs to make a copy himself so that he may read it and consult it (17:18). Moreover, bits and pieces of the *Torah* should appear in every house. Deuteronomy repeatedly enjoins the people to "inscribe them on the doorposts of your house" (6:9; 11:20). In this way, every Judahite would be reminded of the written injunctions of the teaching, or *Torah*. It was written on the doorposts of the house. This must have initially been a means to introduce the orthodoxy of this written text to Judean society. The *mezuzah*, as this writing on the doorposts came to be known, was a reminder of the orthodoxy of the written *Torah*. I have already pointed to two extra-biblical examples – the silver amulets from Ketef Hinnom that cite Deuteronomy 7:9–10 and the priestly blessing in Numbers 6:24–26 – that suggest the religious authority and orthodoxy of texts in the late Judean monarchy. To be sure, not every Judahite would have been able to read, especially at any level higher than a very mundane one, yet the written text had become the basis of religious authority in Judean society.

What was the purpose of writing in Deuteronomy and the Josianic Reforms? The written word authorized the religious reforms of the rural elders and leaders who had been disenfranchised by the centralization of power in the city of Jerusalem and the person of the king. Deuteronomy placed remarkable limits on the power of the king through the written word and the "levitical priests":

> When (the king) has taken the throne of his kingdom, he shall have a copy of this *Torah* written for him in the presence of the levitical priests. It shall remain with him and he shall read in it all the days of his life, so that he may learn to fear YHWH his God, diligently observing all the words of this law and these statutes, neither exalting himself above other members of the community nor turning aside from the commandment, either to the right or to the left, so that he and his descendants may reign long over his kingdom in Israel. (Deut 17:18–20)

This was a radical innovation. The power of the king was being limited. A written *Torah*, deposited with the "levitical priests," ensured that the king did not become too powerful, "exalting himself above other members of the community." In the Near East the king's word tended to be law, but this passage placed the king under equal obligation to the law.

Who was limiting the power of the king? According to the law of the king, the "levitical priests" gave him the law. The next section of Deuteronomy defines this group: "The levitical priests, the whole tribe of Levi, shall have no allotment or inheritance within Israel" (Deut 18:1). The levitical priests were located throughout the land – not just in Jerusalem or in the Temple. In the concluding covenant ceremony of the Book of Deuteronomy, the Levitical priests are placed alongside Moses: "Then Moses and the levitical priests spoke to all Israel, saying: Keep silence and hear, O Israel! This very day you have become the people of YHWH your God" (27:9). It is surely not a coincidence that it is in this very scene in Deuteronomy that the whole writing of the Book of Deuteronomy is described! The narrative develops in 27:1–9:

> Then Moses and the elders of Israel charged all the people as follows: Keep the entire commandment that I am commanding you today. On the day that you cross over the Jordan into the land that YHWH your God is giving you, you shall set up large stones and cover them with plaster. You shall write on them all the words of this *Torah* when you have crossed over, to enter the land that YHWH your God is giving you, a land flowing with milk and honey, as YHWH, the God of your ancestors, promised you.... You shall write on the stones all the words of this *Torah* very clearly. Then Moses and the levitical priests spoke to all Israel, saying...

According to this version, "this *Torah*" is written only after the Israelites have crossed the Jordan. Moses' speech in Deuteronomy was thus written down later, apparently by the levitical priests. The old tribal leaders mentioned in Deuteronomy 27, first "the elders of Israel" and then "the levitical priests," had been marginalized by the centralization and urbanization of the late Judean monarchy. Now, however, they imposed upon the king the written orthodoxy of the text that limits royal power. Ironically, although writing spread in Judah through government bureaucracy, it was turned against the power of government in the Deuteronomic legislation. The Josianic Reforms became a defining moment for the role of writing in biblical texts. Before the late Judean monarchy, writing was a marginal phenomenon in ancient Israel. It served the royal court. It was used to keep temple records. It appeared in magic and had a role in the myths of creation. During the late Judean monarchy, writing became a mundane part of the social fabric. Knowledge was preserved and authority conferred by written texts. The importance of the written word would be felt in all post-Josianic literature. Indeed, the role of writing in society had dramatically changed.

The impact of the text culture introduced by the Josianic Reforms is evident, for example, in Jeremiah. Evidently, the prophet's ministry began at the same time that the priest Hilkiah found the scroll (2 Kgs 22:2, 8). The prophet confesses, "*Your words were found*, and I ate them, and your words became to me a joy and the delight of my heart" (Jer 15:16), alluding both to the finding of the scroll and to Jeremiah's own call (Jer 1:9). The prophet himself was not a scribe, but his close friend Baruch was and wrote down his oracles. So, for example, when YHWH commands Jeremiah to write down a prophetic message (Jer 36:1–2), the prophet calls on Baruch to transcribe his dictation (v. 4). This description of the process of writing down a prophet's words is the first and the only account of the writing process.

A New Social Location for Writing

Not only had writing spread since the days of Hezekiah, it now had a new social location. Writing was no longer essentially a prerogative of the state, but it had spread to various non-scribal classes as well, as can be seen in the inscriptional evidence discussed earlier. To understand just how the social location of writing had changed, let us return to the famous discovery of the scroll: "*The high priest Hilkiah* said to Shaphan the secretary, 'I have found the scroll of the law *in the house of YHWH.*'" That it was the high priest who found the scroll in the temple is critical for understanding the new social location of writing: the priests and the temple. This is a movement away from the traditional control of writing by the state. To be sure, writing had always had a role in the temple, but now the priests utilized the written text as a tool for enforcing a program of religious reform. Writing was no longer simply a magical way to discern whether, for example, a married woman has had an adulterous affair (as in Num 5); it has become a tool for enforcing a certain kind of religious vision upon both the people and the monarchy.

Why should the social location of writing shift so radically at this particular moment in history? To begin with, the increase in literacy opened up the possibility that writing could have a new function in society. As anthropologists have argued, literacy made possible the orthodoxy of the book. More than this, however, political events allowed the priests and the temple – which were normally subject to the monarchy – to gain the upper hand. Josiah's father was assassinated when Josiah was only eight years old, and the "people of the land" – the rural Judean political group – placed the boy-king on the throne. In so doing, this rural politic overturned entrenched political and religious leadership. The written word was invoked to validate these political and religious reforms. When a priest discovered the written word in the temple, the priests, together with "the people of the land," used this written word to gain a stronger position in the politics of the late Judean monarchy.

Although the priest Hilkiah discovers the "scroll of the covenant" – which is an explicit reference to the legislation of Exodus 20–23 referred to in Exodus 24:7 (see further Chapter 7) – the Josianic Reforms follow the Book of Deuteronomy. Deuteronomy was the Magna Carta of Josiah's political and religious reforms. Ironically, Deuteronomy advocates strong restraints on the power of the king. In Deuteronomy 17:16–18, for example, royal power is curbed:

> (The king) must not acquire many horses for himself, or return the people to Egypt in order to acquire more horses, since YHWH has said to you, "You must never return that way again." And he must not acquire many wives for himself, or else his heart will turn away; also silver and gold he must not acquire in great quantity for himself. When he has taken the throne of his kingdom, he shall have a copy of this *Torah* written for him in the presence of the levitical priests.

These restrictions on kingship would actually be employed in the critique of the venerable King Solomon.[39] The Deuteronomic account of King Solomon's reign describes the king as building great chariot cities for his horses, marrying hundreds of women, and collecting great quantities of gold. In a sly and subtle critique, one Deuteronomic author writes, "All King Solomon's drinking vessels were of gold, and all the vessels of the House of the Forest of Lebanon were of pure gold; none were of silver – it was not considered as anything in the days of Solomon" (1 Kgs 10:21). Consider how the status of Solomon has fallen from the wise king of the golden age of the monarchy to the king who has broken God's law! The Deuteronomists give a damning critique of Solomon – one of the founders of the united monarchy – without explicitly criticizing the old king. Furthermore, the Deuteronomic law of the king requires that the *levitical priests* oversee the writing of a copy of the *Torah* for the king. This written *Torah* then assumes a role of binding authority, checking the king's behavior. Deuteronomy was not the document of a strong monarchy; rather, the assassination of King Amon (r. 642–640 B.C.E.) and the installation by the "people of the land" of the eight-year-old Josiah as king provided the opportunity for the "people of the land" to limit the monarch's power. When Josiah grew older (in the eighteenth year of his reign, according to 2 Kgs 22:3), he initiated wide-ranging religious reforms that would reclaim the king's role as the head of the Temple.[40]

What is a central problem – or, better yet, an innovation – of the Book of Deuteronomy? All biblical literature up to this moment was essentially produced under the auspices of royal power. Yet, the book is not a text produced by royal scribes. It limits the power of the king and advocates for the common people. Deuteronomy serves to check the power of the king. It is a book of social conscience that promotes the power of the rural polity, the disenfranchised, and the rural levitical priests. Thus, Deuteronomy is the literature of the "people of the land" (Hebrew, *'Am Ha'aretz*). Deuteronomy expresses concern for the alien in the land and for those living throughout the land of Israel. One of the characteristic phrases of Deuteronomy is "in all your gates," reflecting the book's broad social concerns. Deuteronomy is not simply the work of the elites in Jerusalem or the Josianic scribes of the royal court. Rather, in its broader social concerns Deuteronomy stands in contrast both to royal literature and to the priestly legislation known from the Books of Leviticus and Numbers.

Thus, the social location of writing expands. Writing not only takes place at the behest of the royal court. If, as I have suggested, a written text has become the basis of religious orthodoxy, how was this written word disseminated? We cannot assume that hundreds of written copies were made and kept in private libraries. There is no evidence of this, and it would have been impractical. Even though I have argued for a rising literacy, it was a mundane literacy that arose with the bureaucracy of the Judean economy. Indeed, public religious writing also was mundane: writing that was ordered to be placed on the doorposts of every Israelite family home (Deut 6:9; 11:20) or that was put on amulets to be worn around the neck. These types of writing were reminders of the *Torah of Moses* as dictated in the Book of Deuteronomy. And the levitical priests throughout the land now took an active role in teaching this written *Torah*.

The Critique of the Book

Writing is not necessarily considered a universal good. For example, in an interesting vignette involving Pharaoh and the god Thoth, Plato criticized the Egyptian god and inventor of writing: "You have invented an elixir not of memory, but of reminding; and you offer your pupils the appearance of wisdom, not true wisdom, for they will read many things without instruction and will therefore seem to know many things, when they are for the most part ignorant and hard to get along with, since they are not wise, but only appear wise" (*Phaedrus*, §275a). The text allows one to read "without instruction" and can also displace the traditional teacher. Yet, one can argue, as Plato does, that it is instruction from the living teacher rather than the text itself that makes one wise. The text undermines the community and does not bring wisdom.

Writing locates authority in a text and its reader instead of in a tradition and its community. Writing does not require the living voice. Thus, writing has the power to supplant traditional modes of teaching and social structures of education. In a pre-literate society authority was entirely dependent upon traditions held by parents and elders and passed down orally from generation to generation. The community held the keys to wisdom and authority. Written texts had *the possibility* of replacing traditional community-centered wisdom. One no longer had to depend on the community for knowledge and wisdom because the written word itself could confer knowledge. Viewed from this perspective, the emphasis on a written text in the Josianic Reforms and in the Book of Deuteronomy was not only a novel development but is also a dangerous one. Although it couched itself in the antiquity of the Mosaic revelation and was originally employed by the Deuteronomic reformers to reassert traditional orthodoxy, the written text also had the power to supplant orthodoxy.[41] The tension between text and tradition, between the written and the oral, is already evident in the Book of Jeremiah. One of the more problematic passages in biblical literature has been Jeremiah 8:8, which recalls Socrates' critique of text-based wisdom: "How can you say, 'We are wise, And we possess the *Torah* of YHWH?' In fact, the false pen of the scribes has made it into a lie!" Some commentators have concluded – reluctantly – that this *Torah* of YHWH is the Book of Deuteronomy or some version thereof. It is natural to look to the Josianic Reforms and the discovery of the scroll of the covenant, which is usually thought to be some pre-canonical version of Deuteronomy. This is hardly an obvious conclusion however. One commentator writes, "This short passage is one of the most difficult to understand in the entire book."[42] He muses that it is not possible that the prophet is referring to some bogus law code or condemning the Book of Deuteronomy itself.

In his popular work *Who Wrote the Bible?* Richard Elliot Friedman argues that the prophet Jeremiah himself was the Deuteronomist. Therefore, Jeremiah 8:8 could not be referring to the Book of Deuteronomy. As a result, Friedman seizes on Jeremiah 8:8 as a Deuteronomic critique of the Priestly document. (The Priestly document, or "P" as it is referred to in the scholarly lingo, is to be found primarily in the Books of Leviticus and Numbers, but scholars also assign passages from Genesis and Exodus to this supposed document.[43]) However, this assumes that the Josianic Reforms are primarily priestly reforms. This also misses a critical aspect of Jeremian critique; namely, it is a critique of a written text or writing itself. One interesting aspect of the priestly school is that the very *written-ness* of the tradition is not at stake (see Chapter 7). At no point in P is there an injunction to write it down. Nor is writing even mentioned as an important component of the so-called P document. While P is obviously a text in its present form (and in most scholarly descriptions), this is not something about which P itself seems to be self-conscious. Deuteronomy, in contrast, is quite conscious of itself as a written revelation. Thus, Jeremiah's critique of writing and a written text seemingly could not apply to priestly literature.

The reference to a "lie" (*sheqer*) in Jeremiah 8:8 recalls one of Jeremiah's more trenchant comments concerning the days of Josiah: "Yet for all this her false sister Judah did not return to me with her whole heart, but only by a lie (*sheqer*)" (Jer 3:10; see vv. 6–10). Clearly, there was some dissatisfaction with Josiah's Reforms. The inter-textual allusion between Jeremiah 3:10 and 8:8 to the pretense of Judah's return during the Josianic Reforms utilizes the same Hebrew vocabulary, it was a *sheqer* – a lie.

The wider context of the Jeremiah passage, however, puts it into perspective. In Jeremiah 8:7–9, this written *Torah* of YHWH is juxtaposed with different types of oral tradition:

> 7 Even the stork in the heavens knows its times; and the turtledove, swallow, and crane observe the time of their coming; but my people do not know the tradition (*mishpat*) of YHWH. 8 How can you say, "We are wise, and the Law (*Torah*) of YHWH is with us." In fact, the false pen of the scribes has made it into a lie? 9 The wise shall be put to shame, they shall be dismayed and taken; since they have rejected the word (*davar*) of YHWH, what wisdom is in them?

Critical to the proper interpretation of this passage from Jeremiah are the Hebrew terms (italicized in parentheses in the translation) *mishpat*, *Torah*, and *davar*. Clearly, the *Torah* of YHWH refers to a written text, though scholars usually debate which text. Some think that it refers to Deuteronomy; others suggest that it refers to already written (and false) interpretations of Deuteronomic law. I think the issue is not *which text*, but the authority of any written text as opposed to oral tradition. The context clears up the issue. Verse 9 refers to the "word (*davar*) of YHWH"; this is a technical term in Biblical Hebrew literature that refers to the oral word of God given to the prophets.[44] Wisdom is associated with the oral tradition of the community and proclamations of God's messengers, so how could one reject them and still be wise?

The term *mishpat* in verse 7 is a bit more fluid in meaning; however, it may be translated as "the *tradition* of YHWH" or "the *custom* of YHWH."[45] *Mishpat* is often found in biblical literature in places where it appeals to no known written tradition, yet there is obviously a well-established custom or tradition at work. So, for example, a new king is installed in a traditional procedure and place, "according to the custom (i.e., *mishpat*) of the king" (2 Kgs 11:14). The prophet Samuel warns Israel about "the ways (i.e., *mishpat*) of a king" (1 Sam 8: 9, 11). The use of *mishpat* as a legal term does not reflect written texts, but rather legal judgments. In most cases, there is no written text as such that could even form the basis of the *judgment* (e.g., Gen 18:25; Lev 19:15). Both the social context of Jeremiah's day and the immediate literary context suggest that Jeremiah 8:8 is a protest against the authority of the written texts that were understood as subverting oral tradition and the authority of the prophets.

There is both continuity and contrast between oral tradition and text. Most scholars have stressed a continuum between orality and literacy. On one level, there indeed is a continuum, but on another level, oral and written stand in sharp contrast. Traditional societies relied on oral tradition and the community as the bases for authority. Written texts would eventually challenge and even supplant these sources of traditional wisdom. Jeremiah 8:7–9 illustrates the clear distinction between oral and written authority. In the end, the written text replaced the prophets and oral tradition. In the Second Temple period, the "word of God" would become the written text rather than the oral proclamation of prophets. Yet, the conflict between oral and written was not easily or quickly resolved. The tension between oral and written tradition would be played out in Second Temple Judaism between the Pharisees and Sadducees (among others). Although the oral tradition continually reasserted itself (as it did in Jeremiah's complaint), eventually it was subverted and supplanted.

7

How the Torah Became a Text

The writing of the five books of the Torah is a prominent example of the textualization of ancient Israelite religion. On the one hand, the Book of Exodus, and particularly the revelation at Mount Sinai in Exodus 19–23, serves as a powerful illustration of the Bible's disinterest in its own *textuality*. On the other hand, the Book of Deuteronomy integrates the textuality of the Torah as a pivotal part of the revelation at Mount Horeb (not Mount Sinai as in Exodus). These differing accounts of the revelation reflect a historical process of the textualization of Israelite culture and religion. Although scholars have usually analyzed the Torah from the perspective of who wrote what (using source criticism), this chapter begins with a different approach, asking the question: how does the Torah relate to its own textuality?

The central figure of the Torah's textuality is Moses. There is a literary history to the textualization of Torah that follows Moses' own role in the revelation. Moses is first the deliverer of Israel. Next, he receives and speaks the revelation at Mount Sinai. Moses is given the stone tablets. According to Exodus, these tablets seem to contain the plans for the tabernacle. According to Deuteronomy, these tablets are the Ten Commandments. Finally, Moses grows into an author and the authority for the Jewish religion. The writings and traditions attributed to Moses continued to expand long after his death. They grew to include the entire Torah. Hellenistic Jews between 300 B.C.E. and 300 C.E. continued to write works like the Book of Jubilees pseudepigraphically in Moses' name. After the destruction of the Second Temple, Rabbis such as Akiva and Judah the Prince collected the oral legal traditions into a series of books known as the Mishnah, the Tosefta, and the Talmud. All these works ultimately trace their authority back to Moses: "Moses received Torah at Sinai and passed it on to Joshua, Joshua to elders, and elders to prophets, and prophets passed it on to the men of the great assembly" (M. Avot 1:1).

Before turning to the textualization of the Torah, I must warn the reader that what follows flies in the face of over a century of biblical scholarship. I especially take issue with much of the last few decades of Pentateuchal scholarship, particularly in Europe, which has increasingly located the composition of the Pentateuch in the Persian period. Scholars like Erhard Blum, a professor at Tübingen University, or Rainer Albertz, a professor at Münster University, have continually pushed the composition of the Pentateuch later and later. I cannot even begin to number all the scholars and studies upon which this chapter will touch (as there has been no end to the writing of books on the Pentateuch), but in a few notes, I will detail some of my objections to selected scholars within the academic guild. Ultimately, however, my conclusions are so different because my approach has been so different. To that extent, we have to discuss methodology before turning to details.

My approach to the formation of biblical literature began with an assessment of the practical aspects of writing and the social contexts of writing as they developed in ancient Israel and early Judaism. For example, very complex models of the composition, redaction, and editing of biblical literature into multiple layers by many different hands appear to me not only to be unreasonably subjective but also to require sophisticated concepts of textuality and quite developed Hebrew scribal schools that just cannot be warranted based on the external evidence from archaeology and inscriptions. Even if such unlikely models of multiple authors, redactors, and editors could be justified within the social, economic, and political contexts of ancient Israel, we do not have the tools to convincingly unravel the hypothetical strands. More fundamentally, however, the role of writing and social history point to much simpler models for the composition and growth of biblical literature.

The Word "Torah"

It is noteworthy that the Hebrew word *chodah* (חודה) itself originally meant "teaching" or "instruction," implying an oral collection of tradition. The word comes from the Hebrew root *YRH*, meaning "to instruct." The word *torah* is found widely in biblical literature with this meaning. At the same time, there is a central body of *teaching* contained in the first five books of the Bible, which came to be known as *the Torah*. As Moshe Weinfeld has pointed out, "The transition from Torah as a specific instruction to the sacred 'Book of the Torah' of the Josianic period marked a turning point in Israel's spiritual life."[1] Still, the original meaning of the Hebrew word *torah* as "teaching" underlines its *orality*. The word meant to teach or to instruct orally and had nothing to do with written texts. Part of my intent in this chapter is to show how "teaching" becomes sacred text.

The use of the word *torah* within the Torah itself – that is to say, the use of the term "teaching" within the Pentateuch – betrays the early non-technical meaning of *torah*. In Genesis, for example, God promises to make Israel a great nation because "Abraham obeyed Me and kept My charge: My commandments, My laws, and My *teachings*" (26:5). The word *torah* is part of a frequently used triplet: commandments, laws, and teachings (i.e., *torah*). Moreover, *torah* was not necessarily God's teaching. As we see in the Book of Proverbs, the *torah* could be the teaching of a parent to a child: "My son, do not forget my teaching [*torah*], and let your mind retain my commandments" (Prov 3:1), and "My son, keep your father's commandment; and do not forsake your mother's teaching [*torah*]" (Prov. 6:20). We could multiply such examples, but these suffice to show that *torah* was first part of the oral world of ancient Israel. So how does Torah become the written text par excellence?

Before answering the question of how the Torah becomes a text, it is worthwhile to reflect on the use of the word in the Pentateuch (or "Torah") itself. Scholars usually divide the Pentateuch into at least four sources; these include the "Priestly" and the "Deuteronomic" sources. To simplify this, we may generalize that the Books of Leviticus and Numbers are priestly and that the Book of Deuteronomy is (obviously) Deuteronomic. According to post-Wellhausian scholarship, the priestly writings are supposed to be the last of the four documents. It is thus unexpected that the Hebrew word *torah* never explicitly refers to a text in the Books of Leviticus and Numbers. In Leviticus and Numbers, *torah* retains its meaning as "instruction, teaching," indicating that the Pentateuchal priestly writings are not self-conscious about their own textuality. This may be directly contrasted with the literature of the Persian or Hellenistic periods, which were mostly written by priests, where *torah* is a text. Thus, for example, the written *Torah* (with a capital "T") is central to the religious program of the Persian period as reflected in Ezra-Nehemiah. In Neh 8, for example, a great show is made of the presentaion of the scroll of the Torah of Moses, which is read, studied, and obeyed. This textualization of *Torah* is also evident in the Book of Chronicles, where the term *Torah* can mean a text without qualification (see, e.g., 1 Chr 16:40; 2 Chr 15:3). This sense of the *Torah* as a text began with Deuteronomy and the Josianic writers.

The First Revelation at Sinai

Our modern perceptions of the story of the revelation and writing of the Torah tend to be conflations of a variety of texts and traditions, including the famous scene on the mountain of God from the movie *The Ten Commandments*. However, a quite different picture emerges if we focus on the first tale of God's revelation on Mount Sinai as it appears strictly in the Book of Exodus, chapter 19.

What are the words used to describe the initial revelation on Sinai? They have to do with *speaking*, not with *writing*. They have to do with *orality*, not with *textuality*. This is to be expected given the nature of early Israelite tribal society. To begin with, the people apparently hear the sounds of thunder on the mountain. A wonderful ambiguity in the Hebrew serves the story well. The Hebrew word *Qol* can mean "voice," "sound," or "thunder."[2] As the people ascend the mountain, they hear *Qol* and see lightning flashes. We assume that *Qol* here means thunder since it is accompanied by lightning. However, in Exodus 19:16, the narrative goes on to say that "Moses would speak and God would answer him in thunder/by a voice." In turn, Moses transmits what God has spoken, orally, to the people. So, for example, the Ten Commandments are prefaced by Moses' saying that "God *spoke* all these words" (20:1). The people ask Moses to *speak* to them, to tell them what God has *said* because they are afraid of God's speaking to them directly (Exod 20:19). God instructs Moses to remind the Israelites of what they have seen for themselves – that God spoke with the people from heaven (Exod 20:22).

It is a truly astonishing observation that writing has no role in the revelation at Mount Sinai in Exodus 19. Writing has no role in the description of the giving of the Ten Commandments in Exodus 20. Writing has no role in the so-called Covenant Code in Exodus 21–23. Somehow the story of the revelation in Exodus 19–23 seems unaware that the Torah is a text. This fact will become all the more remarkable when we see how later traditions will be obsessed with telling the story of the *writing* of the Torah.[3] The theme of God's writing of the stone tablets first appears not in Exodus 19 or Exodus 20, but after the covenant ceremony has been completed in Exodus 24. As almost an afterthought in 24:4, the narrator notes that *Moses* himself wrote these things down. Moses wrote them down, not because God had explicitly commanded him to do so in the narrative, but apparently because it just seemed the thing to do.

So, it is Exodus 24 that introduces writing into the Sinai event. This, however, is a very strange chapter. Exodus 24 has been a puzzle to the last century of biblical source critics and an enigma to the last millennium of pious readers.[4] As we shall see, part of this quandary arises simply from the fact that Exodus 24 deals with such central events and ideas. To facilitate a literary analysis of Exodus 24, I have formatted the translation that follows with paragraphing, indentation, and bracketed notes that indicate some of the basic literary units and problems within the story.

1 Then he [no subject indicated] said to Moses, "Come up to YHWH, you and Aaron, Nadab, and Abihu, and seventy of the elders of Israel, and worship at a distance. 2 Moses alone [change in who goes up the mountain] shall come near YHWH; but the others shall not come near, and the people shall not come up with him." 3 Moses came and told the people all the words of YHWH and all the ordinances; and *all the people answered with one voice, and said, "All the words that YHWH has spoken we will do."* 4 And Moses wrote down all the words of YHWH. He rose early in the morning, and built an altar at the foot of the mountain, and set up twelve pillars, corresponding to the twelve tribes of Israel. 5 He sent young men of the people of Israel, who offered burnt offerings and sacrificed oxen as offerings of well-being to YHWH. 6 Moses took half of the blood and put it in basins, and half of the blood he dashed against the altar. 7 Then he took the scroll of the covenant [this same scroll is apparently found in 2 Kgs 23:2], and read it in the hearing of the people; and *they said, "All that YHWH has spoken we will do, and we will be obedient."* 8 Moses took the blood and dashed it on the people, and said, "See the blood of the covenant that YHWH has made with you in accordance with all these words."

9 Then Moses and Aaron, Nadab, and Abihu, and seventy of the elders of Israel [the same group mentioned in verse 1] went up, 10 and they saw the God of Israel. Under his feet there was something like a pavement of sapphire stone, like the very heaven for clearness. 11 God did not lay his hand on the chief men of the people of Israel; also they beheld God, and they ate and drank.

12 YHWH said to Moses, "Come up to me on the mountain, and wait there; and I will give you the tablets of stone (also, the law [*tôrah*] and the commandment [*mitzvah*]), which I have written for their instruction." 13 So Moses set out with his assistant Joshua, and Moses went up into the mountain of God...

There has been a general agreement among scholars that this chapter is a composite of different sources and shows evidence of some reworking. There has been little agreement on how to understand the compositional development. Indeed, I would argue that the centrality of events and issues raised in Exodus 24 are just the reason for this chapter's complexity. Here we ascend Mount Sinai, Moses writes down the Torah, the people make a covenant of blood with God, the elders actually see God, and God himself promises to write on "tablets of stone" and give them to Moses. How could any priestly redactor, any Deuteronomic editor, or indeed any modern commentator resist such a chapter? It is just this type of text that attracts editors, commentators, and interpreters. Before the notion of the text as sacred and unchangeable had developed, editors or commentators would simply insert annotations into the text itself. Some of the most simple of these types of comments may be illustrated by explanatory glosses like 1 Samuel 9:9: "Formerly in Israel, anyone who went to inquire of God would say, 'Come, let us go to the seer'; *for the one who is now called a prophet was formerly called a seer.*"[5] The italics mark an explanatory gloss by a later scribe who felt the need to clarify the meaning of the old Hebrew term "seer." We also get a small glimpse into the historical layering of a text in this example: a later scribe interprets something that is thought to be obscure or difficult by adding an explanatory clause. More theologically or ideologically sensitive topics would attract even more attention as biblical texts were copied and transmitted.

The question is, how can we navigate this morass? I do not wish to debate the redaction and editing of Exodus 24 on the basis of the same old critical methodologies of source criticism, redaction criticism, or tradition history. To do so, would just be adding another voice to the many voices that were heard on Sinai. To get any further with this chapter, we need to try a new approach. My observations about Exodus 24 are guided by the development of textuality itself. My approach takes as its presupposition that the very development of the notion of the written and then of the sacred text must be central to analysis of the composition and editing in Exodus 24.

As a literary text, Exodus 24 stands apart. It begins abruptly without a subject in verse 1, leading to the conclusion that the chapter is removed or truncated from its original context. There is actually some tension with the assumption that the implied speaker of verse 1 is YHWH, who would naturally have told Moses to come up to him on the mountain. The problem with that interpretation is that the narrative is told with YHWH in the third person, thus "*he* said, 'Come up to *YHWH*,'" and not "*YHWH* said, 'Come up to *me*.'" So who said, "Come up to YHWH"? In addition, verse 1 does not easily connect to Exodus 23. Perhaps it should be read as picking up from Exodus 20:22, where the laws of the Covenant Code (Exodus 21–23) begin. But this still would not explain the mysterious and missing subject of the first verse.

Furthermore, literary analysis would suggest that verses 2–8 represent a different source or a major shift in the narrative. This is evident from the change in the group that is supposed to go up to YHWH. In verses 1 and 9, quite a large group – including Moses, Aaron, Nadab, and Abihu, and seventy elders of Israel – are instructed to ascend the mountain. Verse 2 reverses this: Moses should ascend alone. This brings the story of Moses' ascent up the mountain in line with the earlier account in Exodus 19:3 (also v. 20) where Moses also goes up the mountain alone.

To make matters more complex, within this digression in verses 2–8 there seem to be two literary layers. These are indicated by repetition of the oath of the people in verses 3b and 7b: "All the words that YHWH has spoken we will do" (verse 7b starts, "All that..."). This type of repetition is usually an editorial marker that comments or additions have been inserted, as I pointed out with an example from 1 Kings 14:25–28 and 2 Chronicles 12:2–9 (discussed in Chapter 1). The first oath harkens back to Exodus 19:5–8, where Moses had set the "words of God" before Israel and Israel had responded, "All that YHWH has spoken we will do." In this way, verses 2–3 have now connected Exodus 24 back to the original story of the revelation in Exodus 19.

Verses 4–8 add a Deuteronomic interpretative layer to the covenant ceremony. The two parts of Exodus 24:2–8 can be divided as follows:

[Allusion to Exodus 19:5–8] 2 Moses alone shall come near YHWH; but the others shall not come near, and the people shall not come up with him." 3 Moses came and told the people all the words of YHWH and all the ordinances; and *all the people answered with one voice, and said, "All the words that YHWH has spoken we will do."*

[Deuteronomic addition] 4 And Moses wrote down all the words of YHWH. He rose early in the morning, and built an altar at the foot of the mountain, and set up twelve pillars, corresponding to the twelve tribes of Israel. 5 He sent young men of the people of Israel, who offered burnt offerings and sacrificed oxen as offerings of well-being to YHWH. 6 Moses took half of the blood and put it in basins, and half of the blood he dashed against the altar. 7 Then he took the scroll of the covenant, and read it in the hearing of the people; and *they said, "All that YHWH has spoken we will do, and we will be obedient."* 8 Moses took the blood and dashed it on the people, and said, "See the blood of the covenant that YHWH has made with you in accordance with all these words."

The repetition of the oath ceremony in verses 2–8 certainly seems redundant. While the oath in 24:3 essentially follows the very first oath sworn by the people in Exodus 19:5–8, the oath in 24:7 is inspired by Moses writing down the revelation and then reading "the scroll of the covenant" to the people. Verse 4 notes that "Moses wrote down all the words of YHWH." What an understatement! Moses is not commanded to write down the revelation; he just does. In a simple literary reading, this verse would suggest that Moses had written down both the "Book of the Covenant" (Exod 21–23) and the Decalogue (Exod 20). Moses then makes a covenant of blood that reaches its climax in the reading of the "scroll of the covenant" and the repeated oath of the people. It is important to remember here that the people had already heard these words orally and swore to faithfully perform them (v. 3). For this reason, we recognize verses 4–8 as a secondary digression within verses 2–8, which textualizes an oral ceremony.

How should we understand these two sections within verses 2–8 in the context of the composition of the scroll? The first digression ties the story to Exodus 19. Therefore, verses 2–3 are part of the narrative thread of the Book of Exodus as a whole. Verses 2–3 are part of the process that creates one prose narrative out of the disparate stories, oral traditions and liturgies that make up the Book of Exodus. The original story of Sinai, however, is not self-conscious about its own textuality. That is, it did not narrate an account of its own writing. Instead, verses 4–8 narrate an account of Moses writing down the "scroll of the covenant." This scroll, however, was lost, according to the account in 2 Kings 22–23 about Josiah's religious reforms. The high priest Hilkiah finds a scroll that turns out to be this same "Book of the Covenant" – note that Exodus 24:7 and 2 Kings 23 are the only places in the entire Hebrew Bible where the exact expression "the scroll of the covenant" are found.

Where else does Moses write in the Bible? After all, we usually witness Moses as one who receives the divinely written tablets, not as a writer himself. It should not be a surprise that the one other place where Moses is described as a writer is in the conclusion of the Book of Deuteronomy. As part of the commissioning of Joshua as Moses' successor, we read, "Then Moses wrote down this law, and gave it to the priests, the sons of Levi, who carried the ark of the covenant of YHWH, and to all the elders of Israel" (Deut 31:9). This chapter is part of the editorial framework of the Book of Deuteronomy that ties it with the Book of Joshua and into a larger narrative that scholars have called the Deuteronomistic History. Even the casual reader will see, for example, that Deuteronomy 31 and Joshua 1 repeat the story of the commissioning of Joshua, thereby tying the two scrolls – Deuteronomy and Joshua – together, with the repetition serving as the literary thread.[6] It is also important to note that the passages in Exodus 24:4 and Deuteronomy 31:9 both use the editorial device of repetition to frame the portrayal of Moses, the writer of Torah. We may surmise that it is here, in the final editing of the Bible, that Moses becomes a writer. Parenthetically, I should also point out that this editing of the Bible is probably taking place in the late Persian or Hellenistic period.

Exodus 24:4–8 incorporates an important inter-textual connection with Josiah's religious reforms narrated in 2 Kings 22–23. The written document in Exodus 24:7 receives the title "the scroll of the covenant" (*sefer ha-brît*). This is the exact title of the book that Hilkiah, the priest of Josiah, finds in the temple. This is more than a coincidence. Indeed, the expression "scroll of the covenant" is found only here, in Exodus 24:7, and in the story of the discovery of a scroll that prompts the Josianic Reforms (2 Kgs 23:2, 21). The use of this unique expression points to an intentional literary connection between the Sinai revelation in Exodus and the scroll that is mysteriously found in the Jerusalem temple during the renovations undertaken by King Josiah: "Then the high priest Hilkiah said to the scribe Shaphan, 'I have found a scroll of the *Torah* in the house of YHWH.' And Hilkiah gave the scroll to Shaphan, who read it" (2 Kgs 22:8). In 2 Kgs 23:2 and 21, the narrator identifies this "scroll of the *Torah*" (*sefer ha-torah*) with the "book of the covenant" (*sefer ha-brît*). Of course, it would have been difficult to identify this scroll with the Sinai revelation if Moses had not finally written it down as we learned in Exodus 24:4. In point of fact, however, Josiah's reforms do not closely parallel the "Covenant Code" of Exodus 21–23, but they do compare to the Book of Deuteronomy (which might be partially characterized as an interpretation of the Covenant Code).

Let us return now to the description of the narrative in Exodus 24. Verse 9 resumes the narrative thread from verse 1, which had been interrupted by verses 2–8. Note, for example, the explicit resumption of the subjects, "Moses and Aaron, Nadab, and Abihu, and seventy of the elders of Israel," who are going up the mountain. With this restatement of the same list of subjects as in Exodus 24:1 the story returns to where it was before the long digression. The narrative then continues with the remarkable statement that upon going up the mountain, the group "saw the God of Israel." Thereupon, God gives Moses the tablets of stone.[7]

The introduction of the stone tablets at this point in the chapter raises some questions. Exodus 24 has two accounts of writing. The first account, in 24:4, casually notes that Moses had written down the words of God. I have already discussed this account. The second account, in 24:12, portrays God himself as writing on tablets that God gives to Moses. How do these two writings relate to one another? What were the contents of the two tablets described in the second account? These are questions that astute readers should ask as they read Exodus 24.

In its current literary form, Exodus 24 textualizes the Torah in significant ways. This textualization is most closely tied to the language of Deuteronomy and the Deuteronomistic History. First, it adds the statement, "Moses wrote down all the words of YHWH" (v. 4). Second, Moses takes the "scroll of the covenant" and reads it before all the people (vv. 7–8). Surely, it is no coincidence that the expression "scroll of the covenant" (Hebrew, *sefer ha-brît*) occurs only here in Exodus 24:7 and in the story of Josiah's religious reforms (2 Kgs 23:2, 21). A ritual reading of the text in Exodus 24:7–8 is then the basis for the confirmation of the covenant between God and Israel, just as we also find in 2 Kings 23.

In sum, the revelation of the Covenant Code in the Book of Exodus was originally depicted as an oral revelation. There was no reading of texts. There was no writing of texts. The whole revelation reflected the orality of ancient Israel. The Book of Deuteronomy would make textuality central to the revelation. Deuteronomy would also have to address the apparent tension between this newly introduced text that Moses wrote down and the tablets of stone "written by the finger of God." When the Exodus and Sinai traditions were incorporated into the Pentateuch and connected with the Deuteronomistic History (Deuteronomy–Kings), an account of the writing of the "book of the covenant" was introduced by the interpretative repetition in Exodus 24:4–8. When did this textualization of the Torah happen? *Since the "scroll of the covenant" is central to the Josianic religious reforms, the formation of the Pentateuch as we know it must have begun in the late seventh century* B.C.E.

The Tablets of Stone

The tablets of stone take us back to divine origins of writing. These tablets, "written by the finger of God," are central to one of the most provocative texts of the Hebrew Bible. Moses, Aaron, and the elders of Israel go up again to Mount Sinai where they actually see the God of Israel and Moses receives the tablets of stone. The story is recounted in Exodus 24:9–18:

> Then Moses and Aaron, Nadab, and Abihu, and seventy of the elders of Israel went up, and they saw the God of Israel. Under his feet there was something like a pavement of sapphire stone, like the very heaven for clearness. God did not lay his hand on the chief men of the people of Israel; they beheld God, and they ate and drank. YHWH said to Moses, "Come up to me on the mountain, and wait there; and I will give you the tablets of stone, and the law (i.e., *torah*) and the commandment, which I have written for their instruction." So Moses set out with his assistant Joshua, and Moses went up into the mountain of God.... Then Moses went up on the mountain, and the cloud covered the mountain. The glory of YHWH settled on Mount Sinai, and the cloud covered it for six days; on the seventh day he called to Moses out of the cloud. Now the appearance of the glory of YHWH was like a devouring fire on the top of the mountain in the sight of the people of Israel. Moses entered the cloud, and went up on the mountain. Moses was on the mountain for forty days and forty nights.

An odd collection of Israelites – Moses, Aaron, Nadab, and Abihu, and seventy of the elders of Israel – apparently hold a banquet with God on Mount Sinai. This gathering stands in contrast to the revelation in Exodus 19, where Israel was not allowed on the mountain and saw God only in the form of rumblings. The theological difficulty this physical sighting of God created was made clear by the obfuscation of the text when it was translated into Aramaic in the second century C.E. in Targum Neophiti:[8] "they saw the Glory of the Shekinah of YHWH, and they rejoiced over their sacrifices, which were received *as if they ate and drank*." In this early Jewish interpretation, the group did not actually see God, nor did they sup with him. It only seemed like they did. This attempt to explain away this text not only highlights its strangeness to later sensibilities but also suggests the antiquity of the tradition. After the strange picnic described in Exodus 24:11, Moses again goes up to the mountain where God promises Moses the tablets of stone.

What did these tablets of stone contain? One way of answering this question would be to look at the narrative that follows. Exodus 25–31 is primarily a description how to build the desert tabernacle where YHWH would dwell. Exodus 24:12, the giving of the two tablets, begins a literary unit that comes to a neat conclusion in Exodus 31:18. The closure of this literary unit is marked by an *inclusio* – that is, by a literary repetition that recalls the opening of the literary unit and intentionally brings the literary unit to a close. Thus, the narrative that begins in Exodus 24:12 is closed off by recalling this verse in Exodus 31:18:

[24:12] YHWH said to Moses, "Come up to me on the mountain, and wait there; and I will give you the tablets of stone, with the law and the commandment, which I have written for their instruction."

...(plans for the tabernacle and the Sabbath commandment)...

[31:18] When God finished speaking with Moses on Mount Sinai, he gave him the two tablets of the covenant, tablets of stone, written with the finger of God.

The narrative is closed by one of the most powerful and inspiring anthropomorphic images of Scripture. According to Exodus 31:18, God literally wrote the tablets with his own finger. This description is confirmed by Exodus 32:16: "The tablets were the work of God, and the writing was the writing of God, engraved upon the tablets." But what was on these tablets? We naturally assume that the contents of Exodus 25–31 – that is, both the Sabbath commandment and the plans for building the tabernacle – would be on these tablets. Indeed, archaeological and comparative research indicate that the plan and conception of the tabernacle is quite ancient.[9] Thus, the biblical narrative here simply frames and justifies an ancient religious artifact. According to this natural reading of the text, neither the legal code of ancient Israel nor the Decalogue was written on the famous two stone tablets; rather, God had revealed the plans for his own tabernacle and its facilities, as well as the Sabbath commandment to worship at the tabernacle.

What of the fact that the second revelation asserts that God wrote these tablets with his own finger? The best ancient analogy for such a claim would be the Mesopotamian Tablets of Destiny, discussed in Chapter 2. The Tablets of Destiny are a divine writing produced at the creation of the world. It may be that the powerful image of divine writing, the "finger of God," used in Exodus 31:18 is appropriate precisely because it is also a metaphor for creation, as is suggested by Psalm 8:3: "I behold Your heavens, the work of Your fingers, the moon and stars that You set in place." It might be inferred from this that divine writing had its origins in the creation of the world. After all, nothing in either Exodus 24:12 or 31:18 necessitates that God wrote the tablets while Moses waited on the mountain. One might easily assume that the tablets had been written earlier. It should be no surprise that later Jewish tradition explicitly claimed that the Torah was pre-existent (cf. Gen. R, 1:1, 4; b. Pes 54a).[10] Such a claim was hardly invented *ex nihilo* by the Rabbis. Indeed, it was also suggested by the association of Torah with Wisdom, which was created by God in the beginning (e.g., Prov 8:22–30; Ben-Sira 1:1–5). Thus, the Rabbis followed a well-trodden path of interpretation.

This brings us back to the question of what was written by the finger of God? Evidently, the plans for God's dwelling place on earth, not the legal codes or the Decalogue of early Israel. At least this is the simple reading of Exodus 24:9–31:18. After promising to give Moses the tablets, the narrative describes the various aspects of building the tabernacle and concludes with the proscription for the Sabbath service in the tabernacle. After a digression about the Golden Calf (Exod 32–34),[11] the remainder of Exodus (chapters 35–40) is a description of the actual building of the tabernacle. The culminating event is the placing of the two stone tablets into the Ark of the Covenant and situating the ark within the tabernacle (Exod 40:20–21). At precisely this point the presence of God descends to earth and God takes his seat, enthroned above the ark on the wings of the cherubim within the tabernacle. As God promises in Exodus 25:22, "There I will meet with you, and I will speak to you – from above the cover, from between the two cherubim that are on top of the Ark of the Pact – all that I will command you concerning the people of Israel." Actually, this would suggest that *torah is received only after the ark with the tablets is completed and placed in the tabernacle.*[12] After the tabernacle is built, God comes to dwell in the tabernacle (as is reflected in Exod 40). From God's dwelling place in the tabernacle, he speaks to the people of Israel. In this reading, *torah* would be literally the speaking of God from his dwelling place teaching Israel, not a written text (i.e., the *Torah*). Now, it might seem a rather curious thing to seal the tablets within the ark, especially if the tablets were intended to be read and used as a moral and legal guide. On the other hand, if the tablets contained the building plans for the tabernacle, their purpose had been served once the tabernacle was constructed.[13] At that point they could be sealed within the ark as evidence, so to speak, that the dwelling of God on earth was built through divinely revealed and inscribed plans.

So what was revealed to Moses on the mountain? In the narrow context of Exodus 24:12–31:18, the most obvious answer is that the tablets were engraved with the divine instructions for building God's tabernacle. This early story, however, has been woven into the current narrative so that there are two accounts of writing in Exodus 24. Still, when we read Exodus 24 without the interpretation of Deuteronomy and later interpretative tradition, it is not clear what exactly Moses wrote (Exod 24:4) and what exactly God wrote (Exod 24:12). There are two discrete things that could have been written. First, God speaks the Ten Commandments (Exod 20:1–17), and then God speaks again and reveals the Covenant Code (Exod 20:22–23:33). Deuteronomy assumes that it is the Ten Commandments that are written by the finger of God, although this is never made explicit in Exodus 24. One might think that it should have been. The Deuteronomist apparently thought so.

A divine plan of the tabernacle finds parallels in Near Eastern literature and elsewhere in the Bible. The Book of Chronicles, for example, applies this notion of God's written instructions for the Solomonic temple as well. When David hands over the commission to build the Temple, he includes *inspired* written plans. David commands Solomon as follows in 1 Chronicles 28:10–12:

> David gave his son Solomon the plan of the porch and its houses, its storerooms and its upper chambers and inner chambers; and of the place of the Ark-cover; *and the plan of all that he had by the spirit*: of the courts of the House of YHWH and all its surrounding chambers, and of the treasuries of the House of God and of the treasuries of the holy things . . .

According to the Book of Chronicles (a Persian period text), the plan of the Temple was allegedly given to David "*by the spirit*," which undoubtedly intended to indicate the divine origin of the plans. Just as it was critical to its legitimacy for the tabernacle to have divinely inspired and *written* plans, so also was it critical for the Jerusalem Temple to have inspired and *written* plans. 1 Kings 8:4 (//2 Chr 5:5) notes that the tabernacle was brought to the Temple at the time of its dedication. This certainly suggests that the divine home was transferred from the tabernacle to the Temple. In fact, the Holy of Holies mirrors some of the features of the tabernacle – most notably the central place of the Ark of the Covenant. Later tradition saw the Temple as incorporating the tabernacle.[14] This is reflected particularly in the Psalms (e.g., 26:8; 27:4; 61:4).

The tabernacle and the later Jerusalem Temple lacked the authority of antiquity as compared to contemporary temples in the ancient world. They could not claim the veneration accorded the god Marduk's temple in Babylon, which could trace its origins to the creation of the world. Still, the Mosaic tabernacle could claim authority *and* antiquity in other ways. Although the tabernacle was not "lowered from heaven" at the creation of the world (as the Babylonian temple had been in the *Enuma Elish*), the central ritual of the tabernacle service – namely, the Sabbath – had also been ordained at the creation of the world.[15] It is surely not coincidental that the Sabbath is included in the prescriptions for the building of the tabernacle (Exod 31:12–17).[16] Thus, God concludes the description for building the tabernacle by reminding Israel: "it shall be a sign for all time between Me and the people of Israel. For in six days YHWH made heaven and earth, and on the seventh day He ceased from work and was refreshed" (v. 17). By including the Sabbath prescription in the magical tablets written by God that describe the design of God's resting place on earth, a claim is made for the antiquity of the tabernacle through its association with the Sabbath.[17]

The centerpiece of the tabernacle plans in Exodus 25–31 was the specifications for building the Ark of the Covenant, which would afterward house the stone tablets. It is indeed of note then that one of the great mysteries of the Bible is the disappearance of the Ark of the Covenant.[18] Along with the ark, the stone tablets disappear. Even more remarkable is the seeming lack of concern for the disappearance of the ark and the tablets. Many theories have been proposed to account for the disappearance of the ark, from the tenth-century invasion by Shishak to the destruction or capture of the ark by Nebuchadnezzar. But we grope because the Bible is seemingly unconcerned with its disappearance! The search for the lost ark is more a modern search, memorialized by Hollywood, than it was a concern of the ancient Israelites. Conveniently, it was just this disappearance of the ark that allowed later Deuteronomic writers to argue that those missing tablets had the Ten Commandments written on them.

The disappearance of the Ark of the Covenant is not just a historical curiosity, it is also a literary phenomenon. Surprisingly, the Ark of the Covenant practically vanishes in the Book of Deuteronomy, where it appears in only two contexts (10:1–8; 31:9, 25–26). This contrasts with the prominent role that the ark plays in the description of the tabernacle in Exodus (where the Hebrew term *arôn*, translated as "ark," appears 26 times), and then in the wilderness wanderings, the conquest-settlement narratives, and the early monarchy. The ark is also central to the founding of the Jerusalem Temple (2 Sam 6, 15; 1 Kgs 2:26; 3:15; 8:1–21). After Solomon dedicates the Temple in 1 Kings 8, however, the ark is never again mentioned in the historical narrative of Kings. The ark seems passé. Whatever significance it bore (e.g., the presence of God), apparently transferred to the Temple.

The reference to the ark in the Book of Jeremiah raises questions about the contents of the ark. In Jeremiah 3:16–17 we read:

> When you have multiplied and increased in the land, in those days, says YHWH, they shall no longer speak of the ark of the covenant of YHWH. It shall not come to mind, or be remembered, or missed; nor shall another one be made. Rather, at that time Jerusalem shall be called the throne of YHWH, and all nations shall gather to it, to the presence of YHWH in Jerusalem.

Why will Judah no longer speak of the ark? Why will no new ark be built? The ark was the symbol of the divine presence on earth – particularly, of God's presence in the tabernacle and then in the Jerusalem Temple. This text suggests that the city of Jerusalem as a whole will replace the ark (and the Temple) as the locale of God's presence. We may recall Jeremiah's Temple Sermon, where Jeremiah warns the citizens of Judah: "Do not trust in these deceptive words: 'This is the temple of YHWH, the temple of YHWH, the temple of YHWH'" (Jer 7:4). Jeremiah warns that the divine nature of the Temple will not save Judah. The ark was both a symbol and the promise of God's protection of the Temple. Jeremiah rejects this adoration of the Temple, but in doing so the prophet hints that the power of the ark was its authorizing the Temple as God's dwelling place. This passage in Jeremiah, of course, does not tell us what was written on the tablets in the ark, but it does cast doubt that the contents were originally understood as the Ten Commandments and the "book of the covenant." By associating the Mosaic law with the ark, the written Mosaic Torah could also become wrapped up with the myth of the tabernacle and the Sabbath. Since the Sabbath was part of the creation of the world according to Genesis, both the tabernacle and the Torah could claim the antiquity of creation by their association with the Sabbath.

In sum, the original contents of the stone tablets written by God seem to have been the divine plans for the tabernacle and Temple. This type of writing is consistent with the role of writing in early, mostly non-literate societies. The revelation to Moses then would have been an oral revelation, as was befitting early Israel. The very fact that Exodus 19–31 describes the teaching as oral and the plans of God's sanctuary as divinely written is rather ancient. For the most part, Exodus 19–31 reflects rather early conceptions about the role of writing in Israelite society. In Exodus 24, however, an account of the writing of the revelation would have been inserted by later editors who were interested in the textualization of religious orthodoxy. This addition notes that Moses wrote down this revelation into the "book of the covenant." This is identified with the same "book of the covenant" that the priest Hilkiah would discover in the temple that led to the Josianic religious reforms. This addition, however, also made it necessary to clarify the relationship between the scroll that Moses wrote and the two stone tablets that God wrote. The Book of Deuteronomy will clarify this for us.

The Second, Written Law at Horeb

The movie vision of Moses with the Ten Commandments on two stone tablets is a product of the Book of Deuteronomy. In English, the word *deuteronomy* means the "second law,"[19] and this title aptly describes the book. The Book of Deuteronomy contains Moses' speeches to Israel just before they cross over into Canaan. These speeches include a lengthy retelling of the Sinai revelation that contains a slightly "improved" version of the law – a law that is now written. We see the written aspect repeatedly mentioned in Deuteronomy, beginning in 4:13: "He declared to you his covenant, which he charged you to observe, that is, the ten commandments; and he wrote them on two stone tablets." Then, in Deuteronomy 5:22: "These words YHWH spoke with a loud voice to your whole assembly at the mountain, out of the fire, the cloud, and the thick darkness, and he added no more. He wrote them on two stone tablets and gave them to me." Deuteronomy 4–5 serve as an explicit retelling (and even commentary) on Exodus 19–20.[20] This becomes a premise of Deuteronomy that is referred to explicitly or implicitly throughout the book (see

Deut 9:10; 10:2–4; 17:18; 27:8). The literary form of Deuteronomy mixes oral and written. Its framework is Moses' farewell *speech* to the people of Israel. The speech recalls the divine revelation as part of a treaty that YHWH made with Israel. It is this latter form – the treaty – that forces the revelation to become fundamentally a written text.

The treaty is a quintessential written text in the Near East. Treaty texts are known from as early as the third millennium B.C.E. in Mesopotamia. The evidence of treaties illustrates an aspect of the complexity of textuality in the ancient Near East. The literary genre of treaties and their binding authority long precedes the Josianic Reforms.[21] In other words, the concept of textual authority is not completely novel. Yet, the power of the written treaty seems to be in invoking the gods as witnesses; that is, there is a numinous and dangerous power to the written treaty. In this respect, the power of the written treaty relies on the magical properties that written texts could have.[22] Scholars have pointed out that the literary form of the Book of Deuteronomy has parallels with the vassal treaties of Esarhaddon, king of Assyria, who ruled from 681–669 B.C.E. Whereas the contents of the Mosaic covenant are divine law and the sworn pledge refers to God, the vassal treaty concerns political stipulations and refers to a human suzerain. Yet, the covenant ceremony formally resembles the situation found in Esarhaddon's treaty. One of the most striking parallels is in the covenantal scene, where in both the entire people are gathered (Deut 29:9–11//Vassal Treaty of Esarhaddon 4–5). In both scenes the gathered take the pledge not only for themselves but also for the future generations (Deut 29:14//Vassal Treaty of Esarhaddon 6–7; also see the Sefire treaty, I A 1–5).[23]

Now we can ask, why is textuality so prominent in Deuteronomy, while it is almost absent in Genesis through Numbers? Fundamentally, it is Deuteronomy that makes the textuality of the Torah a centerpiece of Jewish religion. It is Deuteronomy that makes Judaism a religion of the book. In Exodus, *torah* is oral teaching, whereas in Deuteronomy the *Torah* is written law. Only when we read Exodus through the refracted light of Deuteronomy's interpretation does the significance of a written law become apparent in Exodus 19–24. The Book of Deuteronomy is usually associated with the religious reforms of King Josiah mentioned in 2 Kings 22–23. Central to these religious reforms is the discovery of a scroll – "the book of the covenant" (cf. 2 Kgs 23:2 and Exod 24:7) – which becomes the basis for these religious reforms. Since the reforms seem to correspond quite closely with the religious orthodoxy advocated in Deuteronomy, scholars have often assumed that it was some form of a scroll of Deuteronomy that was discovered in the temple and that became the basis of these textually based religious reforms. From the previous two chapters, we have good reason to believe that the textuality of the Torah actually did become important in the seventh century B.C.E. A rise in literacy followed on the heels of the urbanization of Jerusalem. This rise in literacy profoundly shaped the development of Judean culture in the seventh century and corresponded to seminal changes in the character of Judean religious practice, particularly the emergence of *authoritative written texts*. Thus, written authority could become the basis of religious critique.

The Book of Deuteronomy evidences throughout its reliance on a textual model that presupposes a textual culture.[24] In contrast, the revelation in the Book of Exodus reflects a fundamental orality in Israelite culture. In Deuteronomy, writing is central to the revelation of the Torah, whereas in Exodus, speaking is central to the revelation of the Torah. The Josianic period did indeed mark a turning point in Israel's spiritual life. Although the scribe Ezra circulated and publicized the Book of Torah in the early Second Temple period (Ezr 7:6, 11; Neh 8:1, 4), this was only "an intensification of the process already started at the time of Josiah."[25]

The Continuing Textualization of the Torah

The textualization of the Torah was an ongoing process. For example, the Book of Jubilees, which was written in the mid-second century B.C.E., presents itself as an account of the words revealed to Moses on Mount Sinai. It begins by referring to the tablets given to Moses: "I will give you two stone tablets of the law and of the commandment, which I have written, so that you may teach them" (Jubilees 1:1).[26] Writing is a central element of the process of revelation and gets repeated mention. God tells Moses, "Set your mind on every thing which I shall tell you on this mountain, and write it in a book" (Jub 1:5). Moses is even given an angelic helper who assists in the textualization of the revelation: "And write down for yourself all the matters which I declare to you on this mountain: what (was) in the beginning and what (will be) at the end, . . . And he said to the angel of the presence: 'Write for Moses from the first creation until my sanctuary is built among them for all eternity'" (Jub 1:26–27).

The angel takes the divine tablets (Jub 1:29) and becomes the direct intermediary: "the angel of the presence spoke to Moses by the word of the Lord, saying, 'Write the whole account of creation...'" (Jub 2:1). Moses is copying down things that were first written in heaven: "And you, Moses, write these words because thus it is written and set upon the heavenly tablets as a testimony for eternal generations" (Jub 23:32). The content of the Book of Jubilees loosely follows the narrative from Genesis 1 through Exodus 20. The narrative of Jubilees closes by accounting for both the divine writing and Moses' writing. While exhorting the people to keep the Sabbath, the book ends, "just as it was written in the tablets which he placed in my hands so that I might write for you the law of each time and according to each division of its days" (Jub 50:13). The Sabbath law was written on the original heavenly tablets, and Moses wrote down the expansion and application of this divine law. In this way, Jubilees accounts for both the divinely written tablets and the Mosaic composition in a much more elegant and premeditated way than the Book of Exodus or even Deuteronomy.

Another example of textualization of Torah is the so-called Temple Scroll, which was found among the manuscripts of the Dead Sea Scrolls.[27] This text was apparently written by the religious sectarians who came to live in the region of Khirbet Qumran during the mid-second century B.C.E. The text is apparently an early composition of that community. The contents of the text largely parallel the canonical Book of Deuteronomy, although there is a striking change in the voice. The Book of Deuteronomy is cast as a speech of Moses, written in the third person. Thus, the Book of Deuteronomy is an account of Moses' farewell speech where Moses summarizes the Exodus experience and the content of God's revelation to him on Mount Sinai. Deuteronomy has only Moses' account of God's revelation on Mount Sinai. But what did God literally say to Moses? The Temple Scroll fills in this gap. Like the Book of Jubilees, the Temple Scroll textualizes an important gap in the revelation from Mount Sinai.

The writing down of the Mishnah, that is, the oral Torah, in the third century C.E. is paradoxically another example of the textualization of the revelation at Mount Sinai. According to the *Sayings of the Fathers*, "Moses received Torah at Sinai and handed it on to Joshua, Joshua to elders, and elders to prophets, and prophets handed it on to the men of the great assembly" (M. Avot 1:1). This is the oral *Torah*, but it is now a text. The *Sayings* might have continued that the oral Torah was committed to writing by Rabbi Judah, the prince, in the third century C.E. The ideology of orality implicit in the oral Torah kept it from being textualized until the third century C.E., but, in the end, even the oral Torah is textualized (see Chapter 10). The irony is that this later textualization of oral Torah in Rabbinic Judaism recalls the earlier textualization of revelation from Exodus to Deuteronomy. Perhaps this is the tyranny of writing, namely, that it continually imposes itself on oral tradition.

The process of textualization (as I have described it) is certainly more complicated than the simple diachronic development. It is not a simple linear historical process. The roles of text and oral tradition in ancient Israel and formative Judaism are complex. There is also an ongoing relationship and tension between oral tradition (eventually, oral Torah) and written Torah. This tension reflects the different social communities of ancient Israel and formative Judaism. As I suggested in the previous chapter, the Josianic (and Deuteronomic) reform was a backlash against the urban and priestly elites by the "people of the land." The *Torah* was critiqued as deriving from "the lying pen of the scribes" (Jer 8:8). On the other hand, oral tradition (i.e., "custom," *mishpat*, Jer 8:7) and the oral prophetic word (*davar*) were hailed as the true wisdom (Jer 8:9). In other words, the prophet Jeremiah was already sensitive to the rising importance of the written Torah, which was used by the religious elites (the lying scribes) to control orthodoxy. The written texts naturally completed and eventually replaced oral tradition. Although the oral tradition would continually reassert itself, it would always be supplanted by the process of textualization.

8

Writing in Exile

The Babylonian exile is where the waters part in the history of Israel. In a series of military campaigns, the Babylonian armies decimated Judah, burned the city of Jerusalem, and ravaged the economy of the region. The first campaign came in 597 B.C.E. At that time, the Babylonians deported a large number of Judeans (2 Kgs 24:14), including the royal family of Jehoiachin (v. 12). A second campaign resulted in the burning of Jerusalem and the countryside in 586 B.C.E. (2 Kgs 25:8–12). The Babylonians set up a provisional government, and in 581 B.C.E. the Babylonians returned and took another group of Judeans into exile (Jer 52:30). Throughout the exile, however, the Judean royal family lived in comfort in the royal citadel of Babylon. They were supplied generous rations by the Babylonian government, and they maintained their claims as the legitimate rulers of Judah. Although the Babylonian conquests and exiles decimated the Judean people, the scribal infrastructure of the royal family remained intact during the Babylonian exile and into the early Persian period. In the troubled days following the Babylonian invasions writing returned to state control under the exiled royal family in Babylon.

The "exile" divides history. Even the terminology – we speak of pre-exilic and post-exilic periods – reflects this division. Although the Babylonian exile is often thought of as one event, it was a long and devastating process. According to Jewish tradition, prophecy ends shortly after the destruction of the Temple and the end of the Hebrew kingdom. The exile also will be a watershed for the collecting and editing of ancient Israelite literature into a book that we call the Bible. Has too much been made of the exile? Can too much be made of the exile? Was the exile a formative period for the composition of the Bible or a dark age? Did the crisis of the exile result in the collecting and editing of biblical literature?

One of the most influential higher critics of the nineteenth century, Julius Wellhausen, used the exile as a defining event in his analysis of Israelite religion and the composition of the Bible. Wellhausen's historical and literary analyses helped elevate the exile to its dominating role in biblical criticism. One biblical scholar has even suggested that it would be fair to say that Wellhausen discovered the exile.[1] The exile was also a turning point for the Hebrew language. Biblical texts written before the exile are described as "Classical Hebrew," or "Standard Biblical Hebrew," whereas later biblical texts (such as Ezra-Nehemiah, Daniel, and Esther) are categorized as "Late Biblical Hebrew."[2] The exile radically altered the political, religious, and cultural institutions of ancient Israel.

Over the past century, scholars have tended to see the exile as the formative period for the writing, collecting, and editing of biblical literature. In his classic work *Exile and Restoration*, Peter Ackroyd contended that the exilic period was marked by intense and creative literary activity.[3] Supposedly, the exile provoked a creative burst of literary energy, part of which was a reaction to the pathos of the destruction of Jerusalem. But the catastrophe also led Judeans to preserve the traditions of society through writing. However, this seems an overdrawn construction. One would expect exile to invite retrenchment rather than intense literary activity. Moreover, the suggestion that writing was a natural response to the attempt to preserve culture is clearly a modern outlook, the reaction of a culture that presumes textuality. Ancient Israel, however, was a society of emerging textuality at the end of the Judean monarchy. Writing was not necessarily the natural cultural response to catastrophe as it would become in a post-Gutenberg world.

Before addressing the role of writing after the exile directly, we must take some time to sketch a picture of the exilic period in Judah. What were Jerusalem and Judah like during the Babylonian period? Outside of the Bible itself, do we have evidence that would suggest that the social setting existed for an intense and creative literary flourishing? The sixth century in Judah – that is, the exilic period – has been associated with what has been called the axial age of ancient civilizations.[4] Scholars have long considered the sixth century one of the more creative periods in world history.[5] It is also the time during which the Greek philosophers and such biblical figures as Jeremiah and Ezekiel were active. The Babylonian exile certainly was a catalyst for dramatic changes in the history of the

Jewish people, but did it make for a period of intense literary activity? Probably not.

Even though traditional scholarship has emphasized the importance of the exile, some scholars have always questioned whether too much has been made of the period. No critic of the exile and its place in biblical scholarship has been more fierce than C. C. Torrey, especially in his work *Ezra Studies* published in 1910. Torrey argued that the exile was essentially a fiction created by Jewish scribes of the late Persian period. He wrote, "The terms 'exilic,' 'pre-exilic,' and 'post-exilic' ought to be banished forever from usage, for they are merely misleading, and correspond to nothing that is real in Hebrew literature and life."[6] Torrey's interpretation has been resurrected in several recent works. For instance, in *The Myth of the Empty Land,* Hans Barstad cautiously invokes Torrey's conclusions, although he often considers them extreme.[7] Torrey also resurfaces in the volume of essays from the European Seminar in Historical Methodology entitled *Leading Captivity Captive: "The Exile" as Ideology and History.* Perhaps Torrey's most vocal supporter in this volume is the biblical scholar Robert Carroll, who writes that he would like to have the sentence of Torrey's quoted earlier "emblazoned on all biblical history textbooks."[8] Carroll – a fiery Irish scholar – was particularly sensitive to the potential for biblically centered approaches to history to politically and socially marginalize groups. He was concerned that such an approach left out much of the social and cultural history of Palestine as well as of the Jewish people. Indeed, although the conventional nomenclature of the academic disciplines has been framed by the Bible, there is much more to the history of Palestine than is found on the pages of the Bible. This is one contribution that this approach can offer. Still, when we consider carefully the growing archaeological evidence, it is foolhardy to downplay the enormous impact of the Babylonian conquest and exiles upon life in Judah and upon the writing of biblical literature.

The Fury of Babylon

Recent archaeological investigations have increasingly laid bare the fury of the Babylonian destruction of Jerusalem, Judah, and the entire Levant. The literary evidence also points to the devastating impact of the Babylonians upon the Levant. The archaeologist Ephraim Stern, a professor at the Hebrew University in Jerusalem, contrasts the Babylonian presence with the Assyrian presence in Palestine:

> The Babylonians waged far fewer military campaigns for the domination of Palestine than the Assyrians, and the number of written sources at our disposal describing these is likewise much smaller. However, the results of the Babylonian conquest were, by all measures, far more destructive, and brought the once-flourishing country to one of the lowest ebbs in its long history.[9]

From Jerusalem's perspective, "the fury that was Babylon" might be an apt retitling of the Assyriologist H. Saggs's classic work, *The Greatness that Was Babylon*. Despite recent tendencies to dismiss or downplay the exile,[10] the scope and ferocity of the Babylonian conquest are becoming clearer with each new archaeological investigation.

There was some continuity after the Babylonian exiles. We know, for example, that the Babylonians appointed a provisional governor over the province in 586 B.C.E. A provisional center in the town of Mizpah was set up to the north of Jerusalem, which – unlike the rest of Judah – was largely unscathed by the Babylonian military campaigns; Mizpah apparently functioned throughout the short period of Babylonian rule.[11] According to 2 Kings 25:12, the Babylonians left "the poorest of the land to be vinedressers and tillers of the soil." Nebuchadnezzar appointed a certain Gedaliah ben Ahikam over the region after the destruction of Jerusalem and the Babylonian exile (see 2 Kgs 25:22–23; Jer 40:7).[12] Gedaliah, however, was assassinated shortly after he was installed (2 Kgs 25:25; Jer 41:1–3). Fearing Babylonian reprisals, the conspirators eventually fled to Egypt. Mizpah apparently continued to serve as a regional capital, and when the Persians overthrew the Babylonian Empire, many returnees settled in this region north of Jerusalem (e.g., Ezra 2:21–28; note Neh 3:7).

The biblical scholar Hans Barstad had this continuity in mind in his important and oft-cited monograph with its provocative title, *The Myth of the Empty Land*. Barstad emphasizes the continuity in the material culture of Judah during the Babylonian period (ca. 586–538 B.C.E.). He suggests that most of the people remained in the region after the campaigns of Nebuchadnezzar.[13] Robert Carroll takes an even more extreme position: "At this juncture in history the land lost some people; very much a minority of people, even important people of status were deported. *Most people lived on in the land as if nothing, except the burning of Jerusalem, had happened*" [emphasis added].[14] If this were actually the case, then it would follow that substantive production of biblical literature could have taken place in Judah during the Babylonian period.[15] The problem is that this was not actually the case.

After 586 B.C.E. did life really continue in Judah in much the same way as before? Is it true that the Babylonian conquests and exiles of Judah had only a minimal impact on the Judean people? Two assumptions underline critiques of the exile. The first assumption is that the majority of the people were left in the country at the end of the Babylonian period – in other words, that the demographic picture changed very little. The second assumption is that the life of the Judean people continued much as usual. Neither proposition stands up to scrutiny. In fact, the demographic changes in Judah were quite profound, reflecting a massive depopulation.[16] The land was not emptied, but it was depopulated. Moreover, every cultural institution of Judean life changed. There was no more Davidic king. There was no Temple. According to biblical tradition (Dan 1:3–4), the scribal infrastructure was exiled as well. Even the language that the people spoke changed, from Hebrew to Aramaic. To be sure, the everyday life of the peasant in Yehud was perhaps not much different under the Babylonians or Persians than it had been under the Davidic kings – that is, the life for those few peasants who were not either killed in war, exiled to Babylon, or forced to flee from economic blight and social chaos.

The trauma of the Babylonian conquest and exile was profound in Judah. Although the material culture definitely continued after 586 B.C.E., the end of the Davidic monarchy and the destruction and pillaging of the Jerusalem Temple alone suggest that basic social organizations did not remain the same. Government and religious institutions were transformed. In his comparative sociological studies of the exile, Daniel Smith-Christopher shows just how far-reaching and profound the experience of exile was for ancient Israel.[17] Prophets like Ezekiel and literature like the Book of Lamentations express the deep psychological impact of the trauma of exile. Furthermore, Barstad's work underscores the way that the later collective memory of the Jewish people creates the event of the exile and emphasizes the totality of this catastrophe. This telescoping of the exile into a single event reflects psychological and ideological factors in later literature; however, the acute psychological trauma, the social dislocation, and the economic devastation were profound and lasting.

The land was much emptier by the end of the Babylonian period than recent critics of the exile have realized. As a result, it is difficult to imagine that there were the social conditions in antiquity that would encourage a great literary flourishing. The Babylonian invasions were savage and ruthless.[18] The Babylonians then largely abandoned the ravaged land, in contrast to the Assyrians, who re-populated exiled regions.[19] It took centuries to recover.

Archaeologists have done extensive surveys of settlement patterns for this period. From these surveys, a relative assessment of the demographics can be made. For example, in the seventh century B.C.E. (at the end of the monarchy), there were at least 116 settled sites (cities, towns, and villages) in Judah. In the sixth century B.C.E. (the Babylonian period), the number drops to 41 sites. Even more striking is that 92 of the 116 sites of the late monarchic period were abandoned in the Babylonian period.[20] Eighty percent of the cities, towns, and villages were either abandoned or destroyed in the sixth century. Many of the towns and villages of the Persian period (42%, i.e., 17 of 41) were settled at previously virgin locations, reflecting a profound disjunction in the population. Moreover, the average size of the sites has shrunk, from 4.4 hectares to 1.4 hectares – a 70 percent reduction. Not only was Jerusalem burned, but most large cities disappear from Judah proper. In general, there is a population shift from the cities to villages.

Excavations of cities such as Jerusalem, Lachish, Gezer, and Megiddo testify to great conflagrations set by the Babylonians in Palestine.[21] And the depopulation trend continued throughout the Babylonian period.[22] Moreover, pottery assemblages and distribution patterns change dramatically at the beginning of the Babylonian period.[23] Only a few sites north of Jerusalem show significant continuity, particularly Mizpah, the center of the Babylonian provincial government. In short, by the end of the Babylonian period few people lived in Judah. Those who remained were "the poorest of the land" and lived in small towns and villages. The economy was essentially one of subsistence farming and pastoralism.

The Babylonian policy in their campaigns to the west was brutal.[24] Rather than attempt to implement a policy that would exploit the region as a province,[25] the Babylonians systematically pillaged the land. Evidence of Babylonian destruction in Judah and the surrounding area is overwhelming. In the last days of its monarchy, Judah was a relatively densely populated, economically prosperous, urban state.

Everything changed in the Babylonian period. The region had little to make it economically viable outside of pastoralism and marginal agriculture.[26] Nor could the region sustain its seventh-century population so the deportations were compounded by economic flight, mostly to Egypt where large Jewish communities suddenly appear. Did life continue in *much the same way*? I think not.

Was the Babylonian period in Judah really the social setting for intense and creative literary activity? This hardly seems likely. Another measure of the changes brought on by the Babylonians was the precipitous decline in public works. Likewise, there is also a decline in luxury items indicative of a prosperous economy.[27] This is precisely the type of archaeological evidence that would indicate the existence of the social infrastructure necessary for writing. In antiquity, writing needed a prosperous urban economy in order to thrive. There is no evidence of such a flourishing urban economy in the Judean hills before the third century B.C.E. Thus, we have very little inscriptional evidence of writing (particularly Hebrew writing) during the Babylonian period.[28] This is as we would expect since most of the settlements in Judah proper were no more than small agrarian or pastoral villages.

The possibility of major literary activity during the exilic period gets bleaker as we delve deeper. Conventional approaches to the history of Syria-Palestine leave out much of the social and cultural history. In particular, the conventional nomenclature of "exile" has failed to account for all the facets of the process of destruction and depopulation that occurred in the sixth century B.C.E. following the Babylonian invasions. We must paint a much broader picture of the "exile" than did the biblical authors. Archaeology must take a leading role in enlarging our canvas. To be sure, the archaeology of the Babylonian period is tricky business, especially since the era lasts less than fifty years. Archaeology is often not well suited to isolating such short periods or identifying events; it is better suited to describing processes. Literature tends to enshrine events, like the falling of the Berlin Wall as the end of the Cold War, whereas archaeology helps us uncover the underlying and more complex processes.

What kind of government infrastructure did the Babylonians put in place in Judah? Could it have provided the context for substantial literary activity in Judah? We know very little about this period in Israel. It was the beginning of a dark age for the history of the region. In the present context, the absence of evidence indicates the general

Babylonian lack of interest in developing the region economically. According to the Book of Kings, the Babylonians set up a provisional government under Gedaliah in 586 B.C.E. (2 Kgs 25:22–26; Jer 40:5–41:18). According to the Book of Jeremiah, Gedaliah was among the supporters of the prophet Jeremiah (Jer 39:14), and Jeremiah had advocated submission to the Babylonians. Gedaliah's provisional government was in Mizpah because Jerusalem had been completely destroyed. But Gedaliah's support for the Babylonians soon caused his demise: a group of Judean rebels assassinated Gedaliah and killed the Babylonian troops stationed at Mizpah (Jer 41:1–2). These events all seem to have transpired in the same year that Gedaliah was appointed. A few years later, around 581 B.C.E., the Babylonians apparently ordered a third deportation (Jer 52:30). Other than these gleanings from biblical literature, we have little direct knowledge about events in Judah during the sixth century until the beginning of the Persian rule. Is there any evidence for writing in Hebrew during the exilic period in Judah? Outside of alleged texts in the Bible, the answer is no. There are no Hebrew inscriptions that have been dated conclusively to the Babylonian period (586–539 B.C.E.).[29] Whichever poor Judeans remained in the land would have been fortunate to eek out a marginal subsistence. They certainly were not part of any great literary flourishing.

"Mozah" Stamps point to changes in the administrative language of the region. They are a significant corpus of the impressions of the word "Mozah" that were stamped on wet clay pots before the pots were fired. Mozah, a small town northwest of Jerusalem, was known for its clay and probably was a center of pottery production. "Mozah" Stamps are sometimes dated to the neo-Babylonian period in Judah; however, competent scholars have given dates ranging from the sixth century to the fourth century B.C.E.[30] The main argument for a neo-Babylonian date for them is simply that the stamps have been found mostly in excavations of the city of Mizpah, which was the center of government in the Babylonian period. However, Mizpah continued to be an administrative center in the Persian period, so this is not a decisive argument. Most likely, the stamps date to the late sixth century and the early fifth. More interesting for this study is that the stamps use Aramaic (not Hebrew) script, even though they were produced locally. This points to the transition from Hebrew to Aramaic as an administrative language, which had already began in the neo-Babylonian period. In other words, scribal schools in the sixth through fourth centuries B.C.E. would be teaching young apprentices to write and to read Aramaic.

By the Rivers of Babylon

The plight of Judah was bleak, but was the situation in exile much better? Could Babylonian exile have been the setting for a literary flourishing? Perhaps not, but there certainly seems to have been some literary activity during the exilic period.

In his recent book on the exile, Daniel Smith-Christopher identifies a tendency among scholars "to presume a tame, even if not entirely comfortable existence...."[31] The great German biblical scholar Martin Noth, for example, points out that the exiles were not prisoners, but merely a compulsorily transplanted population who could move about freely in their daily life.[32] It has also been argued that the exiles were not slaves – at least from the perspective of Babylonian jurisprudence.[33] An often cited, but largely irrelevant, source for the exilic period is the Murashu Archive.[34] The Murashu Archive is an important corpus of late fifth century B.C.E. legal documents from the city of Nippur in central Mesopotamia. The archive contains records of business transactions by the Murashu family or by their employees. These texts, written in Aramaic and Akkadian, mention about eighty distinctively Jewish personal names (Shabbatai, Minyamin, Haggai). These people are presumed to be descendants of the Judean exiles who were still living in Babylonia in the late fifth century B.C.E. (i.e., in the days of Ezra and Nehemiah). Little seems to distinguish them from other people mentioned in the archive,[35] but these texts are so much later than the exile that they are only relevant for understanding Persian rule in the middle Euphrates region during the late fifth century.

The neo-Babylonian empire required the deportation of massive populations for its building programs. Robert McCormick Adam's archaeological survey of central Mesopotamia discovered pronounced increases in the population of the region. He concluded that these increases were due to massive involuntary transfers of people from the Babylonian conquests. These transfers apparently included three separate deportations of Judeans to Babylon (Jer 52:28–30). The Babylonians seem to have tried to rehabilitate this desolate region by populating it with captives. We now have Babylonian texts that confirm that at least some of the Judean exiles were deported to the central Euphrates region.[36] Babylonian sources suggest that these exiles lived together in a "Judean village." They were not citizens of the empire; they were isolated in a type of labor camp.

Biblical descriptions of the exile hardly suggest that the experience was benign. Smith-Christopher has compiled what he calls the "lexicography of trauma" from biblical literature. Here he points to the frequent use of words like "bonds" (*môserâ*; Nah 1:13; Is 52:2; Ps 107:14) and "fetters" (*zîqqîm*; Nah 3:10; Isa 45:14; Ps 149:8; Jer 40:1) to describe the exile. The terms for imprisonment and bondage become metaphors for it. Moreover, the slavery in Egypt becomes an increasingly important historical metaphor for the experience of the Babylonian exiles.[37] The despair of the exiles is captured by the psalmists. In Psalm 137:1–4, for instance, we read:

> By the rivers of Babylon – there we sat down and there we wept when we remembered Zion. On the willows there we hung up our harps. For there our captors asked us for songs, and our tormentors asked for mirth, saying, "Sing us one of the songs of Zion!" How could we sing YHWH's song in a foreign land?

It is difficult to imagine that the situation for the exiles was anything but gloomy. The psalms depict the exiles as prisoners and slaves, tormented by their overlords. Psalm 79 gives a graphic emotional depiction of the experience:

> 1 O God, the nations have come into your inheritance;
> they have defiled your holy temple;
> they have laid Jerusalem in ruins.
> 2 They have given the bodies of your servants to the birds of the air for food,
> the flesh of your faithful to the wild animals of the earth.
> 3 They have poured out their blood like water all around Jerusalem,
> and there was no one to bury them.
> 4 We have become a taunt to our neighbors,
> mocked and derided by those around us....
> 11 Let the groans of the prisoners come before you;
> according to your great power preserve those doomed to die.

Likewise, the entire Book of Lamentations depicts the destruction of Jerusalem and the trauma of the exile. The exiles are described as completely demoralized:

> Judah has gone into exile with suffering and hard servitude;
> she lives now among the nations, and finds no resting place;
> her pursuers have all overtaken her in the midst of her distress. (Lam 1:3)

> My eyes are spent with weeping; my stomach churns;
> my bile is poured out on the ground because of the destruction of my people, because infants and babes faint in the streets of the city. (Lam 2:11)

Why have you forgotten us completely?
Why have you forsaken us these many days? (Lam 5:20)

The five chapters of Lamentations are an extended liturgical dirge bemoaning the fate of Jerusalem and its people after the Babylonian destruction.[38] Such literature must be taken as a reflection of the pathos of people traumatized by exile and destruction. Many such songs of the a people's despair were likely composed during the exile. But songs don't require scribes. When this dirge and other psalms were actually written down is another problem. It is impossible to say. They did not necessarily require pen and parchment. These songs merely required the pathos of a people.

The Royal Family and the Royal Archives in Exile

Biblical poetry captures many heartfelt expressions of the exilic period. What is missing, however, is a sustained prose account of the exilic period.[39] The social condition of the exiles simply did not lend itself to encouraging sustained prose narratives. Rather, we have oral literature. We have the poetry of the psalms and the prophets that describe the plight of the exiles – "If I forget you, O Jerusalem, let my right hand wither!" (Psalm 137:5). There are three brief prose accounts dealing with aspects of and individuals in exile. The first, which I mentioned earlier, is the brief story of Gedaliah, who was appointed by the Babylonians as governor of the region after Jerusalem's destruction and assassinated a few months later. The second is the short account of King Jehoiachin at the end of the Book of Kings (with an almost exact parallel account at the end of the Book of Jeremiah). Finally, there is the story of the prophets Jeremiah and Ezekiel, which will be tied to the fate of King Jehoiachin in Babylon. Where did this literature come from? How and why was it preserved?

The critical figure for answering the what, how, and why questions about writing during exile is King Jehoiachin. The Book of Kings ends with a short prose account of the fate of the last kings of Judah. Central to the narrative is the fate of King Jehoiachin in Babylon. In fact, the Book of Kings ends with this king's release from prison. The question is why? Why is the fate of King Jehoiachin, a prisoner in Babylon for some thirty-seven years before his release in 550 B.C.E., so important to this narrative of the exile? The obvious answer is that this same Jehoiachin was behind the writing of the Bible during the exile.

Who is this Jehoiachin, and how does he figure in the writing of the Bible? The answers to these questions begin with an understanding of some of the political intrigues at the end of the Judean monarchy that continued into the exile. Josiah's opposition to Pharaoh Neco, when Neco marches to battle against the Babylonians at Carchemish in 609 B.C.E., allies Josiah with King Nebuchadnezzar (II) of Babylon. After Pharaoh Neco kills King Josiah at Megiddo in 609 B.C.E., the "people of the land" place Jehoahaz on the throne in Jerusalem (2 Kgs 23:30). Jehoahaz, the son of Josiah, who was himself placed on the throne by popular acclaim, apparently shared his father's anti-Egypt sentiments. As a result, the Egyptians replace Jehoahaz with Jehoiakim. Jehoahaz is taken to Egypt where he dies, apparently under house arrest (2 Kgs 23:33–34). Jehoiakim remains the loyal vassal of Egypt, setting up a larger rivalry between Egypt and Babylon over control of the Judean throne.

Jehoiakim reigned eleven years in Jerusalem, from 608–597 B.C.E. His allegiances flip-flopped between Egypt and Babylon. He began as a loyal vassal of the Egyptians, who had set him up on the throne. After the Egyptians lost a battle at Carchemish to the Babylonians in 605 B.C.E., Jehoiakim switched his allegiance to the Babylonians. Later in his reign, with Egyptian support, Jehoiakim rebelled against the Babylonians. But Jehoiakim died shortly before the Babylonian siege of Jerusalem in 597 B.C.E. This left his son, Jehoiachin, as king in Judah with the Babylonian army approaching the gates of Jerusalem. According to the Book of Kings, "King Jehoiachin of Judah gave himself up to the king of Babylon, himself, his mother, his servants, his officers, and his palace officials" (2 Kgs 24:12). The Babylonians placed Jehoiachin's uncle, Zedekiah, on the throne in Jerusalem while the king, the royal family, the servants of the royal family, and the palace officials accompanied Jehoiachin into captivity in Babylon. (Remember that Jehoiachin's grandfather, Jehoahaz, was apparently still a prisoner in Egypt.) The Book of Kings ends by telling the reader about the eventual release of Jehoiachin (2 Kgs 25:27–30):

> In the thirty-seventh year of the exile of King Jehoiachin of Judah, in the twelfth month, on the twenty-seventh day of the month, King Evil-merodach of Babylon, in the year that he began to reign, released King Jehoiachin of Judah from prison; he spoke kindly to him, and gave him a seat above the other seats of the kings who were with him in Babylon. So Jehoiachin put aside his prison clothes. Every day of his life he dined regularly in the king's presence. For his allowance, a regular allowance was given him by the king, a portion every day, as long as he lived.

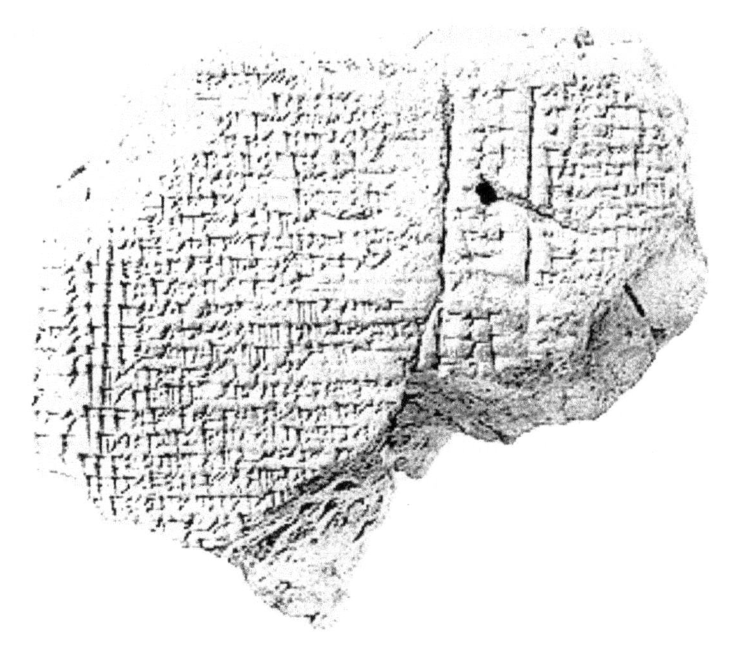

Figure 8.1. Cuneiform Tablet (Babylon 28178) Listing Rations for Jehoiachin (after Weidner)

Clearly, the Book of Kings considered Jehoiachin the true king of Judah. But there were apparently three living kings! Jehoiachin was exiled in Babylon, Jehoahaz was exiled in Egypt, and Zedekiah was king on the throne in Jerusalem. This situation would overshadow the preservation and writing of biblical literature during the sixth century B.C.E. For the royal family of Jehoiachin and the palace scribes would shape the collection, editing, writing, and preservation of biblical literature.

The biblical account of the fate of Jehoiachin and the royal family was essentially corroborated by an archive of 290 clay tablets excavated in the 1930s (see Figure 8.1).[40] These texts, written in cuneiform, were found in the vaults below one of the public buildings near the famous Ishtar Gate leading into the city of Babylon. They date from the years 595 to 570 B.C.E. and list payments of rations in oil and barley to prominent political prisoners from Nebuchadnezzar's military campaigns. Most important for us is the record of payments to "Jehoiachin, king of Judah" (or, as it is transcribed from the Akkadian cuneiform writing, *ana* ^{I}*ya'ukinu šarri ša* ^{KUR}*yaḫudu*). These texts continue to call Jehoiachin "the king of Judah." He was treated as royalty, even though he was under house arrest by the Babylonians. Rations are supplied to Jehoiachin, the princes of Judah, and the royal Judean entourage. One representative list (Figure 8.1) may be translated as follows:

6 liters[41] (of oil) for J[eh]oiachin, king of the land of Judah
2 1/2 liters for the 5 princes of Judah
4 liters for the 8 men of Judah

These individuals are given monthly rations in oil, which was an exchange commodity that could be traded. It served the same function as money. Most importantly, the king of Judah receives a substantially larger amount of oil than the standard ration, which probably reflects both his relative status and the size of his household. In addition, the Judean princes and the royal entourage still receive a standard ration. The standard allotment throughout the lists seems to have been 1/2 liter of oil per month. According to the Babylonian lists, the five young Judean princes have an attendant named Keniah, who received the supplies for them. The royal entourage includes "8 men of Judah." Presumably, some of these were the servants, officers, and palace officials who surrendered to Nebuchadnezzar and were placed under house arrest along with Jehoiachin. This royal entourage may have lived in the southern citadel of Babylon (see Figure 8.2).[42] Jehoiachin probably also served as a counselor to King Nebuchadnezzar, giving information as required about this remote region of the Babylonian Empire. It is out of this royal family, and the support afforded them in the Babylonian court, that the preservation and writing of biblical literature continued, though on a limited basis, in the exilic period.

The fate of Jehoiachin is the central theme to the end of the Book of Kings. Second Kings 24–25 are essentially a late appendix to the Book of Kings. This ending focuses on the fate of the two last Judean kings – Jehoiachin and Zedekiah. It begins with Jehoiachin's exile to Babylon. Zedekiah, the uncle of Jehoichin, is then set up as puppet king by the Babylonians, but he rebels against the Babylonians and meets a gory fate. The Babylonians "slaughtered the sons of Zedekiah before his eyes, then put out the eyes of Zedekiah; they bound him in fetters and took him to Babylon" (2 Kgs 25:7). Jehoiachin, in contrast, had surrendered to the Babylonians. As a result, according to the last verse of the Book of Kings, this king of Judah dines at the table of the Babylonian kings. Who is telling this tale? Why is it being told? This appendix to the Book of Kings justifies Jehoiachin's apparent

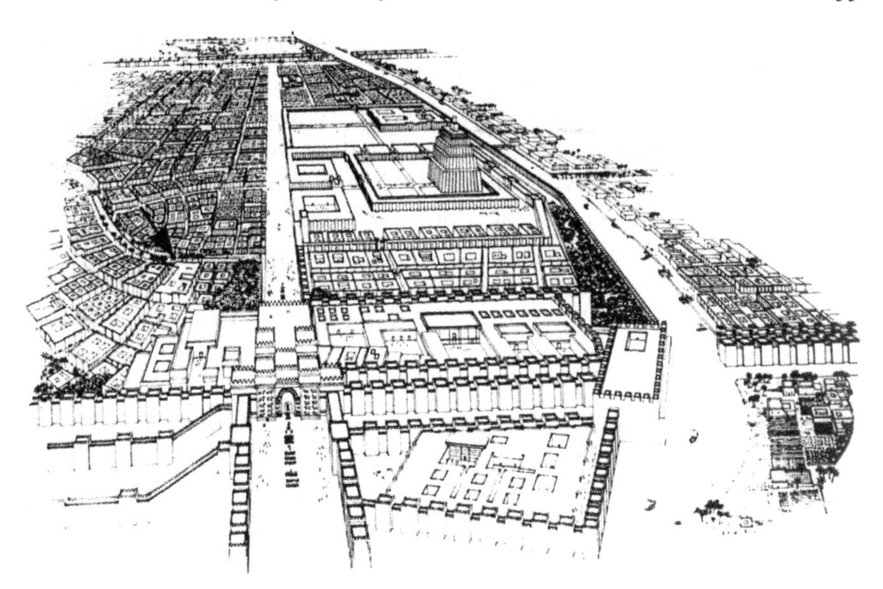

Figure 8.2. Home of the Royal Judean Family (arrow) in Babylon (adapted from the original drawing by Vic Mitchell and published by A. Millard, *Treasures from Bible Times* [Herts, Eng.: Lion Publishing, 1985], p. 135)

cowardice. Instead of standing up against the Babylonians like his father and uncle, he surrenders and receives the royal treatment in Babylon. Eventually, even his freedom is restored.

The historical narrative in the Book of Kings had originally concluded with the account of King Josiah. Scholars have made this determination based on several considerations. First, the book's rigid narrative structure of ascension formulas and death-burial changes before the death of Josiah. Apparently, Josiah's death was not part of the original narrative. When the appendix was added, completing the narrative of the monarchy and telling the fate of Jehoiachin, the new writer uses a different narrative structure. This is further borne out by the fact that the prophetess Huldah, a central figure supporting Josiah's reforms in the Book of Kings, had predicted that Josiah would die peacefully (2 Kgs 22:19–20). Josiah, however, dies in battle (2 Kgs 23:29). From a narrative point of view, Josiah's death disrupts the rigid structure of the placement of the death-burial notices that had characterized the Book of Kings until this point in the narrative. What does the appendix contribute? The new ending of the Book of Kings essentially absolves Jehioachin from wrongdoing, justifies his surrender to the Babylonians, and confirms his status as the legitimate king of Judah even while dining in the palace of Babylon.

One curious aspect about the ending of the Book of Kings is its relationship with the Book of Jeremiah; 2 Kings 24:18–25:21 is largely paralleled by Jeremiah 52. In Modechai Cogan and Hayim Tadmor's commentary on the Book of Kings, they note that "the Deuteronomistic evaluation of Jehoiakim (Jer 52:2) and the manner in which the punishment by exile is presented (Jer 52:3, 7) are hallmarks of the Book of Kings and not Jeremiah."[43] This still does not answer the question of why? Why does Jeremiah 52 largely copy the ending of the Book of Kings?

One of the strangest stories in the composition of biblical literature is the Book of Jeremiah. We essentially have two different "books of Jeremiah." *A* book of Jeremiah (not *the* canonical Book of Jeremiah) was completed before the third Babylonian exile of the Judeans in 582 B.C.E. This book is actually hinted at within the canonical Book of Jeremiah itself: "I will bring upon that land all the words that I have spoken against it, everything that is written within this scroll, which Jeremiah prophesied against all the nations" (Jer 25:13). This scroll of Jeremiah then suffered two different fates. One (shorter, non-canonical) book of Jeremiah was apparently edited in Egypt and later became the basis for the Greek translation of the Book of Jeremiah (known as the "Septuagint," or LXX). This non-canonical version will not concern us here. The longer, canonical Jeremiah was edited in Babylon under the auspices of the exiled Judean royal court.

The editing of Jeremiah can be instructive for understanding the composition of biblical literature during the exile.[44] For this reason, it is worthwhile to delve into some technical observations. Let us begin by looking at the shaping of the Book of Jeremiah that is represented in most English Bible translations. This version is about one-sixth longer than the Greek version of Jeremiah. Verses present in this Masoretic Hebrew text but missing in the Greek Septuagint include Jer 2:1; 7:1; 8:11–12; 10:6–8; 11:7; 17:1–4; 25:13b–14; 27:1, 7, 13, 17, 21; 29:6, 16–20; 30:10–11, 22; 33:14–26; 39:4–13 (//Jer 52:4–16); 46:1; 49:6. The order of Hebrew (MT) and Greek (LXX) texts is largely the same until chapter 25. At this point, the Greek text is organized in a significantly different way. Table 8.1 summarizes the organizational differences between the Hebrew (MT) and Greek (LXX) texts.

The fact that for both versions chapters 1–25 are identical in their order suggests that this arrangement of the composition was already

Table 8.1. *Differences in the Hebrew Masoretic Text (MT) and the Greek Septuagint (LXX) of Jeremiah*

Hebrew (MT)	Greek (LXX)
1–25:13a	1–25:13a
25:13b–38	32:13b–38
26–45	33–51
46	26
47	29
48	31
49:1–6	30:17–21/22
49:7–22	30:1–16
49:23–27	30:29–33
49:28–33	30:23–28
49:34–39	25:14–20
50–51 Babylon	27–28
52	52

set when the second half of the book began to be edited after the exile. The order in the second half of the book is dramatically different, although the content of the oracles is largely identical. Since the text of the oracles is practically the same in both the Hebrew and Greek, they must have been already written down but not arranged into a complete literary composition when the two "books" of Jeremiah went their separate ways. The additions in the longer (and canonical) version of Jeremiah thus should be instructive as to the setting of the composition.

In the conclusion of the Book of Kings, Jehoiachin is depicted as essentially following the counsel of Jeremiah. According to the Book of Jeremiah, the prophet had foreseen the eventual destruction of Jerusalem and Judah by the Babylonians (Jer 21). He advised that destruction was inevitable because of the sins of King Manasseh:

> Then YHWH said to me: "Even if Moses and Samuel stood before me, yet my heart would not turn toward this people. Send them out of my sight, and let them go! . . . I will make them a horror to all the kingdoms of the earth because of what King Manasseh son of Hezekiah of Judah did in Jerusalem." (Jer 15:1, 4)

Jeremiah and the appendix to the Book of Kings share this explanation of Judah's exile. This explanation is made clear from the very beginning of the appendix to Kings: "Surely this came upon Judah at the command of YHWH, to remove them out of his sight, for the sins of Manasseh, for all that he had committed" (2 Kgs 24:3).[45] Additionally, an explanation of Manasseh's sins is introduced into the conclusion of the prose narrative of Josiah's reign to account for why Josiah's wonderful reforms could not avert the disaster of the Babylonian exile (2 Kgs 23:26).[46] Someone was apparently interested in denying the culpability of the last kings of Judah for the exile of Judah. Who could this be? The only logical answer is the royal court of Jehoiachin in Babylon. They had not only the vested interest but also the means to write and preserve this literature.

The prophet Jeremiah apparently supported the royal family in exile even before the fall of Jerusalem. According to Jeremiah 29, during the reign of Zedekiah (before the final destruction of Jerusalem) the prophet wrote a letter to the exiles in Babylon encouraging them to "seek the welfare of the city where I have sent you into exile, and pray to YHWH on its behalf, for in its welfare you will find your welfare" (v. 7). Jeremiah is presented as supporting the exiled royal family, "I know the plans I have for you, says YHWH, plans for your welfare and not for harm, to give you a future with hope" (v. 11). In Jeremiah 29, a Babylonian interpretative addition (vv. 16–20) to Jeremiah's prophecy is evident when we compare the Hebrew and Greek texts. Verses 16–20 are missing in the Old Greek text reflecting an earlier and shorter Hebrew text. These verses must have been added when the scroll of Jeremiah was edited in Babylon for the exiled royal family. They reflect an interpretative addition that contextualized Jeremiah's prophecy for the royal family in Babylon by critiquing their rivals who remained in Jerusalem.

[Babylonian addition] 16 *Thus says YHWH concerning* the king who sits on the throne of David, and concerning all the people who live in this city, your kinsfolk who did not go out with you into exile: 17 Thus says YHWH of hosts, I am going to let loose on them sword, famine, and pestilence, and I will make them like rotten figs that are so bad they cannot be eaten. 18 I will pursue them with the sword, with famine, and with pestilence, and will make them a horror to all the kingdoms of the earth, to be an object of cursing, and horror, and hissing, and a derision among all the nations where I have driven them, 19 because they did not heed my words, says YHWH, when I persistently sent to you my servants the prophets, but they would not listen, says YHWH. 20 But now, all you exiles whom I sent away from Jerusalem to Babylon, hear the word of YHWH:

[Original oracle] 21 *Thus says YHWH of hosts, the God of Israel, concerning* Ahab son of Kolaiah and Zedekiah son of Maaseiah, who are prophesying a lie to you in my name: I am going to deliver them into the hand of King Nebuchadrezzar of Babylon, and he shall kill them before your eyes.

The addition not only is clear when comparing the Old Greek and Masoretic Hebrew texts but also is marked by the repetition of the phrase "Thus says YHWH concerning" (in italics in excerpt), a common editorial technique of biblical writers.[47] The thrust of this addition is to condemn the royal pretender (i.e., Zedekiah) who remained on the throne of David in Jerusalem. The original core narrative (v. 21) was a critique of Jeremiah's personal prophetic adversaries. In fact, at this particular moment in the text Jeremiah tied the activities of these false prophets (and not kings Manasseh or Zedekiah) to the eventual exile of the Judean people. For this reason, it seems likely that the Book of Jeremiah (as we now know it through most English translations from the Masoretic Text) received its final form during the exile and under the general auspices of the exiled royal court of Jehoiachin.

The prophet Ezekiel was apparently, along with Jehioachin, among those exiled in 597 B.C.E. (cf. Ezek 1:2; 2 Kgs 24:15). Unfortunately for Ezekiel, he was not taken to Babylon to live in the royal palace like Jehoiachin and the royal family. Ezekiel was settled along with the other exiles in a work camp along the Chebar canal, just north of Babylon. The Book of Ezekiel shares many things with Jeremiah. Most importantly, Ezekiel acknowledges the legitimacy of Jehoiachin as the king of Judah. In keeping with this, from its beginning the book is dated according to the ruling years of Jehoiachin rather than of Zedekiah (Ezekiel 1:2). Some have suggested that Ezekiel may have held out hope that the imprisoned king would one day return to rule.[48] But such date formulas are part of the editorial structure; thus, they reflect the views of the editors, that is, the exiled Judean royal family in Babylon – views of their own legitimacy. Within the Book of Ezekiel, the prophet's ministry is dated primarily between 593 and 585 B.C.E. – that is, after the first exile (in 597 B.C.E.) but before the third exile (in 581 B.C.E.). Like his contemporary, Jeremiah, Ezekiel counsels acquiescence to the Babylonians (12:1–15; 17:1–22; 21:18–32). The exile was inevitable. Moreover, the royal regent in Jerusalem, Zedekiah, is reviled by Ezekiel as "the vile, wicked prince of Israel" (Ezek 21:25). Ezekiel also apparently blames the exile on the sins of Manasseh (as we observed with Jeremiah and the conclusion to the Book of Kings), although the point is made less directly.[49] All this points us again to the exiled Judean royal family's role in editing and preserving literature that (1) supported their royal claims, (2) absolved Jehoiachin from direct blame for the Babylonian exiles, and (3) counseled submission to the Babylonians.

The Continuing Influence of Jehoiachin's Family

Prominent in the Babylonian ration lists are five princes of Judah, the sons of Jehoiachin. The lineages of the Judean royal family in the line of Jehoiachin are repeatedly recounted in biblical texts (e.g., Ezr 3:2, 8; 5:2; Neh 12:1; Hag 1:1, 12; 1 Chr 3:17).[50] According to these biblical genealogies, Jehoiachin eventually had seven sons, including a certain Shealtiel, the father of Zerubbabel. This Zerubbabel becomes an important figure in the early Judean restoration after the Persian conquest of the Babylonian Empire in 539 B.C.E. The continuing centrality of the royal Davidic family of Jehoiachin forces us to fundamentally reorganize the exile. The centrality and influence of the royal family continues from the exilic period proper into the first years of Persian rule in the late sixth century B.C.E.

Shortly after Cyrus's conquest of the Babylonian Empire, he issued a general decree for the deported peoples to return to their homeland. In a Persian text known as the Cyrus Cylinder we read, "I gathered all their [exiled] inhabitants and returned to them their dwellings.... May all the gods whom I settled in their sacred centers ask daily of Bel and Nabu that my days be long and may they intercede for my welfare."[51] Cyrus thus endeared himself to the exiles by restoring their temples and ancestral lands. Scholars have long recognized that the last part of the Book of Isaiah, chapters 40–66, is an addition to the original corpus of the book. This addition obliges Cyrus's request, actually calling him "his messiah ('anointed'), whose right hand I have grasped to subdue the nations before him" (Isa 45:1). Scholars debate the exact time and author(s) of these chapters. In critical scholarship, the chapters are separated into "Second" Isaiah (chapters 40–55) and "Third" Isaiah (chapters 56–66). Second Isaiah supposedly reflects a Babylonian context, whereas Third Isaiah was written in Jerusalem after the return. This division is probably overwrought. Both "Second" and "Third" Isaiah must have been written down with the support of the royal family of Jehoiachin, whether actually in Babylonian or after the family sends Zerubbabel to reestablish the their claims in Jerusalem.

One of the major scholarly issues concerning the Book of Isaiah has been "authorship." However, there are no authors in the Book of Isaiah. Authorship is not even a concept that is raised by the book itself. Authorship is a Hellenistic or modern issue; it was never an issue in the editing of the book. Rather than an author, the Book of Isaiah has the character of the eighth-century prophet Isaiah. Although the Book of Isaiah was shaped by editing in the Judean royal court during the exile, the initial editing of Isaiah's oracles began in the days of Hezekiah in the late eighth century B.C.E. The power of Isaiah's poetry coupled with his visionary support of the Judean royal family gave the prophet an enduring voice that was preserved and fleshed out in the Judean royal court over the centuries.

Isaiah 61 is often understood as reflecting the voice of a prophetic disciple, "Third" Isaiah. This seems to be a misreading of the text. We find in verses 1–4 these famous words:

> The spirit of YHWH GOD is upon me,
> because YHWH has anointed me;
> he has sent me to bring good news to the oppressed,
> to bind up the brokenhearted,
> to proclaim liberty to the captives,
> and release to the prisoners;
> to proclaim the year of YHWH's favor,
> and the day of vengeance of our God;
> to comfort all who mourn;
> to provide for those who mourn in Zion –
> to give them a garland instead of ashes,
> the oil of gladness instead of mourning,
> the mantle of praise instead of a faint spirit.
> They will be called oaks of righteousness,
> the planting of YHWH, to display his glory.
> They shall build up the ancient ruins,
> they shall raise up the former devastations;
> they shall repair the ruined cities,
> the devastations of many generations.

These words do not refer to a prophet, however. Elsewhere in the Hebrew Bible, the spirit came upon leaders (not usually prophets), especially as they were about to assume their leadership roles (e.g., Deut 34:9; Judg 3:10; 6:34; 11:29; 13:25; 1 Sam 11:6). The anointing was part of the ritual that marked the installation of a king or a high priest. Prophets, in contrast, did not hold an institutional office into which they could be installed. The spirit comes upon the "anointed" (Hebrew, *messiah*) king so that the appointed leader can carry out royal duties, including humanely treating the oppressed, setting free prisoners, and rebuilding the ancient ruins of Jerusalem. Such were the duties of a righteous king. This description, then, was likely taken as a reference to one of the exiled princes in Babylon who was being called to restore Jerusalem.

The Book of Isaiah ends by advocating the universality of God and trying to marginalize the temple (and therefore also the priests). The last chapter of "Third" Isaiah begins:

> Thus says YHWH:
> Heaven is my throne and the earth is my footstool;
> what is the house that you would build for me,
>   and what is my resting place?
> All these things my hand has made,
>   and so all these things are mine, says YHWH. (Isa 66:1–2)

The text justifies a certain reluctance by the royal family to put all their assets into rebuilding the Jerusalem Temple. After all, YHWH was the God of the entire universe. Was the entire universe meant specifically to refer to Babylon, where most of the royal Judean family lived (even after the Persian king Cyrus's decree of return)? This universalistic prophecy then would continue to justify the exiled royal family in Babylon, even while the royal family apparently established a foothold back in Jerusalem. Notably, the text alludes to a well-known text in ancient Israel – the Promise to David in 2 Samuel 7. There, in an oracle of the prophet Nathan, God questioned David's desire to build the Temple: "Shall you [David] build me a house to live in?" (v. 5). Isaiah 66 fleshes out this idea by suggesting that a house could not be built for YHWH since he dwelled in heaven. It is important here to recognize that this allusion to 2 Samuel 7 acknowledges a central story within Israelite culture. This is not simply an erudite reference to an obscure text by a learned scribe.[52] Rather, it represents an ongoing dialogue about the Temple within the Judean royal family that began with the allusion to the well-known story in 2 Samuel 7.

Another allusion to 2 Samuel 7 is found in the book ascribed to the late-sixth-century prophet Haggai. In contrast to Isaiah 66:1–2, reference allowed for a covert critique of the Judean royal court's reluctance to rebuild the Temple. The book begins, "Thus says YHWH of hosts: These people say the time has not yet come to rebuild YHWH's house. Then the word of YHWH came by the prophet Haggai, saying: 'Is it a time for you yourselves to live in your paneled houses, while this house lies in ruins?'" Although the prophecy is superficially aimed at "the people," it would have been the governor Zerubbabel who dwelled in a paneled house, not the people. Zerubbabel was a descendant of Jehoiachin and the royal Davidic dynasty. His reluctance to build the temple is directly contrasted with King David's desire to do so. The whole temple-building narrative in 2 Samuel 7 begins with David saying to the prophet Nathan: "See now, I am living in a house of cedar, but the ark of God stays in a tent." David sees himself living in a luxurious house and is prompted to build the Temple. Zerubbabel is living in a fine house while the Temple lies in ruins, yet he apparently does not think the time has come for temple building.

The narrative in Ezra 1–6 tells the story of the early return of the Judean royal family.[53] This prose narrative of the early post-exilic period continues the story of the Judean royal family but introduces an increasingly important role for the priests. The priests stand beside Zerubbabel rebuilding the Temple. Eventually, the rebuilt Temple will marginalize the royal family in the politics of post-exilic Jerusalem as the priests become the leaders of the Second Temple Jewish community. Cyrus's edict of return is personalized for the Jews in Ezra 1:1–4:

> In the first year of King Cyrus of Persia, in order that the word of YHWH by the mouth of Jeremiah might be accomplished, YHWH stirred up the spirit of King Cyrus of Persia so that he sent a herald throughout all his kingdom, and also in a written edict declared: "Thus says King Cyrus of Persia: YHWH, the God of heaven, has given me all the kingdoms of the earth, and he has charged me to build him a house at Jerusalem in Judah. Any of those among you who are of his people – may their God be with them! – are now permitted to go up to Jerusalem in Judah, and rebuild the house of YHWH, the God of Israel – he is the God who is in Jerusalem; and let all survivors, in whatever place they reside, be assisted by the people of their place with silver and gold, with goods and with animals, besides freewill offerings for the house of God in Jerusalem."

The promise of restoration is described as fulfilling the prophecy of Jeremiah – that favorite prophet of the royal family.

The royal regent Zerubbabel leads a contingent of exiles back to the Persian province of Yehud (Ezra 2:1–2). It is worth noting that Zerubbabel is a fairly common Babylonian name that means "seed of Babylon." Another prominent member of the royal family, Sheshbazzar, also has a Babylonian name; he is listed as the first governor of Yehud in the Book of Ezra (1:8; 5:14; cf. 1 Chr 3:18).[54] These Babylonian names probably reflect the close and perhaps even fond connection that the Judean royal family had with the city of Babylon. Zerubbabel, appointed governor by the new Persian king Cyrus, begins to rebuild the city of Jerusalem, its Temple, and Jewish life in the land (Ezra 3:2–8):

> Then Jeshua son of Jozadak, with his fellow priests, and Zerubbabel son of Shealtiel with his kin set out to build the altar of the God of Israel, to offer burnt offerings

on it, as prescribed in the law of Moses the man of God.... They kept the festival of booths, as prescribed, and offered the daily burnt offerings by number according to the ordinance, as required for each day, and after that the regular burnt offerings, the offerings at the new moon and at all the sacred festivals of YHWH, and the offerings of everyone who made a freewill offering to YHWH. From the first day of the seventh month they began to offer burnt offerings to YHWH. But the foundation of the temple of YHWH was not yet laid.... In the second year after their arrival at the house of God at Jerusalem, in the second month, Zerubbabel son of Shealtiel and Jeshua son of Jozadak made a beginning, together with the rest of their people, the priests and the Levites and all who had come to Jerusalem from the captivity.

Zerubbabel, representing the exiled Judean royal family, returns to Jerusalem. It is interesting, however, that the only member of the Judean royal family that is mentioned as returning from Babylon is Zerubbabel. There are extensive lists of returnees in the Book of Ezra, but there is no indication after Zerubbabel that the Judean royal family ever returned to Jerusalem.

The situation in Jerusalem in the early Persian period (the late sixth century B.C.E.) was bleak. There were no major cities in the central hill country. The population in cities and villages had declined by as much as 85 percent during the sixth century. The Persians defined the borders of the province that they named "Yehud" (or, Judah) quite narrowly.[55] The province was completely confined to rugged hills and most suitable for subsistence farming and pastoralism. It had poor access to trade routes. It was depopulated from the Babylonian invasions and the economic blight that followed. Zerubbabel had left the luxury of Babylon, where he had lived in the royal citadel complex, to return to a backwater on the fringe of the empire. Although he apparently managed to build for himself a "paneled house," the economic situation would not easily recover. The prophet Haggai (ca. 520 B.C.E.) speaks of the situation: "You have sown much, and harvested little; you eat, but you never have enough; you drink, but you never have your fill; you clothe yourselves, but no one is warm; and you that earn wages earn wages to put them into a bag with holes" (Hag 1:6). Haggai blames these conditions on the returnees' lack of faithfulness, but to be fair the economic situation did not lend itself to prosperity. Both archaeological investigations and literary sources suggest that the economic blight extended well into the fifth century B.C.E.[56]

With the support and sometimes goading of priests and prophets, Zerubbabel helps rebuild the Jerusalem Temple. The Book of Haggai justifies Zerubbabel's position as the legitimate royal leader, while goading him to complete the Temple. I recalled earlier that the book opens by encouraging the building of the Temple:

> In the second year of King Darius, in the sixth month, on the first day of the month, the word of YHWH came by the prophet Haggai to Zerubbabel son of Shealtiel, governor of Judah, and to Joshua son of Jehozadak, the high priest: "Thus says YHWH of hosts: These people say the time has not yet come to rebuild YHWH'S house. Then the word of YHWH came by the prophet Haggai, saying: 'Is it a time for you yourselves to live in your paneled houses, while this house lies in ruins?'"

Although the prophet's words are couched as a message to Zerubbabel and the priest Joshua, it is essentially the king's responsibility to rebuild the Temple. The prophet diffuses the directness of the critique of Zerubbabel with the statement that "*these people* say the time has not yet come to rebuild YHWH's house." However, it was not *these people* who were living in paneled houses, but the governor Zerubbabel and perhaps the high priest. The contrast with the venerable King David's desire to build YHWH's Temple is striking. Zerubbabel, of course, does build the Temple, thereby legitimating his claim to leadership over the Jewish community.

The short prophetic Book of Haggai closes by reiterating the hope for the restoration of Jehoiachin's family line through Zerubbabel (Hag 2:20–23):

> The word of YHWH came a second time to Haggai on the twenty-fourth day of the month: "Speak to Zerubbabel, governor of Judah, saying, I am about to shake the heavens and the earth, and to overthrow the throne of kingdoms; I am about to destroy the strength of the kingdoms of the nations, and overthrow the chariots and their riders; and the horses and their riders shall fall, every one by the sword of a comrade. On that day, says YHWH of hosts, I will take you, O Zerubbabel my servant, son of Shealtiel, says YHWH, and make you like a signet ring; for I have chosen you, says YHWH of hosts."

At this point in the historical record, however, Zerubbabel disappears. Some scholars have suggested that the Persians imprisoned or killed him. According to a much later Jewish tradition from the sixth century C.E. (*Seder 'Olam Zuta*), Zerubbabel returned to his prominent position in Babylon, where he died and was buried. There is no good evidence to say for certain what happened to Zerubbabel. We know only that he disappeared. The entire Judean royal family will also vanish from the historical record at this point. From archaeological and literary evidence, it seems that the economic catastrophe wrought by the Babylonians in Jerusalem lingered. Of course, it may simply have been that Zerubbabel preferred to return to the privileged position held by the royal family in Babylon rather than remain in the squalor of Persian Yehud.

Fundamentally, the writing of the exilic period was an extension of writing by the state. It was writing by and for the Judean royal family. The royal family is the only social setting suitable for writing substantive literature during the exile. The literature of pre-exilic times was likely preserved by the royal family in Babylon and then returned to Jerusalem when the royal heir Zerubbabel returned and rebuilt the Temple. The biblical literature produced during the sixth century B.C.E. reflects the interests of the Judean royal family. Thus, writing during the exile and the early post-exilic period was largely not a response to the Babylonian destruction and exile in the traditional sense. Rather, it was a return to the more traditional setting of writing in antiquity – as a production of the government, even a government in exile. The great literature of the exile was oral literature, the psalms and the lamentations of the people. But when and how this oral literature was finally put down on parchment remains difficult to say. There is no reason to suppose that they were written down until much later.

9

Scripture in the Shadow of the Temple

The Persian period brings an end to royalist-centered biblical literature. The Davidic kings vanish from the scene, and the leadership of the Jewish community in Jerusalem passes to the priests. The identity of the Jewish people will be centered increasingly in the Jerusalem Temple. The composition and editing of biblical literature will be located in the Jerusalem Temple. The production of written literature will be controlled by the priests. The sons of David are not forgotten, but they are dispossessed. The priests are no longer interested in the sons of David as princes of Israel. Rather, David and his sons become patrons of the temple, its priests, and its services. In David's place, the priest and scribe Ezra arises. With the hand of God upon him, like a second coming of Moses, Ezra leads the post-exilic community. At the center of the priestly leadership will be the Book of Moses. The priests become the guardians of the Mosaic Torah and the sacred writings of ancient Israel. The oral word of God through the prophets comes to an end as the temple priests and scribes will *textualize* the word of God.

This chapter will deal with writing in the fifth through third centuries B.C.E., that is, from the mid-Persian into the Hellenistic period. Although the Persian period proper begins with the Persian king Cyrus's conquest of Babylon in 539 B.C.E., the continuing role of the Davidic royal family made for continuity into the first years of Persian rule in Jerusalem in the late sixth century B.C.E. The Davidic royal family disappears by the end of the sixth century B.C.E., and leadership apparently transfers to the priests. These are dark times for Jerusalem and the Persian province of Yehud. In past generations, it was "dark" simply because we knew so little about this period of history. Increasingly, archaeology has filled in the void but has painted a very bleak picture of a depopulated and impoverished region. Yet, this period has long been considered by scholars as a formative period for the writing of the Bible. Supposedly, a great burst of literary activity inspired by the catastrophe of the Babylonian exile continued into the "restoration" period. Giovanni Garbini writes, "... under the domination of the Achaemenids, Hebraism knew its magical moment and Hebrew Literature its golden age."[1] Rather than a golden age, however, the archaeological record points to the economic deprivation of Jerusalem and its surroundings. Rather than the great flourishing of biblical literature, this would be a time of retrenchment. In the present chapter, I will argue that the priests and scribes were preserving the literature of Israel rather than creating it. Writing was quite limited and reflected the Aramaic linguistic world of the Persian Empire.[2]

The composition of little, if any, biblical literature can be placed in this period with certainty. The most likely books composed in the Persian period would be the Book of Chronicles and Ezra-Nehemiah.[3] Other books like Esther and perhaps Ecclesiastes may have been composed in the fourth or third century B.C.E. The final composition of the Book of Daniel is usually placed in the mid-second century B.C.E.[4] All this literature shows the marked linguistic influence of the Aramaic world imposed by the Persian Empire. Although most of the biblical psalms were composed earlier, the Book of Psalms itself was not yet complete. The priestly levitical singers helped shape the Book of Psalms, but this songbook of ancient Israel is perhaps the most fluid book in the entire canon.[5] Part of the retrenchment process was the collecting and editing of biblical literature. Thus, for example, a prose tale is added to the archaic poetry of the Book of Job to give the book its final form.[6] Editorial activities of the priests include adding superscriptions, providing editorial glosses, and shaping biblical literature into books and groups.[7] A collection of the smaller prophetic scrolls, the "minor" prophets (Hosea, Joel, Amos, Obadiah, Jonah, Micah, Nahum, Habakkuk, Zephaniah, Haggai, Zechariah, Malachi), was edited into a larger scroll of "the twelve."[8] Although the Pentatuech was essentially composed in the pre-exilic period, its final editorial shaping took place in the Jerusalem Temple. It is difficult to be certain that all of this editing and shaping of the biblical canon was actually taking place in the Persian period, especially given the social context. It is entirely reasonable that some of these editorial processes be dated to the third century B.C.E. during the early Hellenistic period. The third century was a period of relative stability, of royal Egyptian support for scribes and texts, and of recovering economic prosperity.

The Recent Trend

My thesis here challenges the recent trend to date the composition of all biblical texts later and later. Since the rise of historical criticism in the nineteenth century, it has been assumed that the Persian period was a time of literary production. The recent fashion changes only one element, arguing that almost all (if not all) biblical literature is the product of the Persian and Hellenistic periods. This recent trend revisits one from the early twentieth century when a few scholars argued that the Bible was essentially a product of the Persian, Hellenistic, *and Hasmonean* eras.[9] The discovery of the Dead Sea Scrolls has placed a *terminus ad quem* on this theory because some of the biblical manuscripts discovered among them already date to the third century B.C.E. However, one can still ask whether the Bible is a Hellenistic "book."[10] That is to say, the Bible as a "book" is quite late. As a "book," the Bible actually awaits the technological innovation of the codex, which gave it the physical form of a book.

A more disparaging slant on this trend is to call the Bible an "invention" of Persian and Hellenistic scribes, asserting that Jewish nationalists were creating an identity and a connection with the land through literary invention.[11] Not only is it asserted that David and Solomon were literary fictions, but even that Ezra and Nehemiah were invented generations later to justify ideological and religious claims by Hellenistic Jews. These assertions supposedly arise from the observation that we have no explicit evidence outside the Bible for figures such as David and Solomon, or even Ezra and Nehemiah.[12] In his measured critique, James Barr notes that "since so little is known of the Persian period, we come to rest in the Greek period."[13] But Barr goes on to observe that "If this kind of argument were applied consistently to everything, there could be no knowledge of anything."[14] This is a classic case of the reduction to absurdity. The suggestion that Ezra and Nehemiah are merely fictions invented by later writers is instructive, however. It points to how little we know about the Persian period. In the absence of evidence, everything becomes a vapor. These are the real dark ages in history of the Jewish people. There is enough light, however, to make our way in the darkness.

The Dark Shadow of the Persian Empire

So, what kind of historical context was the Persian period for the writing of biblical literature? The Babylonian destruction of the Judean kingdom cast a long and dark shadow over the post-exilic period. Perhaps the most striking archaeological discovery has been just how depopulated the land became during the Babylonian and Persian periods. This insight was first brought to bear on the period in a study by Kenneth Hoglund, *Achaemenid Imperial Administration in Syria-Palestine and the Missions of Ezra and Nehemiah* (1992). It has now been brought up-to-date in the important and thorough archaeological study done by Charles Carter, *The Emergence of Yehud: A Social and Demographic Study* (1999). Carter estimates that the population of the entire province of Yehud was only about 13,350 at the end of Babylonian period in the late sixth century B.C.E.[15] Although this population would grow to about 20,650 by the end of Persian rule in the mid-fourth century B.C.E., these are amazingly modest figures. According to archaeologists, the city of Jerusalem itself never had a population of more than 1,500 during the Persian period![16] It should be emphasized that these are merely estimates and that population in antiquity is notoriously tricky to estimate. But the basic picture is clear. The land was sparsely populated. Jerusalem was a small town. These figures must give us pause when we reassess the view that the Persian and Hellenistic period was marked by the great literary flourishing that resulted in the wholesale creation of the vast corpus of biblical literature.

The depopulation of Yehud, in fact, is suggested in the remarks of a Greek traveler, Hecataeus of Abdera, who lived about 300 B.C.E. Hecataeus suggests that the Jews came originally from Egypt but were expelled from there and settled in Judaea, "which is not far distant from Egypt and was at that time utterly uninhabited."[17] Hecataeus cannot be taken too seriously here, as he reflects typical mythical Greek descriptions of settlement of new countries in an empty land. However, later Hecataeus reinforces this description with the observation that Jews were forbidden to sell their land lest doing so "bring on a scarcity of manpower."[18] Implicit in this observation is again the problem of a depopulated Yehud. There were apparently too few people to fully work the land.

Biblical literature paints a similar portrait of an economically impoverished Yehud. When Nehemiah, a minor Persian official and one of the leaders of the post-exilic Jewish community, arrived in Jerusalem in the mid-fifth century B.C.E., the economy was still in the ruins left by the Babylonians. Although Zerubbabel completed rebuilding the temple in 515 B.C.E., the Judean royal family seems to have vanished by then. Nehemiah found the walls of Jerusalem still in ruins (Neh 1–2). Carter notes that "taxation and tribute levied upon the populace of Yehud by imperial policy contributed to Yehud's economic difficulties."[19] The people were weighed down by the burden of imperial taxation and local administrative abuses (Neh 5:1–19). The levitical priesthood had apparently abandoned the city of Jerusalem because it was not economically viable (cf. Neh 13:10–13).[20] Thus, the biblical depiction of the general economic situation accords well with the situation reconstructed by archaeologists.

Nehemiah also hints at the general depopulation of Jerusalem. In his memoirs, he wrote, "The city was wide and large, but the people within it were few and no houses had been built" (Neh 7:4). It is important to realize that the city that Nehemiah calls "wide and large" was only about thirty acres (as compared to about 150 acres in the seventh century B.C.E. and then later in the second century B.C.E.). On a relative basis, Jerusalem not only was small, it also was depopulated.

The situation gradually, but not dramatically, improved over the three centuries of Persian rule. The sixth through fourth centuries B.C.E. in Yehud have three distinct phases. In the first phase of Persian rule, the country lacked the proper infrastructure to build any sort of coherent administrative structure or economy. The population was insufficient. The Israeli archaeologist Ephraim Stern observes that "even if there was a formal intent to create it, the country lacked the proper conditions."[21] In 488 B.C.E. and again in 459 B.C.E., Egypt revolted against the empire. This marked the beginning of a second phase of Persian rule in Syria-Palestine. The empire began to take a more active role in its administration in the west, including the tiny province of Yehud. The missions of the biblical figures of Ezra and Nehemiah seem to follow in the wake of these Egyptian revolts.[22] The Persians build a series of forts and ports along the coast of Syria-Palestine to deal with threats from both Egypt and Greece. In spite of this, Yehud remains relatively isolated in the central hills, and the economic and demographic recovery proceeds rather slowly. The last phase began with the Egyptian revolts in 400 B.C.E., when Egypt succeeded in regaining its independence. In the early fourth century B.C.E., Palestine became the battlefield for conflicts between a resurgent Egypt and the Persian Empire. Archaeological excavations have uncovered evidence of a wave of destruction on the Judean coast and in the foothills west of Jerusalem during the early fourth century B.C.E. The Persians were pressed not only by Egypt on the south but also by the Greeks

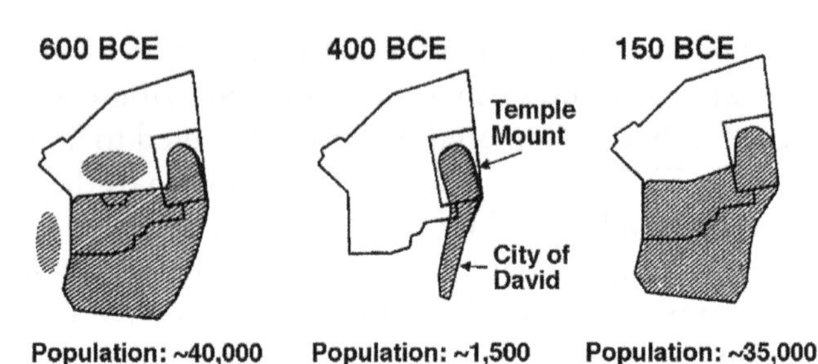

Figure 9.1. The Size of Jerusalem from 600 B.C.E. through 150 B.C.E.

on the west and by Babylonian revolts internally. Eventually, the Persian Empire crumbled in the wake of Alexander the Great and a new Macedonian Empire. Jerusalem was spared conquest by surrendering to Alexander in 333 B.C.E. However, Alexander died only a decade later and his generals fought over parts of his kingdom. Stability and prosperity would begin to return to Jerusalem only at the beginning of the third century B.C.E. under the rule of the Ptolemies in Egypt.

This is a brief sketch of the historical picture of Palestine as we know it in the sixth through fourth centuries B.C.E. At the end of the fourth century, Jerusalem's population was still less than fifteen hundred persons. At that time, the northern part of the city (or the Temple Mount) was dedicated to the Temple and settlement was confined to the tiny City of David. This is in stark contrast to Jerusalem during the late monarchy or the reign of the Hasmonean kings (see Figure 9.1). The economy continued to be hampered by the city's disadvantageous geographical position in the remote hills of central Palestine. The economy of Yehud remained dependent upon subsistence farming and pastoralism. Other than that of the few priestly elites and Persian administrative officials in Jerusalem, it is unlikely that there was substantive literacy. Writing, as we will see, does serve a major role in the Persian imperial administration, but this writing was in Aramaic. This is hardly a picture that encourages us to envision the magical moment of biblical literature.

The archaeological and literary record of the sixth through fourth centuries presents a problem for the traditional view that this was a creative period for Biblical Hebrew literature. The archaeologist Charles Carter was quite aware of this problem: "If Yehud was this small and this poor, how could the social and religious elite sustain the literary activity attributed to the Persian period?"[23] He asks how the city of Jerusalem, which had shrunk to very small proportions with a population of less than fifteen hundred, could support such prolific literary production? Not just prolific literary production, but prolific production *in the classical Hebrew idiom.* Another question asks why the inhabitants of Jerusalem would want to support such prolific literary production. This was not the modern world. When we search for possible anthropological analogies, we must realize that changing writing technologies make these analogies inappropriate. A Jewish girl, Anne Frank, could write her diary in a closet in Amsterdam during World War II, but she had the advantage of over two millennia of major technological and cultural advances in writing.

One favorite solution of the past generations, namely, to push much of biblical literature into the Hasmonean period (167–63 B.C.E.), is no longer an option. As mentioned before, the Dead Sea Scrolls give us biblical manuscripts dating to the mid-third century B.C.E. Moreover, the Hebrew language of the second century B.C.E. is so distinctively different from biblical literature that it is not a plausible solution. This would be like saying that Shakespeare wrote his works in the 1990s! So, this narrows the window for the vast, diverse, and complex compendium of writings that make up the Hebrew Bible.

Another solution is to simply rewrite Persian history. The British scholar Philip Davies, for example, suggests, "The view of Judah in the Persian period as a cultural backwater and as economically poor perhaps needs to be reconsidered."[24] Why does it need reconsidering? Because the great amount of scribal activity that many assume flourished in the Persian period is clearly inconsistent with the portrait of the Persian province of Yehud upon which archaeologists, historians, and biblical scholars have agreed. As if aware of this problem, Davies goes on to remark that "the later we move in date, the easier it is to conclude that the temple could sustain a number of scribal schools with a vigorous scribal activity." Davies rightly insists on not just one scribal school, but a number of schools, which of course would be necessary to generate the quantity and variety we find in biblical literature. In the same vein, Anthony Saldarini, the late professor of Early Christianity at Boston College, suggests that "scribal activity by a variety of groups (priests, prophets, visionaries, scribes, and other community leaders) must be postulated in order to account for the composition and editing of the biblical collection during the exilic and postexilic periods."[25] We have to assume a variety of groups or schools to account for the composition of biblical literature in these periods *only if we also assume that biblical literature must have been composed primarily in the Persian period.* This is an assumption that requires the postulation of vigorous scribal activities at a time when such scribal activities in the Hebrew language seem implausible.

Such scribal activities become more plausible as we press into the Hellenistic period, particularly in the third and second centuries B.C.E. Of course, as we do press later, we run into the problem of the Qumran biblical manuscripts that date back into the third century B.C.E. And, what shall we make of Jewish literature like Jubilees or Ben-Sira? They are written in Hebrew, but in a much later literary style and linguistic strata of the Hebrew language. These are Jewish literary compositions widely understood to date to the third and second centuries, but they differ vastly in language and spirit from the Bible. On the one hand, everything we know about the Persian province of Yehud makes it an unlikely candidate for such a vast flourishing of a number of scribal schools – as scholars have correctly assumed were needed in order to account for the astonishing literary diversity of the Hebrew Bible. On the other hand, it is difficult to assign this vigorous scribal activity to the later periods because of the Qumran biblical texts, the Septuagint, and the apocrypha and pseudepigrapha. Where can we go? Back to the late Judean monarchy. Back to the days of King Hezekiah and King Josiah. Back to the times of the prophets Isaiah and Jeremiah. Then, the social and economic conditions favored the flourishing of literature. There, an abundance of writing in Hebrew during the late Judean monarchy has been uncovered in archaeological excavations. It is there that biblical Hebrew literature found its magical moment.

Priestly Leadership

Who were the leaders of the Jewish community after the exile? The sons of David disappear in the Persian period. As a result, the Persian period marks the end of royalist-oriented biblical literature. The Book of Ezra-Nehemiah is one of the few examples of literature from the Jewish community in Jerusalem during this period, and Ezra-Nehemiah has only Babylonian and Persian kings. Notably, the book reduces the venerable King David to a person who establishes the Temple and its personnel (Ezra 3:10, 8:20; Neh 12:24, 36, 45–46). With the disappearance of the royal Davidic family from Yehud, the

Table 9.1. *Governors of Yehud*

Governor	Date
Sheshbazzar	538 B.C.
Zerubbabel	520 B.C.
Elnathan	late sixth century B.C.E.
Nehemiah	445–433 B.C.E.
Bagohi	408 B.C.E.
Yehezeqiah	fourth century B.C.E.
Yehezer	(uncertain)
Ahzai	(uncertain)

leadership of the community was left in the hands of the priests. The rebuilt Temple provided a focal point for their leadership.

The governors of Yehud during the Persian period become priests. Although the historical picture is piecemeal, Duke University archaeologists Carol and Eric Meyers were able to construct a list of governors of Yehud using archaeological, inscriptional, and literary sources (see Table 9.1).[26]

One of the most striking aspects of this list is that only the first two governors, Sheshbazzar and Zerubbabel, are clearly Davidides. These last two sons of David along with (perhaps) Elnathan are the final extension of the exiled royal family of Jehoiachin (discussed in the last chapter). With them, the royal family's leadership of the Jewish people in Yehud ends. The power passes to the temple that they built and to those who administered the temple. The Persian imperial policy employed a temple economy, utilizing Near Eastern temples as a means of levying and gathering taxes and tribute. Temples naturally gained in prominence and the priests with them. The temple and its attendants – the priests – were the central and defining institution of Judaism as it emerged in this period.

The displacement of the royal Davidic family was complete by the fourth century. It is telling that archaeologists have found coins minted with the inscription of a certain "Yohanan, the priest" dating to the mid-fourth century B.C.E. The most fascinating, if not the most compelling, evidence is the anecdotal report by the Greek traveler Hecataeus of Abdera from around 300 B.C.E. In his treatise on Egypt, he writes:

> Moses picked out the men of most refinement and with the greatest ability to head the entire nation, and appointed them priests.... These same men he appointed to be

judges in all major disputes, and entrusted them to the guardianship of the laws and customs. *For this reason, the Jews have never had a king*, and authority over the people is regularly vested in whichever priest is regarded as superior.[27] [Emphasis added.]

Hecataeus also mentions an old priest by the name of Ezekias, apparently a person of standing in the Jewish community, who was forced to flee to Egypt in 312 B.C.E. This figure might tentatively be identified as a Greek form of the Hebrew Yehezeqiah, who was a governor of Yehud in the late Persian period.[28] Several coins from the mid-fourth century bear the inscription "Yehezeqiah, the governor." These coins suggest again that the roles of the priest and the governor, of sacral and secular leadership, increasingly overlapped in the Persian period. They may also suggest that the Judean priestly leadership participated in one of a series of revolts against Persian hegemony that raged between 366 and 343 B.C.E. This Judean leader is striking coins not only with his own image upon it but also with inscriptions using *the archaic national script of the Jews* (i.e., in paleo-Hebrew rather than imperial Aramaic). As linguistic anthropologists have observed, language and especially script is often encumbered with political and ethnic ideology. These coins point to a nationalist Jewish movement led by the priests.

Hebrew in an Aramaic World

The Hebrew language was under siege during the Persian period. Its very existence was threatened by the pervasive spread of Aramaic that was fostered by the imperial administration of the Persian Empire. The evidence of hundreds of Aramaic inscriptions that have been excavated dating to the Persian period "attest to the extent of Aramaic penetration in Palestine – down to the local rural population."[29]

We have almost no inscriptional evidence for Hebrew writing in the Persian period. What little was written in Hebrew was an ideological assertion trying to preserve the ethnic and cultural identity of the Jewish people. In contrast to the hundreds of Aramaic ostraca, seals, papyri, and other inscribed artifacts, we have precious little to indicate that Hebrew was being written in the Persian period. We can count the evidence on the fingers of one hand. There are, for example, a few coins dating to the fourth century B.C.E. that use the word "priest" or "governor" and are written in the old Hebrew letters. Yet, the fact that we have these few coins reviving the old national Hebrew script indicates that the Hebrew language was not completely lost in the Persian and Hellenistic periods. It also points to the ideological role of Hebrew in the Jewish community of the late Persian period. A little more than a century after the Yehezeqiah coins, the Hasmoneans would also make a point of using Hebrew on coins minted in their own image. The Bar Kochba revolt in the second century C.E. also used paleo-Hebrew on their coins, although by this time such usage was primarily symbolic and the Hebrew writing replete with mistakes.[30] Certainly, the Hebrew language continued to be spoken and read, and there was even some biblical literature written in Hebrew. Third century copies of biblical manuscripts (including the Books of Jeremiah and Samuel) testify to an ongoing tradition of copying and preserving biblical Hebrew literature. No, Hebrew did not cease after the exile, but it would be overshadowed by the pervasive influence of an Aramaic-speaking world.

Aramaic became the native language of most Jews living in Palestine during the Second Temple period. For instance, it is commonly assumed that Aramaic was the native tongue of Jesus of Nazareth. To be sure, Jews continued to speak Hebrew. Hebrew was the language of most of the sacred Jewish scriptures. It was the language of prayer. It was a language of religious teaching, discussion, and debate. The religious sectarians at Khirbet Qumran actually tried to avoid any influence of Aramaic in their own sectarian writings – although not with complete success.[31] Aramaic became the vernacular. It was used in the administration of the vast Persian Empire and was the language of a vast network of scribal schools stretching from Iran to Turkey to Egypt.

There are lots and lots of inscriptions from the Persian period – that is, lots and lots of *Aramaic* inscriptions. Aramaic writing is preserved on clay, metal, stone, and papyrus. We have every possible kind of literature, from marriage deeds to wisdom literature like the words of Ahiqar. There are letters in Aramaic written from an Egyptian Jewish Diaspora community requesting permission to build a temple in Elephantine. There are economic texts and diplomatic texts, treaties, and seals. There are administrative inscriptions. These all reflect local administration rather than the imposition of imperial authority. Charles Carter suggests that "none of the seal impressions from Yehud that date to the Neo-Babylonian or Persian periods indicate anything but a local administrative structure, emanating from Tell en-Nasbeh [Mizpah] in the Neo-Babylonian and early Persian period, and from Jerusalem by the end of the sixth century or the

Latin	A	B	D	E	I	K	L	M
Paleo-Hebrew	𐤀	𐤁	𐤃	𐤄	𐤉	𐤊	𐤋	𐤌
Aramaic	𐡀	𐡁	𐡃	𐡄	𐡉	𐡊	𐡋	𐡌

Figure 9.2. Some Differences Between Old Hebrew and Aramaic Scripts

beginning of the fifth century."[32] Every conceivable type of document written on a wide variety of materials has been discovered dating to the Persian period. Given the use of Aramaic as a bureaucratic language of the empire, it is hardly surprising that we find so much Aramaic. To be fair, the abundance of Aramaic writing is mostly found outside the borders of Yehud. But Yehud also has its fair share of Aramaic inscriptions, especially administrative, economic, and legal texts. Thus, it is completely fitting that large sections of the Books of Ezra and Daniel are composed in Aramaic. Moreover, that this Aramaic language colors late Biblical Hebrew and Rabbinic Hebrew is hardly a shock.

The Aramaic world had an insidious influence on the development of the Hebrew language. Even what is known today as the "Hebrew" alphabet, is actually an Aramaic alphabet (see Figure 9.2).[33] The science of paleography (i.e., the study of the development of the shape and form of letters) has demonstrated that the Jews adopted Aramaic script during the Persian period. In Joseph Naveh's classic book *The Early History of the Alphabet*, he calls this Aramaic script "the Jewish script" to distinguish it from the Hebrew script of earlier periods. Paleographers usually refer to the old-style Hebrew alphabet as paleo-Hebrew. Remarkably, the early biblical manuscripts found among the Dead Sea Scrolls are written in Aramaic (*not Hebrew*) script. This change was so pervasive that almost all biblical texts copied in later periods were written in Aramaic letters rather than the old Hebrew script. When inscriptions in the Hebrew language do begin to appear in numbers during the Hasmonean and Roman periods (beginning in the second century B.C.E.), it is usually the Hebrew language written with Aramaic letters.

There was clearly no strong ideology during the Persian period culture that prevented the adoption of Aramaic letters, grammar, and vocabulary. It is important to remember that script is often ideologically and theologically loaded. Later, a strong ideology would develop that reasserted the importance of the paleo-Hebrew script. Nineteenth-century scholars actually had argued that the so-called Hebrew language of Rabbinic literature (usually called "Mishnaic," or "Rabbinic," Hebrew), whose basic features begin to emerge in the Persian period, was actually "merely a Hebraized Aramaic, artificially created by Schoolmen."[34] In his well-known grammar of Mishnaic (or, Rabbinic) Hebrew written at the beginning of the last century, Moshe Segal successfully defended Rabbinic Hebrew as a genuine colloquial Hebrew dialect and not merely Hebraized Aramaic. Still, Segal in his grammar of Mishnaic Hebrew had to acknowledge the pervasive influence that Aramaic had upon Hebrew.

There is almost a complete absence of Hebrew inscriptions from the Persian province of Yehud. Until the mid-third century B.C.E., practically no evidence exists of writing in Hebrew (apart from the Bible). Ironically, this is exactly the time when Biblical Hebrew literature is supposedly exploding, when Biblical Hebrew literature has its magical moment. Some scholars have even suggested that the entire Hebrew Bible was written in the Persian and Hellenistic period. Yet, beyond a few disputed Hebrew inscriptions from the very early Babylonian period (586–539 B.C.E.), we have no substantive Hebrew inscriptions until the second century B.C.E. This absence should be expected. The social and economic conditions of Persian Yehud were not conducive to a great literary flourishing.

The Aramaic language predates the rise of the Persian Empire. Aramaic is the language of the Aramean states that arose in Syria in the tenth century B.C.E. The Assyrian Empire had already adopted Aramaic as an administrative language for its dealings with the west in the eighth century B.C.E.[35] Aramaic is the language of Israel's neighbor and rival to the north. According to biblical tradition, it is also the language of Israel's ancestors: "My father was a wandering Aramean" (Deut 26:5). Aramaic is also a closely related language to Hebrew, and thus it is often difficult to tell the difference between Aramaic influence on Hebrew and the shared linguistic heritage of the two cousin languages.

At the end of the fourth century, the Aramaic-speaking world changed into a Hellenistic, Greek-speaking, world. By the third century B.C.E., the Hebrew Bible began to be translated into Greek by the Jewish community in Alexandria. The Greek translation, known as the Septuagint after a legendary tale of its original seventy translators, came to be used in the Diaspora and then later in Christian liturgy. According to the legend told in the Letter of Aristeas, the translation was made at the behest of Ptolemy II Philadelphus (285–247 B.C.E.), who was collecting books for the famous royal library in Alexandria. Although the legend purports that the seventy translators independently arrived at the exact same translation (thereby suggesting the divine character of the translation), scholars have questioned how well the translators even understood Biblical Hebrew. The eminent Oxford University biblical scholar James Barr is skeptical about how well the Greek translators understood the Hebrew text.[36] Jan Joosten, professor of Hebrew at the University of Strasbourg, points out that the Septuagint translators demonstrate a knowledge of their own contemporary Hebrew, which is distinct from the Hebrew of biblical literature. Joosten points to several anomalies in the Septuagint's translation, observing that "The mechanism leading to the Septuagint's translation appears to be one of unconscious assimilation to contemporary Hebrew."[37] One interesting example is the Biblical Hebrew word *ger*, which means a "resident alien" in all biblical texts. However, as a result of religious developments in the later Second Temple period, the Hebrew word *ger* comes to mean "a religious convert," as attested by Qumran Hebrew texts and Rabbinic literature. The Septuagint reflects the meaning of the word in contemporary (i.e., "late") Hebrew by translating *ger* as a religious convert. The point is that by the third century B.C.E., the Hebrew language itself had changed so much that it represents a completely different phase in the history of Hebrew. For this reason, it is impossible to reconcile the historical development of the Hebrew language with a late Persian or Hellenistic dating for the composition of biblical literature.

Writing and Biblical Literature in the Persian Period

Whereas Hebrew became a marginal language in the Persian period, the role of writing itself became increasingly important. The Persian Empire employed a standard Aramaic lingua franca throughout the Near East. Official Aramaic, as it is called by scholars, was used from Iran to Egypt with negligible variations. The uniformity of Aramaic was testimony to the strong imperial administration and its scribal chancellery. The influence was naturally felt particularly on the biblical literature composed within the borders of the Persian Empire. Most notably, the Book of Ezra includes substantial sections composed in Aramaic. Even where Hebrew was being written, the influence of the Aramaic lingua franca imposed itself on the Hebrew.

As noted earlier in this chapter, Aramaic had a special influence on the latest books of the Bible because of the Aramaic world in which they were written.[38] The dating of many biblical books cannot be certain,[39] as so much depends on the assumptions we make about the composition of this literature. However, the Books of Ezra-Nehemiah, and Chronicles are literary works of the Persian period.[40] The Book of Daniel dates to the Hellenistic period, although the Aramaic stories in the book seem to date back to the Persian period.[41] It is difficult to be precise about the Book of Esther, though it must be dated somewhere between the fifth and second centuries B.C.E. These happen to be the texts for which there has always been wide agreement, because of both language and content, that they were written in the Persian and Hellenistic periods. The Book of Job has a narrative prose introduction (chapters 1–2) that was added in the Persian or Hellenistic period; that is to say, it was edited in a later period, although the large poetic section (chapters 3–41) is earlier. The dating of the books of Song of Songs and Ecclesiastes is in dispute because the linguistic anomalies of these works go far beyond the use of Aramaisms; many scholars have plausibly suggested that they may reflect a different dialect of Hebrew and posit their origin in northern Israel.[42] The assessment of the evidence here – and in other cases – depends quite a bit on the assumptions that we bring to the linguistic data. The ultimate point is, however, that the list of biblical literature that shows the pervasive influence of Aramaic is quite short. Given that the entire scribal infrastructure of the Persian Empire was Aramaic and that the vernacular dialects of Syria-Palestine were related to Aramaic as well, any literature composed in this late period would naturally reflect the pervasive influence of its Aramaic world. But very little biblical literature shows this influence. Why? Simply because this was a period of retrenchment, collecting, and editing rather than creative literary production.

The training of scribes during the Persian period would have been in Aramaic. This is evident in the Book of Ezra-Nehemiah. In Nehemiah 8:8, for example, we read, "So they read from the book, from the law of God, *with interpretation* [or, *translation*]. They gave the sense, so that the people understood the reading." This text assumes that an audience in Jerusalem in the fifth century B.C.E. did not understand the Hebrew of the Torah.[43] It had to *interpreted* or *translated*, as the Hebrew word, *meforash*, in this text suggests (also see Ezr 4:18). In fact, the very Hebrew word employed, *meforash*, is a loanword from Aramaic, where it was a technical term used in the Persian chancellery. In other words, the use of this expression, *with interpretation*, indicates that the author had training by the Persian administration in Aramaic. Not only would the urban and priestly elite in Jerusalem have used Aramaic on a day-to-day basis, but some of them would also have had formal scribal training in Aramaic. This training utilized the resources of the Persian Empire.

In contrast, there were few resources and little infrastructure for scribal training specifically in Hebrew. A colloquial Hebrew continued to be spoken, but with significant Aramaic influence. In fact, Nehemiah laments the complete loss of Hebrew through intermarriage: "In those days also I saw Jews who had married women of Ashdod, Ammon, and Moab; and half of their children spoke the language of Ashdod, and they could not speak the language of Judah, but spoke the language of various peoples" (Neh 13:23–24). The "language of Ashdod" and the "language of various peoples" were varieties of Aramaic. This passage implies both certain continuity in Hebrew as well as significant incursion by Aramaic. It is important to remember, however, that the text of Nehemiah itself is *late Biblical Hebrew*. Nehemiah is not written in the Classical literary idiom. When Nehemiah laments the loss of Hebrew, it is not proposing that this is a loss of the Classical literary idiom. Nehemiah is regretting the loss of the understanding of Hebrew literature and the loss of the ability to speak in the late colloquial dialect of Hebrew.[44]

Biblical literature, and more generally, Jewish literature has historical gaps. The biggest gap is from the sixth century through the second century B.C.E. The Bible contains stories in the Pentateuch of the origins of the Jewish people. It has prose narratives detailing the monarchy until the Babylonian exiles. After this, things get sketchy. Apart from the account of Ezra-Nehemiah, there are no Jewish literary accounts of the sixth through second centuries B.C.E. There is no narrative account after the disappearance of Zerubbabel and his cohort and the completion of the Temple in 515 B.C.E. until the appearance of Ezra, traditionally (although not universally) dated to about

458 B.C.E. Nehemiah is supposed to be Ezra's contemporary. Setting aside for the moment the squabbles about how historical these biblical figures are, it is striking that we have no biblical accounts of the history of the Persian or Hellenistic periods apart from these biographical glimpses. These gaps are not only a feature of biblical literature. We have no contemporary historical accounts of these periods anywhere. As a result, the later Jewish historian Flavius Josephus (in the first century C.E.) is hard-pressed to write the history of this period in his comprehensive book *The Antiquities of the Jews*, which begins with Moses and tells the history of the Jewish people until the author's own day. Jewish literature engages history again only in the second century B.C.E. in the Book of Maccabees. How do we account for this gap? Archaeological and literary sources offer an explanation. This period was simply not one that favored a great flourishing of Hebrew literature in Jerusalem.

When we come to the second century B.C.E., Hebrew literature sees a revival. The Book of First Maccabees, the Wisdom of Ben-Sira, the Book of Jubilees, and the Book of Daniel (among others) are all composed in the second century B.C.E. This revival is certainly spurred on by the rise of the Hasmonean state, which adopts Hebrew as part of its nationalistic agenda. The Hasmoneans try to revive the old Hebrew script, which they use for their coins. The Qumran religious sect makes the use of Hebrew a strong ideological part of their sectarian identity; they compose many new works found among the famous Dead Sea Scrolls. But this Hebrew is markedly different from the Classical Hebrew known from the Bible and inscriptions dating to the seventh century B.C.E. This is the precursor to what comes to be known as Rabbinic Hebrew (sometimes, Mishnaic Hebrew). The Aramaic language continues to influence all facets of the Hebrew language. Indeed, once Aramaic becomes the lingua franca of the Near East during the Persian Empire, its encroaching upon Hebrew is unstoppable.

One basic problem in the modern study of the Biblical Hebrew language can be traced back to the break in the Hebrew scribal tradition between the monarchy and the Persian period. As I pointed out in the last chapter, this tradition continued in a limited way during the Babylonian exile and until the end of the sixth century B.C.E. At that point, however, this scribal infrastructure recoiled within the impoverished and depopulated province of Yehud. A decisive break in the Hebrew language and its scribal institutions occurred. Jon Berquist, in his survey of Persian history entitled *Judaism in Persia's Shadow*, argues that "literacy rates were so low that written law made little sense for most people. Laws were customs rather than written statements demanding adherence to the letter."[45] Particularly in Persian Yehud, whose economy was largely subsistence farming and pastoralism and whose people lived largely in small villages, literacy rates must have been quite low. Yet, writing was a central part of Persian imperial administration.

The Temple Library

According to one late Hellenistic Jewish tradition, Nehemiah founded a library in Jerusalem. We read in 2 Maccabees 2:13–14:

> The same things are reported in the records and in the memoirs of Nehemiah, and also that he founded a library and collected the books about the kings and prophets, and the writings of David, and letters of kings about votive offerings. In the same way Judah also collected all the books that had been lost on account of the war that had come upon us, and they are in our possession.

Nehemiah *founds* a library and *collects* books according to the tradition. Of course, this passage is quite a bit later and attributes to Nehemiah activities that are typically Hellenistic. These are activities that might also be associated with the editing of literary works, as it was to some extent in the founding and building of the great Hellenistic library in Alexandria, Egypt. So, it is difficult to be confident about the historicity of this traditional attribution to Nehemiah of the creation of a library. But a library of biblical literature was created in Jerusalem. The biblical literature of ancient Israel was preserved.

The origins of the Temple library probably go back to the rebuilding of the temple by the last of the Davidic line in the late sixth century B.C.E. The literature of the royal family was probably deposited in the Temple archives at that time. The Temple library was apparently limited to "the holy books." The first-century Jewish historian Josephus speaks of holy books "laid up in the Temple."[46] Interestingly, Josephus emphasized the Temple as a repository for the holy books and not for the more widely distributed profane works. One theme of the Book of Ezra is the search of the archives. Persian officials are repeatedly asked to "search the archives" for the history of the city of Jerusalem, for permission to rebuild the temple, for letters and documents. These notices indicate the general interest in libraries and archives that had begun in the Assyrian Empire and continued into the Persian Empire.

The Texualization of Jewish Religion

The written word is presented as a central concept in the religious program of Ezra and Nehemiah.[47] According to the biblical accounts of Ezra-Nehemiah, the literature of ancient Israel comes to have a special role in establishing the authority and promulgating the reforms of Ezra and Nehemiah. It is worth citing at length the detailed narrative of the reading of the Law of Moses recounted in Nehemiah 8:1–5:

All the people gathered together into the square before the Water Gate. They told the scribe Ezra to bring the scroll of the Law/*Torah* of Moses, which YHWH had given to Israel. Accordingly, the priest Ezra brought the law before the assembly, both men and women and all who could hear with understanding. This was on the first day of the seventh month. He read from it facing the square before the Water Gate from early morning until midday, in the presence of the men and the women and those who could understand; and the ears of all the people were attentive to the scroll of the Law/*Torah*. The scribe Ezra stood on a wooden platform that had been made for the purpose. . . . And Ezra opened the scroll in the sight of all the people, for he was standing above all the people; and when he opened it, all the people stood up.

The narrative slows down to give us the details. Apparently, a special wooden platform, a lectern, is made just for the reading of the *Torah*. Ezra opens the scroll with a great flourish. The people rise out of respect for the word of God. What a scene! No doubt this scene was intended to serve as a pattern for the reading of the *Torah* in the Jewish community. The story is thus programmatic and appears to have achieved its desired effect. The reading of *Torah* invites action as well. In the continuation of the narrative, the *Torah* provides the explicit basis for religious performance:

And Nehemiah, who was the governor, and Ezra the priest and scribe, and the Levites who taught the people said to all the people, "This day is holy to YHWH your God; do not mourn or weep." For all the people wept when they heard the words of the *Torah*. . . . On the second day the heads of ancestral houses of all the people, with the priests and the Levites, came together to the scribe Ezra in order to study the words of the *Torah*. And they found it written in the *Torah*, which YHWH had commanded by Moses, that the people of Israel should live in booths (*sukkot*) during the festival of the seventh month, and that they should publish and proclaim in all their towns and in Jerusalem. . . . And day by day, from the first day to the last day, he read from the scroll of the Law/*Torah* of God. They kept the festival seven days; and on the eighth day there was a solemn assembly, according to the ordinance. (Neh 8:9–15)

Not only does Ezra read the *Torah* out loud to the people, but the people also come together to study *Torah*. This is a new stage in the text's centrality. Also, the narrative is careful to highlight the author of the *Torah*, which came through Moses. In obedience to what they studied in the written *Torah*, the people observe what is known today as the Jewish feast of *Sukkot* (or, "the feast of booths").

The Book of Chronicles is the most extensive literary work of the Persian period. Although Chronicles represents one of the few Persian literary works, it is a poor excuse for literature. Chronicles is largely a retelling of the history of Judah, and it borrows mercilessly from the Books of Samuel and Kings. The book begins with nine chapters of genealogies, with an emphasis on the priestly genealogies of its authors. It then picks up the story of the ancient Davidic kings beginning with the death of Saul. A quick comparison of Samuel and Chronicles shows how closely Chronicles borrows from its sources:

1 Samuel 31	**1 Chronicles 10**
1 Now the Philistines fought against Israel; and the men of Israel fled before the Philistines, and many fell on Mount Gilboa.	1 Now the Philistines fought against Israel; and every man of Israel fled before the Philistines, and many fell on Mount Gilboa.
2 The Philistines overtook Saul and his sons; and the Philistines killed Jonathan and Abinadab and Malchishua, the sons of Saul.	2 The Philistines overtook Saul and his sons; and the Philistines killed Jonathan and Abinadab and Malchishua, the sons of Saul.
3 The battle pressed hard upon Saul; and the archers found him, and he was wounded from the archers.	3 The battle pressed hard on Saul; and the archers found him, and he was wounded by the archers.
4 Then Saul said to his armor-bearer, "Draw your sword, and thrust me through with it, so that these uncircumcised may not come and thrust me through, and make sport of me." But his armor-bearer was unwilling, for he was terrified. So Saul took his own sword and fell upon it.	4 Then Saul said to his armor-bearer, "Draw your sword, and thrust me through with it, so that these uncircumcised may not come and make sport of me." But his armor-bearer was unwilling, for he was terrified. So Saul took his own sword and fell on it.
5 When his armor-bearer saw that Saul was dead, he also fell upon his sword and died with him.	5 When his armor-bearer saw that Saul was dead, he also fell on his sword and died.

6 So Saul and his three sons and his armor-bearer and all his men died together on the same day.	6 So Saul died and his three sons and all his house died together.
7 When the men of Israel who were on the other side of the valley and those beyond the Jordan saw that the men of Israel had fled and that Saul and his sons were dead, they abandoned their towns and fled; and the Philistines came and occupied them.	7 When all the men of Israel who were in the valley saw that the army had fled and that Saul and his sons were dead, they abandoned their towns and fled; and the Philistines came and occupied them.
8 The next day when the Philistines came to strip the dead, they found Saul and his three sons fallen on Mount Gilboa.	8 The next day when the Philistines came to strip the dead, they found Saul and his sons fallen on Mount Gilboa.
9 They cut off his head, stripped off his armor, and sent messengers throughout the land of the Philistines to carry the good news to the houses of their idols and to the people.	9 They stripped him and took his head and his armor, and sent messengers throughout the land of the Philistines to carry the good news to their idols and to the people.
10 They put his armor in the temple of Astarte; and they fastened his body to the wall of Beth-shan.	10 They put his armor in the temple of their gods, and fastened his head in the temple of Dagon.
11 But when the inhabitants of Jabesh-gilead heard what the Philistines had done to Saul,	11 But when all Jabesh-gilead heard everything that the Philistines had done to Saul,
12 all the valiant men set out, traveled all night long, and took the body of Saul and the bodies of his sons from the wall of Beth-shan. They came to Jabesh and burned them there.	12 all the valiant warriors got up and took away the body of Saul and the bodies of his sons, and brought them to Jabesh.Then they buried their bones under the oak tree in Jabesh, and fasted seven days.
13 Then they took their bones and buried them under the tamarisk tree in Jabesh, and fasted seven days.	13 So Saul died for his unfaithfulness; he was unfaithful to the LORD in that he did not keep the command of the LORD; moreover, he had consulted a medium, seeking guidance, 14 and did not seek guidance from the LORD. Therefore the LORD put him to death and turned the kingdom over to David son of Jesse.

The only substantive change in the story is the addition of an editorial comment at the end. Some of the small discrepancies probably reflect a slightly different text in the Chronicler's source. Many small changes that are especially evident in the Hebrew original reflect the continued updating of the language from the Classical idiom to the Chronicler's own late Hebrew idiom. Sometimes updating the language to a more contemporary Hebrew also invited minor interpretative changes.

Sometimes the Book of Chronicles will reorganize chapters from its source. For instance, the story of King David from 2 Samuel 5–24 is completely reorganized in 1 Chronicles 11–21. Negative aspects of David's life – like David's adultery with Bathsheba and his murder of her husband, Uriah – are completely omitted. The reorganization serves to emphasize David's role as temple builder.[48] A long addition in 1 Chronicles 22–29 highlights the establishment of the various temple administrators, singers, and priests. Where we can see that Chronicles had a source (from the canonical books of Samuel and Kings), the text usually follows quite closely, even when it has re-arranged the order of the chapters. Chronicles makes additions in a few places as it suits the purposes of the Jerusalem priesthood of the Persian period. Mostly, the priests add genealogies, and they also introduce a long digression on the building and administration of the Temple. They often include theological comments, such as in 1 Chronicles 10:12–13, which was cited earlier. They also omit what seems irrelevant or does not advance their interests. They are quite concerned to make David and Solomon into pious kings worthy of their role as temple builders. Hence, most of the negative features of these idealized figures is left out. Most impressively, the priests also leave out the entire account of the northern kingdom of Israel as told in the Book of Kings. Sometimes this excision is clumsy and traces of the older literary source come to the fore. For the most part, however, the northern kingdom is missing from the story of the Jewish people in this revised history from the pen of the Jerusalem priests.

The Book of Chronicles has a keen awareness of the idea of sacred written traditions. In this respect, it is possible to characterize the Chronicler as an interpreter of Scripture. The growing prominence of authoritative written texts is apparent throughout Chronicles. For example, when the spirit of God comes upon Azariah in 2 Chronicles 15, Azariah spouts a rambling, somewhat enigmatic, injunction to the people of Judah. Most interesting to the present concern is the statement: "For a long time Israel was without the true God, and without a teaching priest, and without *Torah*" (v. 3). The idea here of a "teaching priest" – no doubt one like Ezra – apparently follows the absence of *Torah*, that is, a written tradition. Although the term *torah* originally meant "instruction" and hence originally had an oral context, this oral *torah*, or "instruction," is transformed into the textual and written *Torah* in Second Temple literature. The transformation is implicit as, for example, in 1 Chronicles 16:40: "according to all that is *written* in the *Torah* of YHWH which he *commanded* Israel."[49] To begin with, the instructions were orally *commanded*, but these commands were subsequently *written* down. Hence, the *Torah* that the priest teaches is now those commands that were written in a document, as we learn in 2 Chronicles 17:9: "And the priests taught in Judah, having with them the *scroll of the Torah of YHWH*, and they went about among all the cities of Judah and taught the people." We see in Chronicles both the sacred written text and the priest who instructs the people from the authority of this sacred text.

More generally, we witness in the Jewish literature written in the Persian and Hellenistic periods the rise of Scripture. The very idea of "Scripture" depends upon a textual culture. In an oral culture the activities of composing, learning, and transmitting blend together. Tradition is constantly reinventing itself. Writing, on the other hand, freezes tradition. As Plato so astutely observes in Socrates' speech to Phaedrus, "written words go on telling you just the same thing forever." Henri-Jean Martin, in his monumental work *The History and Power of Writing*, observes that writing "is not revolutionary, but it appears every time that a revolution in communications prompts a fusion into a larger whole. When this occurs it accelerates the changes set in motion within that society."[50] The Persian Empire did constitute a revolution in writing technology. By standardizing one language and writing throughout an empire stretching from India to Asia Minor to Africa, the Persians spread an official language throughout the Near East. No longer was writing restricted to government affairs; writing was now a part of the cultural system that the Persians disseminated through the known world.

Textualizing the "Word of YHWH" – the Eclipse of Prophecy

The most telling aspect of the change in the religious culture advocated by the priests is in the transformation of the meaning of the technical term, "the word of YHWH." Throughout biblical literature and particularly in the Former Prophets, "the word of YHWH" refers to the words of the prophets. There is no indication in biblical literature that this "word of YHWH" was anything other than the divinely commissioned speech of the prophets, until we get to the late Book of Chronicles. This term is critical to changing the concept of the word of God among the temple priests and scribes during the Persian period.

It is worthwhile to draw out this issue in further detail.[51] The expression "the word of YHWH" appears about two hundred forty times in the Hebrew Bible. Strikingly, "the word of YHWH" is not used to describe the Mosaic revelation in the Pentateuch.[52] In the Pentateuch, God "speaks" to Moses, but the formulas are completely different. Rather, "the word of YHWH" usually appears in stereotyped formulas relating to the oracular and prophetic word. It appears mainly in the Former and Latter Prophetic Books. There are, for instance, a variety of expressions that begin, "and the word of YHWH came to prophet X." There are also frequent summaries of events that conclude, such and such happened "according to the word of YHWH through the prophet X." Thus, "the word of YHWH" is a technical term for the prophetic revelation.

This observation was briefly made in Chapter 6, when I discussed the critique of the written word by the prophet Jeremiah. Jeremiah complained that the scribes and the wise men had rejected "the word of YHWH" and instead had favored the written Torah (Jer 8:7–9). Fundamentally, Jeremiah was complaining that the "wise men and scribes" had displaced the traditional loci of authority – oral tradition and the prophetic word – with a new kind of authority, the written word. *Torah*, which had been "oral instruction," was turned into a textual authority by "the lying pen of the scribes." The priests and scribes of Jerusalem in the Persian period will advance this transformation. The prophet Jeremiah had complained that the meaning of *torah* had been transformed from oral tradition to text. Now, in the Book of Chronicles, "the word of YHWH," has been transformed from the oral word of God spoken by the prophets into the written word of God.

It may seem strange that the Hebrew word for "prophecy" – *nevû'ah* – was coined in the late Persian period. The word appears only in the Books of Chronicles and Ezra-Nehemiah (2 Chr 9:29; 15:8; Ezr 6:14; Neh 6:12), which were written in the Persian period. Why is this? Simply put, the normal term for prophecy had been "the word of YHWH," but this term was co-opted by the textualization of the literary traditions. Since the "word of YHWH" now had come to refer to the Torah of Moses, a new term was needed that would refer specifically to the prophetic word. This neologism, of course, continues to exert an enormous influence on modern religious expression – the "word of God" is now usually thought of as a text.

Biblical prophecy itself disappears (at least formally) in the wake of this transformation.[53] The expression "the word of YHWH" had been central to the description of the prophetic reception of God's word. By appropriating this term, prophecy itself will be subsumed into the written word and disappear. There is a strong Jewish tradition that prophecy ended with the destruction of the Temple in 586 B.C.E. Zechariah, Haggai, and Malachi are considered the last of the great prophets, and they are replaced by the sages. Other terminology also reflects this new emphasis on the written word as an authoritative basis of religion. The word *darash*, "to inquire," and the related noun *Midrash* no longer mean simply "to inquire" but begin to be used for interpretation of a written text.[54] So, for example, "Ezra had set his heart to study (*darash*) the *Torah* of YHWH" (Ezr 7:10). Prophecy will become an increasingly scribal phenomenon. The "prophet" will be the one who understands the mysteries of God encoded in the written word. An explict example of this process is found among the Dead Sea Scrolls, in their commentary on the prophetic Book of Habakkuk. The true interpreter was "the Teacher of Righteousness, to whom God made known all the mysteries of his servants the prophets" (1 QpHab 7:4–5). The prophets themselves did not understand their revelations, but the community's leader, the Teacher of Righteousness, was shown by God the meaning of the prophetic writings. Ironically, the sect did not consider the Teacher of Righteousness a prophet. Rather, he was thought to be the inspired interpreter of the divine word.

The Book of Chronicles uses four formulas for its formal citations of the Mosaic law known from the Pentateuch. The most common way of citing the Mosaic law begins with "as it is written," an expression that is used frequently in Ezra-Nehemiah as well as in Chronicles.[55] The other formulas include "according to the commandments of Moses" (e.g., 2 Chr 8:13), "according to the *Torah* of Moses" (e.g., 2 Chr 30:16), and "according to the word of YHWH" (e.g., 1 Chr 15:15; 2 Chr 35:6). In Chronicles and Ezra-Nehemiah, the reference to written Mosaic legislation appears as a regular feature of the historian's presentation. The last two expressions, "the *Torah* of

Moses" and "the word of YHWH," point to a critical semantic shift from oral to written tradition.

In the Persian and early Hellenistic periods, the writing of biblical literature comes to an end. Already we see in the last writings of such literature development of the concept of the sacred written text. But was the textualization of ancient Israel complete? There were those who would have rejected the displacement of traditional oral authority by the written word. Although prophecy was marginalized by the new orthodoxy, it would reemerge later in new forms like apocalyptic literature. But, fundamentally, the dissent was silenced in history. First of all, it was silenced by the oral locus of the dissent. The oral tradition is not preserved for future generations after the speakers are gone. Ironically, in order for criticism of the written word as we see in Jeremiah to be registered, it had to be written! Thus, an institutional bias exists that limits our awareness of the full extent of the critique of the written word in Second Temple Judaism. Second, the control of writing resided among the temple and political elites. Those who had a vested interest in the shift of authority from the oral tradition to the written text were also those who controlled the means of production of the written word. The more limited the economic resources and restricted the political leadership, the more difficult it would become to produce subversive literary texts. This was especially true in antiquity, before breakthroughs in the technology of writing made widespread literacy more feasible. The silence of the critique of the authority of written texts is a reflection of the dark years of the Persian period. But this silence would be broken in the voices of formative Judaism and Christianity.

The Synopsis

The time has come to review some of the main arguments of this book and to see how I have answered some of the questions that I first posed. When was the Bible written? Why was it written? How did the Bible become a book? I approached these questions from the perspective of the role of written texts in ancient Israel. I pointed out that writing had a restricted role in antiquity. Writing was first of all controlled by the state. Writing was both a display of state power and a tool of state administration. Second, writing was a gift of the gods. As such, writing was part of magical rituals like the Execration texts or the ritual of the bitter water (Num 5). Writing was also something done in heaven, as with the Book of Life or the divine tablets that originally had the blueprints for God's earthly abode. Oral tradition, in contrast, was the medium of cultural continuity. Early Israel sang songs of their ancestors and told stories of their forefathers. Through proverbs and folktales and songs each generation received and passed on the cultural legacy of ancient Israel.

A major transition in ancient Israel began in the late eighth century B.C.E. Writing became both more centralized and more widespread in Judah; as the society became urbanized, the economy more complex and the government more substantial. Writing had always been a projection of royal power, and now this power extended to the collection of a great library in Jerusalem (just as the Assyrians and the Egyptians were doing during this same period). King Hezekiah desired to create a kingdom similar to the legendary (in his days) kingdom of David and Solomon. The oral traditions of ancient Israel were compiled into written texts. The palace archives containing administrative texts of ancient Judah were used in composing histories of the Judean kings. One catalyst for the restoration of the golden age of Israel – that is, the united monarchy of David and Solomon – was the fall of the northern kingdom of Israel. This final destruction vindicated the house of David, which had struggled for centuries with its northern neighbor. As many refugees from the north flooded into Jerusalem, Judah accommodated not only these new citizens but also their traditions. Some of their prophetic traditions, as in the Book of Hosea, were edited in the Judean royal court. These also were understood to vindicate Judah. A history of Israel was written as though Judah and Israel were one kingdom, though even this account acknowledges that the "united" Israel was but a fleeting historical moment. Nevertheless, this ideology of one kingdom of the twelve tribes of Israel was embodied in the literature of the late eighth century. This literature both preserved and created the golden age of David and Solomon. This great literary flourishing, albeit short-lived, was the beginning of biblical literature as we know it. The political vision of Hezekiah took its military expression in a revolt against Assyria in 705 B.C.E. The Assyrian king Sennacherib crushed this revolt in 701 B.C.E. and with it all dreams of a new golden age under the sons of Hezekiah. Judah then struggled as a vassal of Assyria until the demise of the Assyrian Empire in the days of King Josiah (r. 640–609 B.C.E.).

The second major phase in the literary formation of the Bible came in the days of King Josiah in the late seventh century B.C.E. The use of writing for mundane economic and administrative purposes had continued unabated from the days of Hezekiah. Literacy had spread throughout the fabric of Judean society. Soldiers could read and write. Craftsmen were literate. Whereas writing had previously had a restricted role in society, the spread of writing into everyday life meant that now writing could become a tool for subversion of the centralized power of the government. Texts were no longer only the products of the palace or the priests. A turning point for biblical literature was the assassination of King Amon (r. 642–640 B.C.E.); the "people of the land" set up the boy-king, Josiah, at the tender age of eight years old, on the throne in Jerusalem. Influenced by the "people of the land" and his family connections in the rural foothills of Judah, Josiah instituted political and religious reforms that were directly aimed at the cultural influence that urbanization and northernization had had in the days of Hezekiah. Writing became a tool, as in the Book of Deuteronomy, for critiquing the vision of Hezekiah. Solomon was not a great king according to the Deuteronomists, but a king who violated the divine law as recorded in "the book of the covenant" (compare 1 Kgs 11 with Deut 17:14–20). The Deuteronomists advocated a return to the traditional religion of their forefathers. Of course, this tension between the urban and the rural, between the central palace and the rural elders, must have always existed. However, the Deuteronomic revolution gave the rural elders a written voice. Ancient writings, which had been elevated as literary propaganda in the days of Hezekiah, were turned on their head. Writing becomes a typical mode of expression in the latter days of the Judean monarchy. Biblical literature realized its apex in the last decades of the Judean monarchy.

The end of the great independent literary flourishing came swiftly. The lull between the fall of the Assyrian Empire and the rise of the Babylonian Empire lasted only as long as the reign of Josiah (r. 640–609 B.C.E.). When Josiah died in battle at Megiddo at the hands of the Egyptian Pharaoh Neco, with him died the hope for an independent Judean kingdom.

The Babylonians quickly assumed control of the region; three military campaigns, in 597, 586, and 581 B.C.E., were punctuated by destruction and exile. The royal family led by King Jehoiachin submitted to the Babylonians in 597 B.C.E. and were taken into exile where they were apparently treated relatively well. Those who remained and resisted the Babylonians did not fare quite as well. The Babylonians pillaged the region, and Judah was depopulated by destruction, exile, and flight until the land was nearly uninhabited. Judean captives worked as slaves on the canal projects of Babylon while the Judean royal family and their entourage lived in relative ease in the southern citadel in the city of Babylon. Because of all this the exilic period was a period of retrenchment for biblical literature. The writing and preservation of biblical literature returned to the hands of the royal family. The continuity in the royal family of Jehoiachin reached to the end of the sixth century B.C.E. continuing even after the fall of Babylon to the Persian king Cyrus in 539 B.C.E. Under the Persians, a descendent of Jehoiachin, Zerubbabel, assumed leadership of those who returned to Jerusalem in the late sixth century. However, Jerusalem and Judah were but shells of their former selves. The land was ravished by war and depopulated. As part of the royal family's claim to leadership in the restoration, Zerubbabel helped rebuild the Temple (completed in 515 B.C.E.). Shortly thereafter, however, Zerubbabel and the royal family mysteriously disappeared. The biblical literature of the exile and early post-exilic periods mostly complete and update earlier works. The great shift from orality to textuality that began in the late Judean monarchy suffers an enormous setback in the devastation of Jerusalem and Judah. The conditions in which literacy and textuality could flourish disappeared.

The Persian period was a dark age for biblical literature. The Persian province of Yehud was depopulated, impoverished, and geographically isolated. The once great city of Jerusalem remained mostly in ruins, even though some semblance of a temple had been rebuilt. Even the Hebrew language saw a decline, as Aramaic language and letters began to replace Hebrew as the language of the Jews. In the shadow of the Persian Empire, faithful priests who served in the Jerusalem Temple preserved biblical literature. For the most part, the work of the priests was not the composition of literature, but its preservation. This meant that they added the editorial framework to some biblical literature. The great poems of the Book of Job, for example, were given an editorial prologue and conclusion. The priests shaped the Psalms into a five-part book that paralleled the Five Books of Moses (or, Pentateuch). The priest Ezra was an ideal exemplar of the new priesthood. Ezra was both a secular and religious leader who was trained in the courts of the Persian kings and served in Jerusalem with their support. From the Books of Ezra and Nehemiah, which were among the few biblical books actually composed during the Persian period, it is clear that Ezra was trained in the Aramaic scribal chancellery. Ezra and the priestly leadership were both the guardians and the teachers of the sacred texts. As such, they controlled the authoritative texts. This secular priestly leadership continued to the end of the Second Temple period and the Roman destruction of Jerusalem in 70 C.E. It is clear that in the late Second Temple period the priestly leadership explicitly rejected the authority of oral tradition. Undoubtedly, they did so because it undermined the scriptural authority that they could claim as the teachers of Israel. The Rabbinic leadership that followed the destruction of the Second Temple would mark a decisive break with this model of secular leadership by priests and with its rejection of oral tradition.

This brings us to the epilogue of our story. In the third century B.C.E., Jewish literature would again begin to flourish under the cultural renaissance of Hellenism. Egyptian Hellenistic rule brought peace and relative prosperity back to Jerusalem. The city began to grow again. But the canon of biblical literature was largely closed. For the most part, the Bible was no longer being written. Rather, it was being copied, translated, paraphrased, commented upon, and embellished in every conceivable way. The literati were largely composed of the priests and the Levites. By the end of the third century B.C.E., students at Jewish schools in Jerusalem were studying the Scriptures as exemplified in the proverbs of the priestly schoolmaster Sirach. By the mid-third century, the Scriptures were being translated into Greek by priests in the Egyptian Diaspora. The Dead Sea Scrolls include Hebrew manuscripts dating to the third century B.C.E. pointing to the active copying and transmission of the Hebrew Scriptures. Neither Rabbinic Judaism nor early Christianity, in contrast, would number their early adherents from among the scribes. They were not dominated by social elites or by learned priests. Rather, they were lay movements and emerged out of the unlearned and unschooled. As a result, they would reflect the authority of both the oral tradition and the teacher.

10

Epilogue

What would the role of the written word be as Judaism and Christianity emerged in the first centuries? As a way of concluding, I would like to reflect on the relationship between oral tradition and written text in the formation of Judaism and Christianity. Although the heart of this book has been its look at the early development of writing and texts in ancient Israel and at the relationship of writing and these texts to the formation of the Hebrew Bible, it seems worthwhile to suggest how this textualization played out in the formative period for Judaism and Christianity.

Textualization is among the great cultural developments of the first millennium of the Common Era. For instance, textualization certainly is one of the more fascinating aspects in the rise of Islam. In fact, the expression "people of the book" came out of Islam to refer to itself, Judaism, and Christianity. Moreover, in *Veda and Torah: Transcending the Textuality of Scripture* (1996), Barbara Holdrege has reflected on textuality in the Hindu and Jewish traditions during the first millennium C.E. The Vedas were transmitted orally for many centuries. They were transmitted orally not because writing was unknown among the Hindus, but because of the primacy of orality.

Indeed, the concept of the sacred and authoritative written word is already attested in the last books of the Hebrew Bible written in the Persian period. This concept is quite clear in the priestly Book of Sirach, which was composed at the beginning of the second century B.C.E. and already cited a threefold canonical division of the Jewish Bible into the Law, Prophets, and Writings (which Ben-Sira refered to as "the other books").[1] Likewise, the Dead Sea Scrolls also acknowledge the tripartite canon, although the final shape of this canon was still not determined.[2] As long as biblical literature was copied on scrolls, the exact canonical order of the biblical books would not be set. The basic tripartite division of the Jewish Bible was known, but not necessarily which books went in which part. So, for example, the Book of Ruth was sometimes included as part of the Book of Judges within the section that included the Prophets; more usually, it was placed within the third division of the Writings. Thus, the order of books would vary somewhat in the first centuries of the Common Era. More than this, an entirely different canonical order was also taking shape among Jews in the Diaspora, especially in Alexandria. This more historically orientated organization of the individual books eventually became the basis for the Christian canons. But the invention of the codex forced decisions to be made about the set order of the biblical books within the codex. Christians adopted the codex form for their manuscripts from the second century C.E.,[3] and that preference helped shape the canon of Christian literature. Jews, in contrast, continued to favor the scroll as a writing material for many centuries after the invention of the codex.

Although a role was given to the sacred writings by both the early Christians and the Jews, displacement of the oral tradition was not quick and simple among the masses. The written word had been the sphere of the social elites. It guarded the religious orthodoxy of the priestly aristocracy. It was a tool of government and empire. Oral tradition, in contrast, was located in the family and in kinship relationships. Oral tradition was carried along through proverbs, stories, and songs passed down from one generation to the next. Moreover, as William Graham argues in his book *Beyond the Written Word: Oral Aspects of Scripture in the History of Religion*, even the written word is relational. That is to say, "A text becomes 'scripture' in active, subjective relationship to persons, and as part of a cumulative communal tradition. No text, written or oral or both, is sacred in isolation from a community."[4] Likewise, even after oral tradition is textualized, it never completely escapes a fundamental orality. Thus, scholars speak of writing in an oral mode or of scribal orality. Many of the literary forms of writing actually came from an oral setting, including, for example, the ancient Israelite formula used in letter writing. This derivation prompts the use of an oxymoron like scribal orality or oral writing. There is a gray area between orality and literacy. Hence, the term "literate" needs to be carefully defined. Literacy can exist on many different levels – from the mundane literacy of craftsmen and low-level bureaucrats to the high literacy of court scholars and scribes. Orality continues to exert an influence on writing and texts even after people have passed a threshold of literacy.

Although there is an ebb and flow to orality and literacy, orality and textuality stand on opposite and sometimes competing sides of cultural authority. We may take as one example of the tensions between oral tradition and the written word that were part of early Judaism and Christianity a halachic discussion between Rabbi Elazar ben Azaria and Rabbi Akiba. Elazar rejects Rabbi Akiva's scriptural interpretation in favor of oral tradition. Elazar says, "Even if you explicate the verse all day long I won't accept it, rather it is oral *torah* given to Moses from Sinai" (cf. Sifra Tzav, Parashah *he*, Pereq *Yod Alef*, 34b–35a; B. Menahot, 89a). This is a question of where cultural authority lies. It does not lie in the citation and explication of Scriptures. According to Elazar, it lies in the oral tradition passed down from Moses within the community. Although there can also be symbiosis between orality and textuality, there is no continuum. There is a choice to be made here. Does authority rest with the text or with the teacher? Once authority resides in the text, the teacher can be dismissed (even if this does not always happen). It is not coincidental that Martin Luther's refrain *sola scriptura* ("Scripture alone") took root in the fertile soil of the *Gutenberg Galaxy* (to borrow from the title of Marshall McLuhan's seminal book). It is also instructive that the competing claims of orality and textuality have a long history. This history was influenced by both technological innovation and socio-political change.

The appeal to the text did not eliminate the need for the teacher, but it did make literacy a prerequisite. In the Josianic Reforms, for example, the priest Hilkiah finds the scroll and the scribe Shaphan reads it to the king. In the Persian period reforms, the priest/scribe Ezra reads the *Torah* to the people. The Levites – "the guardians of the tabernacle of the Lord" (according to Num 31:30, 47) – also assisted in reading and interpreting the Torah (Neh 8:8–9). The orthodoxy of the text in these settings restricted religious authority to those who had the texts and could read them. Practically, this tended to concentrate religious authority in the temple, where the ancient scrolls were kept, and center it upon the priestly scribes who could read the sacred texts.

As the oral tradition became textualized in Judaism and Christianity, the distinction between the cultural authority of the text and of oral tradition blurred. Beginning in the third century C.E., a central feature of the ancient synagogue became the Torah shrine, which housed the ark containing the Torah Scroll. This tradition continues into the modern synagogue. This ancient architectural feature probably encouraged the retention of the scroll as a preferred writing medium. But the scroll also reflected a fundamental, perhaps ideological, rejection of the concept of the codex. Interestingly enough, the Torah shrine is absent from the earliest synagogues. Until its destruction in 70 C.E., the Jerusalem Temple was the center of the Jewish community within Judea as well as the Diaspora. The teaching of the Torah was carried out daily in the Temple and its courts by priests, Levites, and scribes. The synagogue, in contrast, was primarily a community center where worship would have been conducted probably on Sabbaths and feast days.[5]

The Bible was now written. But the struggle for the Bible was not yet over. In the first centuries of the Common Era, the text still had to press its claim to sole religious authority in Judaism and Christianity, which were in their formative stages. The role of biblical literature as authoritative Scripture would be one of the essential issues as these religious traditions struggled to define themselves. Both Christianity and Rabbinic Judaism emerged out of popular culture. They were not sponsored by the state, nor did they emerge from institutional religion. Because of this, the written word played an uneasy role in early Christianity and formative Judaism.

The Social Location of the Written Word

Critical to the emergence of sacred Scripture was the rise of Hellenism and the cultural revolution that it engendered in the Near East. After the turmoil that characterized the fourth century B.C.E. in Palestine, the political situation stabilized in the third century B.C.E. Palestine was under the control of the Hellenistic rulers in Egypt known as the Ptolemies. Egypt began to prosper. The Nile River valley produced abundant grain, which was traded throughout the Mediterranean world. The Hellenistic rulers began to build again, trying with their grand temples and palaces to recapture the glory of Egypt's past. Egypt experienced a renaissance.

The Ptolemiac rulers considered themselves intellectuals. They established a new capital in Alexandria, the city that Alexander the Great had founded in 331 B.C.E. after his conquest of Egypt. Ptolemy I (also known as Ptolemy Soter, r. 305–282 B.C.E.) established the great library in Alexandria.[6] He also built a museum as a gathering place for writers, poets, scientists, and scholars. Members were given a salary as well as free room and board. Ptolemy Soter himself wrote an authoritative history of Alexander the Great. The library in Alexandria that he founded grew under the lavish patronage of Ptolemy II (Philadelphus, r. 282–246 B.C.E.). Conveniently for the great library in Alexandria, Egypt had a monopoly on the prime writing material of the ancient world – papyrus. According to the Letter of Aristeas, Ptolemy II, king of Egypt, requested that his librarian collect books from around the world for his library. The library supposedly held over 490,000 scrolls.

Ptolemy Philadephus is remembered for his generosity to science and the arts. According to a popular Jewish tradition, Philadephus even commissioned the translation of the Torah into Greek. More generally, he sought to acquire books for his library by any means necessary. He built Alexandria into the cultural capital of the Hellenistic world. He also spread Hellenism into the Palestine, creating such Hellenistic cities as Philadephia (which is today within the city of Amman, Jordan), Philoteria (on the Sea of Galilee), and Ptolemais (just north of the modern-day city of Haifa on the Mediterranean coast). Ptolemy III (Euergetes I, r. 246–222 B.C.E.) was also a patron of literature. Ptolemy IV (Philopator r. 222–204 B.C.E.) was a writer.

Jews were also caught up in the cultural revolution in Ptolemaic Egypt. Although the Letter of Aristeas suggests that Ptolemy commissioned the translation of the Torah, most scholars believe that the translation was done by the Jewish community for the Jewish community in Egypt who no longer understood Hebrew. Most of the Hebrew Bible was apparently translated in the third century in Egypt. It is probably not coincidental that the earliest extant Hebrew biblical manuscripts found among the Dead Sea Scrolls date to the mid-third century. That is, the first non-biblical evidence for the earnest study, copying, and translating of biblical literature is precisely in the third century B.C.E. These manuscripts attest to a lively scribal tradition that developed in the Hellenistic period.

The Priests as Teachers

The priests were the guardians and teachers of the sacred written text in the Second Temple period.[7] They were the teachers of the law. Although writing during the period of the monarchy was primarily an affair of the government and royal scribes, the secular leadership of Israel had transferred to the priests after the Jerusalem Temple was rebuilt in 515 B.C.E. Along with taking over the secular leadership, the priests also inherited the administrative role of writing in the Persian Empire. At the same time, the priests were entrusted with the sacred writings deposited in the Temple and the priests and the Levites charged with teaching and interpreting Scripture. The first explicit statement of this charge to the priests is in a Persian-period composition, the Book of Chronicles, which relates that King Jehoshaphat had appointed priests and Levites "to teach in Judah, having the book of the *Torah* of YHWH with them; they went around through all the cities of Judah and taught among the people" (2 Chr 17:9).

An apocryphal book, *The Wisdom of Sirach*, reflects a priestly, aristocratic school that was earnestly studying the Scriptures in Hebrew by the end of the third century B.C.E. In the second century, a priest known as Yeshua Ben-Eliezer Ben-Sira translated the Hebrew book of his grandfather into the Greek book now known as *The Wisdom of Sirach*.[8] The grandfather, Ben-Sira, had lived in Jerusalem where he had his school (cf. Sir 50:27). This is the first mention in Hebrew literature of a school, and it is sometimes used (quite inappropriately) to project the institution of schools back into ancient Israel. The world of Ben-Sira, however, was a thoroughly Hellenistic world. The institution of schools and study described in Sirach are reflections of Hellenistic culture not remnants of an ancient Israelite school system. According to the preface of the Greek translation:

> Many great teachings have been given to us through the Law and the Prophets and the others that followed them, . . . Now, those who read the scriptures must not only themselves understand them, but must also as lovers of learning be able through the spoken and written word to help the outsiders. So my grandfather Yeshua, who had devoted himself especially to the reading of the Law and the Prophets and the other books of our ancestors, and had acquired considerable proficiency in them, was himself also led to write something pertaining to instruction and wisdom, so that by becoming familiar also with his book those who love learning might make even greater progress in living according to the law.

Within the book of Sirach, the sons of Aaron are praised as the teachers of Israel: "In his commandments God gave him authority and statutes and judgments, to teach Jacob the testimonies, and to enlighten Israel with his law" (Sir 45:17). Although the prologue praises Ben-Sira's erudition in the Hebrew Scriptures, the Hebrew language of the Book of Sirach is quite distinct from that used in biblical literature.[9] Almost three hundred years after Sirach, the late-first-century C.E. Jewish historian Josephus (himself a priest) describes a similar role for the priests as the teachers of Israel. According to Josephus, the Jewish people entrusted writing "to their high priests and to the prophets, ... and these records have been written all along down to our own times with the utmost accuracy" (*Against Apion* 1.6). In another book Josephus notes that Moses "delivered these books to the priests, with the ark, into which he also put the Ten Commandments, written on two tables" (*Ant* 4.8.44). According to Josephus, the priests continue to be responsible for reading the Scriptures publicly (as Ezra had) during the septennial celebration of the Feast of Tabernacles (*Ant* 4.8.12).[10]

Scholars have often assumed that that a group of non-priestly scribes grew up in the wake of Hellenism. These lay scribes would have been the precursors to the Pharisees and then to the Rabbinic sages.[11] As Steven Fraade, professor of Rabbinics at Yale University, points out, there is no evidence from the Second Temple period to support the development of lay teachers at that time. Fraade writes:

First, there is little evidence for the existence of a broad class or movement of non-priestly (and certainly not antipriestly) scribes and sages in this period. Second, the extant sources, right up to and shortly after the destruction of the temple, continue to associate the overall authority to preserve, interpret, teach, and legally apply sacred Scriptures with the priesthood.[12]

The scribes were drawn largely from the priestly class beginning with Ezra, the model priestly teacher and scribe. Rabbinic Judaism, in contrast, rejected the centrality of the priests as the authorities of religious orthodoxy. In fact, one of the most striking omissions in the chain of oral tradition given in *The Sayings of the Fathers* is the priesthood. There were no priests in the chain of oral tradition! In the *Sayings* oral tradition begins with Moses and passes on to the Rabbis without mentioning a single priest. The prophets who received the oracular (and oral) word of God have a privileged place in this line of the oral Torah, but not the priests. Oral tradition would not depend on the priests.

The group that is most closely associated with the priests and the temple at the end of the Second Temple period (i.e., in the first century B.C.E. and C.E.) were the Sadducees. In fact, their name refers to the group's claim to be the descendents of Zadok, a high priest when the Temple was first built by King Solomon. According to the contemporary Jewish historian Flavius Josephus, the Sadducees rejected oral tradition in favor of the written Torah alone:

The Pharisees have delivered to the people a great many observances by succession from their fathers, which are not written in the law of Moses; and for that reason it is that the Sadducees reject them and say that we are to esteem those observances to be obligatory which are in the written word, but are not to observe what are derived from the tradition of our forefathers. (Josephus, *Anti* 13.10.6)

As priests of the Temple, they had special access to the sacred writings. The Sadducees were the priestly aristocracy of the Second Temple period who also served as secular leaders of the Jewish community. The scribes were dependent upon the ruling authorities, both the Romans and the Sadducees for their livelihood.[13] The scribes themselves were probably largely from priestly and levitical lineage. Josephus also contends that the Sadducees were drawn largely from the aristocracy, which supported them: "The Sadducees are able to persuade none but the rich, and have not the populace obsequious to them, but the Pharisees have the multitude of their side" (*Ant* 13.10.6). From this we may surmise – not surprisingly, I might add – that the authority of oral tradition (as opposed to written texts) had its greatest currency among the multitudes.

Oral and Written in the Dead Sea Sect

Among the most famous archaeological discoveries of the twentieth century was the Dead Sea Scrolls. According to the traditional story, the scrolls were first "discovered" by a poor shepherd boy who had lost his sheep. In looking for his lost sheep, he happened upon a cave of treasures – the first Dead Sea Scrolls. What are the Dead Sea Scrolls? They are a group of about nine hundred manuscripts pieced together from thousands of fragments. About 25 percent of these manuscripts are biblical manuscripts. Before the discovery of the scrolls, our earliest Hebrew manuscripts dated to about the tenth century C.E. The earliest biblical manuscripts among the Dead Sea Scrolls dates to the third century B.C.E. Of the remaining 75 percent of non-biblical manuscripts, about half are previously known literature (like the Book of Jubilees) and half hitherto unknown sectarian Jewish literature. The scrolls are associated with a Jewish sect that lived on the northern shore of the Dead Sea from about 135 B.C.E. to 68 C.E. The literature of this sect reflects a highly literate religious culture. The large number of biblical manuscripts in this sectarian community's library suggests the centrality of the biblical text for the sect and substantiates an active reading and study of the Scriptures. Both internal texts describing the activities of the community and external observers like Flavius Josephus testify to the centrality of the written word for the sect.[14]

Just who was this religious group? The group developed their identity in opposition to the Jerusalem priestly aristocracy. One of their main enemies was "the Wicked Priest," which seems to be a reference to the high priest in Jerusalem. They rejected the Jerusalem Temple and looked forward to an eschatological time when God himself would build a new temple in Jerusalem.[15] They read the passage in Isaiah 40:3, "prepare the way of the Lord in the wilderness" as a literal reference to themselves. Their duty in the wilderness was to study "the Torah, which was decreed by God through Moses for obedience" (1QS viii, 14–15). As a result, they established a remote settlement on the north shore of the Dead Sea, where the famed Dead Sea Scrolls would later be found. The scrolls were the library of the sect, but not all of this literature was composed by the sect; nor did all of it necessarily represent the views of the sect. Judging from references within the scrolls, the sect apparently had split with the priestly leadership in Jerusalem.

The group is usually identified with a sect known from the writings of the Jewish historian Flavius Josephus as the Essenes.[16] The religious sect, however, seems to have been an ultra-religious branch or perhaps even a splinter of the Essenes. Professor Lawrence Schiffman of New York University has suggested that this sect was a splinter group of the Sadducees.[17] It may be that the sect was an early group of dissenting Jerusalem priests, who might be called proto-Sadducees (since the "Sadducees" are mostly known from sources from the first century C.E. or later). Indeed, it was this group that seems to have developed into a new priestly sect that Josephus calls the Essenes. But their exact label is less important than their attitude toward texts. I shall call them Essenes, as Josephus apparently did.

The Essenes shared with the Sadducees the rejection of oral tradition. For example, in the Dead Sea Scroll known as Damascus Document the group criticizes the application of oral tradition to the interpretation of religious practice, concluding that their opponents "have corrupted their holy spirit, and with blasphemous language they have reviled the statutes of God's covenant, saying, 'They are not fixed'" (CD v, 11–12). The group's religious practices were based on the written text.[18] One passage in the community's literature illustrates this: "Concerning the Leader it is written, 'he shall not multiply wives to himself' [a quote from Deuteronomy 17:17]; but David had not read the sealed book of the Law in the Ark; for it was not opened in Israel from the day of the death of Eleazar and Joshua and the elders who served the goddess Ashtoret. It lay buried <and was not> revealed until the appearance of Zadok" (CD v, 1–5). The problem for the community was that King David had several wives. This is explained by simply noting that the sacred writings were hidden away the hidden and then found book recalls the discovery of "the scroll of the covenant" during the time of King Josiah. The important thing to notice is the centrality of the text for defining and critiquing religious practice.

The Essenes also chose priests to be the teachers in and leaders of their community. Community organization is addressed in several places. For example, in the Damascus Document, we read:

> The rule for those who live in all the camps [throughout the land of Israel]. All shall be mustered by their names: the priests first, the Levites second, the children of Israel third, the proselyte fourth.... The priest who presides at the head of the Congregation must be between 30 to 60 years old, learned in the Book of Meditation and in all the regulations of the Torah, speaking them in the proper way. (CD xiv, 3–8)

The priests were always first. The sect allowed non-priestly members, but the priests were the leaders and the teachers. Although disenfranchised from the Jerusalem religious aristocracy, they were a priestly and literate group and in many ways were similar to the Sadducees in their orientation to the sacred text and their rejection of orality. The settlement at Qumran, however, was destroyed by the Romans in the Great Revolt in about 68 C.E. Like the Sadducees, the sect did not survive this conflagration.

From Pharisees to Rabbis

The Pharisees have long been a problem for scholars. All we have by way of sources concerning the Pharisees are the words of others talking about them. We have no texts written by the Pharisees themselves. To understand just how poorly the Pharisees are understood, one need only consult the scholarly literature.[19] Scholars have described the Pharisees as both religious leaders and politicians. They have made them into a learned scholarly group as well as a lay movement that competed with the priesthood. It is certainly an oversimplification to place the Pharisees into any single category. In general, however, the Pharisees seem to derive their identity from their opposition to the

Sadducean priestly aristocracy. As already noted, our understanding of the Pharisees comes from what others wrote about them rather than from what they wrote about themselves. Martin Jaffee, professor of Rabbinics at the University of Washington, in his important book *Torah in the Mouth*, makes the observation, "There is not a single text from the Second Temple period that can sustain for long the argument that it was composed by a Pharisee for the purpose of stating a Pharisaic point of view."[20] This is quite a remarkable realization. There are no Pharisaic texts. Why?

The gap in Pharisaic literature is not limited to the Second Temple period. The Pharisees were apparently a loosely associated Second Temple Jewish group that eventually provided the background for the Rabbis of formative Judaism in the first through sixth centuries C.E. Fraade notes that after the destruction of the Temple by the Romans in 70 C.E. for "a historically critical period of over one hundred years during which the rabbinic sage movement took root and underwent significant growth and development, there is not a single clearly datable rabbinic source...."[21] From what we can tell from our sources, the Rabbis did not write until the third century C.E., when a steady stream of Rabbinic documents begins to surface. Beginning in the third century C.E. with the writing down of the oral Torah into a book known as the Mishnah, the Rabbis begin to commit oral tradition to pen and scroll.

This absence of Pharisaic texts is not for lack of Second Temple literature. We have literature, just not literature that expresses a Pharisaic viewpoint.[22] Beginning in the Hellenistic period in the third century B.C.E. a great variety of Jewish literature is written. The Pharisees are noteworthy in the historical account of the Hasmonean dynasty in 1 Maccabees. They are mentioned in the historical writings of Flavius Josephus and in the New Testament writings dating to the first century C.E. The Pharisees are also alluded to in the writings of the Dead Sea sect of Essenes as "those who expound smooth things." These Pharisees are presumed to be the ancestors of Rabbinic Judaism.

Pharisaic and Rabbinic Judaism share an emphasis on oral tradition. The primacy of orality in Rabbinic Judaism is seen in one of its best-known texts from *The Sayings of the Fathers*:

> Moses *received* (oral) torah at Sinai and handed it on to Joshua, Joshua to elders, and elders to prophets, and prophets handed it on to the men of the great assembly. They said three things: "Be prudent in judgment, raise up many disciples, make a fence around the Torah." Simeon the Righteous was one of the last survivors of the

great assembly. He used to say: "On three things does the world stand: "On the Torah, and on the Temple service, and on deeds of loving kindness." Antigonos of Sokho *received* (the oral *torah*) from Simeon the Righteous. He used to say, "Do not be like servants who serve the master on condition of receiving a reward, but like servants who serve the master not on condition of receiving a reward, and let the fear of Heaven be upon you." Yose ben Yoezer of Seredah and Yose ben Yohanan of Jerusalem *received* it from them.... (M. Avot 1:1ff)

This text argues for the continuity between Pharisaic Judaism and Rabbinic Judaism. It also makes a clear distinction between oral tradition and the written text that is reflected in its description of the origins and authority of the oral torah. In my translation, I have tried to emphasize this distinction by translating oral torah with the lower case "t" and the written Torah with a capital "T" (the difference in Hebrew being the use of the definite article to refer to written Scripture). Central to the description of the transmission of oral torah is the role of the teacher. The oral *torah* claimed its authority from Israel's first and greatest teacher – Moses. According to this passage, "Moses *received* (oral) torah at Sinai and *handed it on* to Joshua, Joshua to elders, and elders to prophets, and prophets handed it on to the men of the great assembly." The later Rabbinic sages also "receive" the oral torah.

There can be no mistake that the *torah* referred to in *The Sayings of the Fathers* must be specifically the oral tradition. As Jaffee observes, "M. Abot's use of the term *torah* in particular – without the definite article that would denote Scripture – to indicate the teaching that Sages receive from Moses is not accidental or ill-considered."[23] He sees an implicit connection between *torah* as "oral tradition" and *ha-Torah* as "Scripture." This is reflected in the Rabbinic sayings that refer to *ha-Torah* (or, Scripture).

This interplay between the two meanings of *torah* as oral teaching and written text was presaged by the prophet Jeremiah. As I discussed in Chapter 6, Jeremiah speaks about the transformation of oral *torah* into written *Torah* when he writes, "How can you say, 'We are wise, and the *torah* of YHWH is with us,' when, in fact, the false pen of the scribes has made it (i.e., *teaching/torah*) into a lie (i.e., a written text/*Torah*)?" It was the pen of the scribes that changed the very essence of *torah* ("teaching"), transforming it into *Torah* ("text"). This transition, however, does not have the two Torahs mirroring one another; rather, they are competing with one another. The new written *Torah* locates authority in a different social group – those who called themselves "the wise" (Hebrew, *chakham*). These were the scribes of ancient Israel, and they wrested authority from the traditional groups such as the elders and the prophets. The "wise" were identified with the political leadership of Jeremiah's day. Rabbinic tradition would turn the tables on the definition of the "wise."

From where would religious authority ultimately derive in Rabbinic Judaism? From Scripture or from the oral tradition of the scribes? It is important to remember that there is a significant difference between ancient Israel and Rabbinic Judaism in their respective attitudes toward text. The Rabbinic culture had to assume some authority for the written Torah because it already existed, whereas ancient Israelite culture introduced the authority of the written word and then had to figure out the implications. Thus, Rabbinic Judaism, which depended on oral tradition, had to struggle with its relationship with the ancient textual authority that had been introduced in Israel during Josiah's (seventh century B.C.E.) and Ezra's (fifth century B.C.E.) reforms. This issue was debated in early Judaism, but Rabbinic Judaism would later merge the distinction between the oral and written Torah. In a later Babylonian Talmud tradition, for example, we read, "All the same are the words of the Torah and the words of the scribes" (bYoma 28b). Of course, this merger of oral and written happened at time when the oral tradition, ironically, had already been codified. The commentary of the Babylonian Talmud was a commentary on what had become a written text, even if ideologically it remained the oral *torah*. This was a new stage in the textualization of Jewish religion.

Writing in Early Christianity

It is hardly surprising that early Christianity, with its roots among the common people, should show some distance from writing. In its attitude toward writing, early Christianity is a close sibling of Pharisaic Judaism.

The New Testament writers had various perspectives on the importance of the written word. This may be suggested by the different tactics that the Gospels take to their own textuality. The Book of John, for example, concludes, "But there are also many other things that Jesus did; if every one of them were written down, I suppose that the world itself could not contain the books that would be written" (John 21:25). This is an implicit critique of John's own written work that began by defining the true Word as a person, not a text: "In the beginning was the Word . . . And the Word became flesh and lived among us, and we have seen his glory, the glory as of a father's only son, full of grace and truth" (John 1:1, 14). It is important to contextualize this characterization of Jesus as "the Word of God" with the earlier textualization of the "word of God" in the Book of Chronicles (discussed in Chapter 9). In biblical literature, the "word of God" was invariably the oral prophetic word. In the Persian period, however, the Book of Chronicles textualizes this term so that it refers to the written Torah of Moses. Seen in this context, the Book of John's assertion that the "Word of God" is a person and not a text seems most radical. In contrast, the Book of Luke-Acts, in its introductory statement, seems to place a much higher value on the importance of the written word:

> Since many have undertaken to set down an orderly account of the events that have been fulfilled among us, just as they were handed on to us by those who from the beginning were eyewitnesses and servants of the word, I too decided, after investigating everything carefully from the very first, to write an orderly account for you, most excellent Theophilus, *so that you may know the truth concerning the things about which you have been instructed.* (Luke 1:1–4)

Here the written word will serve Theophilus as a guide to the truth about things that he has heard orally. The Books of Luke-Acts and John thus are quite conscious of their own textuality and the creation of textual authority. The Gospels of Matthew and Mark, however, do not directly address their own textuality. The Book of Matthew, for example, seems to limit the concept of text to the genealogy of Jesus: "An account/book (Bίβλος) of the genealogy of Jesus the Messiah, the son of David, the son of Abraham" (Matt 1:1). Matthew adopts the Pharisaic and Rabbinic model of the authority of the teacher rather than of the text as it concludes: "And Jesus came and said to them, 'All authority in heaven and on earth has been given to me. Go, therefore, make disciples of all nations, baptizing them in the name of the Father and of the Son and of the Holy Spirit, and teaching them to obey everything that I have commanded you. And remember, I am with you always, to the end of the age'" (Matt 28:18–20). Jesus is the authoritative teacher who passes his authority along to his disciples. It is perhaps not a coincidence that Martin Jaffee notes, "Galilean Sages of our period [third-fourth centuries C.E.] claimed access to revealed knowledge that could be learned only through discipleship."[24] Jaffee speaks of Galilean rabbis who are later than Jesus, but this highlights some similarity between early Christianity and Rabbinic Judaism in their treatment of oral tradition and the role of discipleship.

The advantage of books, however, is that they endure when the teacher passes away. The Book of Matthew addresses this by having Jesus pass his authority along to his disciples. The Book of John also addresses this by introducing the Holy Spirit, which becomes a surrogate teacher. We need to be careful not to suggest that there was a rejection of the written Scriptures either in early Christianity or in Judaism. In Matthew, for example, Jesus is quoted as saying, "For truly I tell you, until heaven and earth pass away, not one letter, not one stroke of a letter, will pass from the law until all is accomplished" (Matt 5:18). Similarly, the Gospel of Luke records, "But it is easier for heaven and earth to pass away, than for one stroke of a letter in the law to be dropped" (Luke 16:17). Thus, it is a question not of a rejection of scriptural authority, but of the relationship of the written word to oral teaching. Similarly, Pharisaic Judaism (and later Rabbinic Judaism) did not reject the Scriptures; rather, it would not accede to the written word as sole cultural authority.

Luke-Acts seems to be a proponent of high literate culture. It is in Luke, for example, that we find the classic expression of Jesus opening the Scriptures on the road to Emmaus (Luke 24:13–27). It is noteworthy also that Luke 4:16–30 describes Jesus reading from the Book of Isaiah on the Sabbath day. In contrast, the parallel passages in Matthew 6:1–6 and Matthew 54–58 describe Jesus only as "teaching" in the synagogue. Jesus is generally described in the Gospels as teaching, not as explaining the Scriptures (cf. Mark 1:21–28, 39; Matt 4:23–25; 7:28–29). At the same time, Jesus frequently chides his detractors, demanding, "Have you not read in the scriptures?" (e.g., Matt 12:3, 5; 19:4; 21:16, 42; 22:31; Mark 2:25; 12:10, 26; Luke 10:26). Rather than be an appeal to the Scriptures however, this seems to serve a rhetorical purpose. Jesus' detractors are those who find their authority in the Scriptures; Jesus turns their authority upside down. In Matthew 22:31, Jesus answers the Sadducees, who query him about resurrection which they argue is not found in the Hebrew Scriptures: "You are wrong, because you know *neither the scriptures nor the power of God*." Their argument is derived from the written Scriptures, but Jesus' response implies that they have erred, both from their own perspective of the sole authority of written texts and from the perspective of the greater authority of the oral tradition.

The power of God was to be found in the authoritative teacher and the oral tradition. One of the more interesting texts is Luke

11:52, which speaks of the "key of knowledge." In this passage, Jesus condemns the lawyers (νομικος), that is, those who are being trained in reading and interpreting the Jewish law, "because you have taken the key to knowledge" (ὅτι ἤρατε τὴν κλεῖδα τῆς γνώσεως). One may also translate this expression as "you have kept to yourselves the key to knowledge," that is to say, that they took away the means by which others might gain understanding. The fact that according to this account in Luke-Acts the lawyers held the keys to the written texts can be read in two ways. On the one hand, one might recognize that the written Scriptures held the keys to knowledge. This could be a strong statement for textual authority. On the other hand, one might see the keys to knowledge as being held by a certain social group. The early Christian movement did not arise from the literati. The early Christians were neither priests nor lawyers, but fishermen and the like. This statement hints that the division between textual authority and oral tradition was also a division between the social classes of the Mediterranean world in the first centuries and their access to texts and literacy.

Paul was well educated, yet he too expressed reservations about the written word. Paul could write, although his penmanship apparently left something to be desired: "See what large letters I make when I am writing in my own hand!" (Gal 6:11). In another place, Paul requests that his friend Timothy bring to him both his books and writing material: "When you come, bring the cloak that I left with Carpus at Troas, also the books, and above all the parchments" (2 Tim 4:13).[25] Paul's reservations about writing perhaps can be traced to his training as a Pharisee. According to the Book of Acts, Paul claims, "I am a Jew, born in Tarsus in Cilicia, but brought up in this city at the feet of Gamaliel, *educated strictly according to law of our fathers*, being zealous for God, just as all of you are today" (Acts 22:3). Paul asserts that he was taught by the living voice of Gamaliel (not that he studied) and that he was "educated strictly according to the law of our fathers" (πεπαιδευμένος κατὰ ἀκρίβειαν τοῦ πατρῴου νόμου) – that is, in the oral *torah*. It is for good reason that Paul considers himself a Pharisee of Pharisees (Acts 23:6; Phil 3:5); namely, Paul inherits the Pharisaic emphasis on oral tradition and its focus on the teacher or Rabbi as the bearer of the tradition.

Werner Kelber notes in his book *The Oral and the Written Gospel* (1983) that in early Christianity the transition from oral to written tradition was a movement not of continuity (as the form critics supposed) but of discontinuity. Oral communication is different from written since speaking involved presence and immediacy. Written communication is external, abstract, objective. It is noteworthy that Jesus taught orally and was heard by a rural, largely non-literate audience. When this oral tradition was put into writing in the forms of the Gospels, a fundamental transition resulted. As Paul says, "The letter kills" (2 Corith 3:6). The irony of Paul is that he wrote so much to so many. Like Plato's critique of writing, Paul's critique also had to be written. It may not be a coincidence that Paul wrote letters, not books. Paul advocated for the living voice of the teacher in his letters. He constantly claimed that he was called to preach the gospel; the "gospel" (Greek, εὐαγγέλιον) was first of all an oral proclamation.[26] Paul never claimed that he was called to write.

Birger Gerhardsson, in his important book entitled *Memory and Manuscript* (1961), noted that Jesus received no teaching according to one Gospel (John 7:15) and that the Apostles are described as unlearned men from the commoners (Acts 4:13).[27] As Gerhardsson recognized, these are distinctly dogmatic statements. They reflect a positive attitude about the disciples' lack of learning. Jesus was not a scribe, nor was he a social elite. The disciples were not among the literati. The dogmatism is instructive. It is a reflex of the ideology of the Gospel writers and the early church. This ideology is particularly critical of scribes and book learning. In John 7, for example, Jesus is teaching in the Temple. This context puts him amid the scribes and literati of the Jewish religious elite. Appropriately, Jesus is portrayed critiquing the religious establishment by quoting the Law itself: "Did not Moses give you the law? Yet none of you keeps the law" (v. 19). Jesus, however, shuns textual authority and claims his own authority from "the one who sent him." Put another way, the teacher is more important than the text. Despite Jesus' use of the text to critique the religious establishment, he claims a higher authority that is not textually based.

I have asked a trifling question about how the early Christians mediated between oral and written authority. An even bolder question was asked by John Dominic Crossan and Jonathon Reed: was Jesus even literate? In their popular book *Excavating Jesus: Beneath the Stones, Behind the Texts*, they suggest that Jesus was actually an illiterate peasant.[28] This, however, is a difficult argument to sustain.

After all, Jesus is portrayed as being able to read and write. In Luke 4:16–18, for example, we read:

> When Jesus came to Nazareth, where he had been brought up, he went to the synagogue on the sabbath day, as was his custom. He stood up to read, and the scroll of the prophet Isaiah was given to him. He unrolled the scroll and found the place where it was written: "The Spirit of the Lord is upon me, . . ."

Literacy skills were likely associated with the religious training of young Jewish males. That is, they could read the Scriptures. This is rather limited literacy however. But the suggestion that Jesus was illiterate is really just a rhetorical trope, which highlights the limited literacy of the Mediterranean world of Jesus and his disciples.[29] The ideology of orality may have also limited the acquisition of high-level literacy. The importance of the living voice of the teacher took priority over knowledge that could be gained from books.

How the Bible Became a Book

Throughout this book I have contended that the making of books and the appeal to the authority of writing was largely derived from the institutions of state and temple. Writing was the domain of the royal court and then the priestly aristocracy. Writing was used as a tool of government and then taken over as a tool of religious authority and orthodoxy.

I have not provided a precise dating for every verse of the Bible, nor have I tried to assign each biblical book its exact historical position. These are issues that are bound to be the subject of scholarly debate forever. What I have done is offer some observations about the role of writing within biblical literature as well as in ancient Israelite society. I have demonstrated that writing becomes an important cultural feature of ancient Judah beginning in the late eighth century B.C.E. I have argued that this is attested archaeologically by the data about the development of ancient Israelite society and the role of writing. It is also suggested internally within biblical literature by the development of a self-consciousness about the importance of the written word in the biblical narrative during the Josianic Reforms in the late seventh century.

There was ebb and flow to oral tradition and sacred texts that began with the Josianic Reforms. The written word traveled a rocky road to its eventual place as sacred text and the standard for religious orthodoxy. Two issues shaped the path of this road. The first was the give and take between orality and literacy. As literacy became more prevalent, textuality became more plausible. That is to say, the better people could read, the more the written word could serve as guidepost for religious orthodoxy. The second was the competition between orality and textuality as modes of authority. Orality and literacy were stages along the same road, whereas orality and textuality was the fork in the road. The road more traveled was oral tradition, where the community and the teacher provided education and defined authority as they had for generations. The new road was textual authority. This was a road built by the government with the support of the social and religious elites.

The Great War with Rome destroyed the power of the priests and the social elites. In 66 C.E., the Jewish masses led by messianic Zealots revolted against the Roman Empire. Within four years, the revolt was quelled, the city of Jerusalem destroyed, and the Temple burned in a great conflagration. More importantly perhaps, the aristocratic leadership of the Temple was also destroyed. Although Sadducees did not support the revolt, the destruction of the Temple and Jerusalem destroyed their base of power. Parenthetically, the religious sect at Qumran was also destroyed by the Romans at this time. These two groups that best represented the religious authority of the text were wiped out along with the Temple by the Romans. With their demise, traditional orality would reassert itself.

Both early Christianity and Rabbinic Judaism, which grew of the lay classes, struggled with the tension between the sacred text and the authority of the oral tradition in the aftermath of the destruction of the Temple. Although they acknowledged the authority of the written Scriptures, they also asserted the authority of oral tradition and the living voice of the teacher. Christianity, however, quickly adopted the codex. In fact, early Christianity was quite innovative in its adoption of the codex. This fact probably encouraged the authority of the written Scriptures in the early Church. Judaism, in contrast, was quite slow in adopting the codex and even today it is a Torah *scroll* that we find in a synagogue ark. Eventually, Judaism too would cloak its oral tradition in a written garb. Still, a fierce ideology of orality would persist in Rabbinic Judaism even as the oral Torah and the written tablets were merged into one pre-existent Torah that was with God at the very creation of the world.

Suggested Further Reading

Casson, Lionel. *Libraries in the Ancient World.* New Haven: Yale University Press, 2001.

Crenshaw, James L. *Education in Ancient Israel: Across the Deadening Silence.* New York: Doubleday, 1998.

Demsky, Aaron. "Writing in Ancient Israel and Early Judaism: The Biblical Period." In *Mikra: Text, Translation, Reading, and Interpretation of the Hebrew Bible in Ancient Judaism and Early Christianity*, edited by M. J. Mulder. Assen: Van Gorcum; Philadephia: Fortress, 1988, pp. 2–20.

Elman, Yaakov, and Gershoni, Israel, eds. *Transmitting Jewish Traditions: Orality, Textuality, and Cultural Diffusion.* New Haven: Yale University Press, 2000.

Finkelstein, I., and Siberman, N. A. *The Bible Unearthed.* New York: Free Press, 2001.

Fishbane, Michael. *Biblical Interpretation in Ancient Israel.* Oxford: Clarendon, 1985.

Friedman, Richard E. *Who Wrote the Bible?* San Francisco: Harper & Row, 1987.

Goody, Jack. *The Power of the Written Tradition.* Washington, DC: Smithsonian Institution Press, 2000.

Hallo, William W., and Younger, K. Lawson, Jr. *The Context of Scripture.* Vol. 2: *Monumental Inscriptions from the Biblical World.* Leiden: Brill, 2000.

Halpern, Baruch. *The First Historians: The Hebrew Bible and History.* San Francisco: Harper & Row, 1988.

Havelock, Eric. *The Muse Learns to Write: Reflections on Orality and Literacy from Antiquity to the Present.* New Haven: Yale University Press, 1986.

King, Philip J., and Stager, Lawrence E. *Life in Biblical Israel.* Library of Ancient Israel. Louisville: Westminster John Knox Press, 2001.

Kugel, James. *The Bible As It Was.* Cambridge, MA: Harvard University Press, 1997.

Levy, Thomas E., ed. *The Archaeology of Society in the Holy Land.* New York: Facts on File, 1995.

Martin, H.-J. *The History and Power of Writing*, translated by Lydia G. Cochrane. Chicago: University of Chicago Press, 1994.

Millard, Alan. *Reading and Writing in the Time of Jesus.* The Biblical Seminar. Sheffield: Sheffield Academic Press, 2001.

Naveh, Joseph. *The Early History of the Alphabet: An Introduction to West Semitic Epigraphy and Palaeography.* 2nd ed. Jerusalem: Magnes, 1987.

Niditch, Susan. *Oral World and Written Word: Ancient Israelite Literature.* Library of Ancient Israel. Louisville: Westminister John Knox Press, 1996.

Ong, Walter J. *Orality and Literacy: The Technologizing of the Word.* London: Routledge, 1982.

Pedersén, Olaf. *Archives and Libraries in the Ancient Near East, 1500–300 B.C.* Bethesda, MD: CDL Press, 1998.

Schniedewind, William M. *Society and the Promise to David: A Reception History of 2 Samuel 7:1–17.* New York: Oxford University Press, 1999.

Schniedewind, William M. "Orality and Literacy in Ancient Israel," *RSR* 26 (2000): 327–32.

Sommer, Benjamin. "Revelation at Sinai in the Hebrew Bible and in Jewish Theology." *Journal of Religion* 79 (1999): 422–51.

Notes

Chapter 1

1 W. Graham highlights the disjunction between the modern book culture and the pre-modern world in his important book, *Beyond the Written World: Oral Aspects of Scripture in the History of Religion* (Cambridge: Cambridge University Press, 1987), pp. 11–66.

2 See C. H. Roberts and T. C. Skeat, *The Birth of the Codex* (London: Oxford University Press for the British Academy, 1983).

3 On the impact of the codex, see H.-J. Martin, *The History and Power of Writing* (trans. Lydia G. Cochrane; Chicago: University of Chicago Press, 1994), pp. 59–60.

4 A. Hurvitz, "The Origins and Development of the Expression מגלת ספר: A Study in the History of Writing-Related Terminology in Biblical Times," in *Texts, Temples, and Traditions: A Tribute to Menahem Haran* (ed. M. V. Fox et al.; Winona Lake, IN: Eisenbrauns, 1996), pp. 37*–46* [Hebrew].

5 R. E. Friedman, *Who Wrote the Bible?* (San Francisco: Harper & Row, 1987), pp. 146, 188.

6 Friedman, *Who Wrote the Bible?*, p. 16.

7 S. Fish, *Is There a Text in This Class? The Authority of Interpretative Communities* (Cambridge, MA: Harvard University Press, 1980). See more generally, S. Suleiman and I. Crosman, eds., *The Reader in the Text: Essays on Audience and Interpretation* (Princeton: Princeton University Press, 1980).

8 An interesting book on the evolving interpretation of the U.S. Constitution and its place in our national identity is by Richard B. Bernstein, *Amending America: If We Love the Constitution So Much, Why Do We Keep Trying to Change It?* (New York: Times Books, 1993).

9 See my book, W. M. Schniedewind, *Society and the Promise to David: A Reception History of 2 Samuel 7:1–17* (New York: Oxford University Press, 1999).

10 See Y. Elman and I. Gershoni, eds. *Transmitting Jewish Traditions: Orality, Textuality, and Cultural Diffusion* (New Haven: Yale University Press, 2000), pp. 16–18.

11 E.g., P. Machinist, "On Self-Consciousness in Mesopotamia," in *The Origins and Diversity of Axial Age Civilizations* (ed. S. N. Eisenstadt; New York: State University of New York Press, 1986), pp. 192–95.

12 YHWH is the personal name of the Israelite God, whose vocalization is not completely certain and which is not pronounced by religious Jews in reverence to God.

13 A convenient and readable introduction to the Documentary Hypothesis may be found in Friedman, *Who Wrote the Bible?*; also see the article by J. C. O'Neill,

"History of Biblical Criticism," in *ABD*, vol. 1 (Garden City, NY: Doubleday, 1992), pp. 726–30.

14 See, for example, S. Niditch, *Oral World and Written Word: Ancient Israelite Literature* (Library of Ancient Israel; Louisville: Westminister John Knox Press, 1996).

15 J. L. Crenshaw, *Education in Ancient Israel: Across the Deadening Silence* (New York: Doubleday, 1998).

16 D. Tannen, "The Myth of Orality and Literacy," in *Linguistics and Literacy* (ed. W. Frawley; New York: Plenum Press, 1982), p. 47.

17 Niditch, *Oral World and Written Word*, p. 3.

18 H. Gunkel, *The Legends of Genesis* (trans. W. H. Carruth; reprint [1961] ed.; New York: Schocken, 1901); also see Gunkel, *The Folktale in the Old Testament* (trans. M. Rutter with an introduction by J. Rogerson, ed.; Sheffield: Almond, 1987).

19 See R. Culley, *Studies in the Structure of Hebrew Narrative* (Philadephia: Fortress, 1976); S. Niditch, *A Prelude to Biblical Folklore: Underdogs and Tricksters* (Urbana: University of Illinois Press, 2000). See further my review of recent scholarship on this topic, W. M. Schniedewind, "Orality and Literacy in Ancient Israel," *RSR* 26 (2000): 327–32.

20 See the classic essay by J. Ross, "The Prophet as Yahweh's Messenger," in *Israel's Prophetic Heritage* (ed. B. Anderson and W. Harrelson; New York: Harper & Row, 1962), pp. 98–107.

21 S. Parker, *Stories in Scripture and Inscriptions: Comparative Studies on Narratives in Northwest Semitic Inscriptions and the Hebrew Bible* (New York: Oxford University Press, 1997).

22 Some of Goody's more important works include J. Goody and I. Watt, "The Consequences of Literacy," *Comparative Studies in Society and History* 5 (1963): 304–45; Goody, *The Domestication of the Savage Mind* (Cambridge: Cambridge University Press, 1977); Goody, *The Logic of Writing and the Organization of Society* (Cambridge: Cambridge University Press, 1986).

23 E.g., Tannen, "The Myth of Orality and Literacy," pp. 37–50; the essays in *Literacy and Society* (ed. K. Schousboe and M. Trolle-Larsen; Copenhagen: Akademisk Forlag, 1989).

24 L. Alexander, "The Living Voice: Scepticism towards the Written Word in Early Christian and in Graeco-Roman Texts," in *The Bible in Three Dimensions: Essays in Celebration of Forty Years of Biblical Studies in the University of Sheffield* (JSOTSS, 87; ed. D. Clines, S. Fowl, and S. Porter; Sheffield: Sheffield Academic Press, 1990), pp. 221–47.

25 Galen, *De libr. Propr.* 5, Kühn XIX 33/Scripta Minora II 110.25–27.

26 Cited by Alexander, "The Living Voice," pp. 221–22.

27 On the oral Torah, see M. Jaffee, *Torah in the Mouth: Writing and Oral Tradition in Palestinian Judaism, 200 BCE–400 CE* (New York: Oxford University Press, 2001).

28 H. Soloveitchik, "Rupture and Reconstruction: The Transformation of Contemporary Orthodoxy," *Tradition* 28 (1994): 64–130. Also see M. Friedman, "Life Tradition and Book Tradition in the Development of Ultraorthodox Judaism," in *Judaism from Within and Without: Anthropological Studies* (ed. H. Goldberg; Albany: State University of New York Press, 1987), pp. 235–55.

29 On the impact of technology on writing and literacy, see W. J. Ong, *Orality and Literacy: The Technologizing of the Word* (Padstow, Cornwall: T. J. Press, 1982) and Martin, *The History and Power of Writing.*

30 See A. Millard, *Reading and Writing in the Time of Jesus* (The Biblical Seminar; Sheffield: Sheffield Academic Press, 2000), pp. 69–83.

31 For a summary and critique of this extreme skeptical position, see B. Halpern, "Erasing History," *Bible Review* 11 (1995): 27–35, 47; S. Japhet, "In Search of

Ancient Israel: Revisionism at All Costs," in *The Jewish Past Revisited* (ed. D. N. Myers and D. B. Ruderman; New Haven: Yale University Press, 1998), pp. 212–33.

32 For example, N. P. Lemche, "The Old Testament – A Hellenistic Book?" *SJOT* 7 (1993): 163–93; L. Grabbe, ed., *Did Moses Speak Attic? Jewish Historiography and Scripture in the Hellenistic Period* (JSOTSS, 317; Sheffield: Sheffield Academic Press, 2001).

33 A. Hurvitz, "The Historical Quest for 'Ancient Israel' and the Linguistic Evidence of the Hebrew Bible: Some Methodological Observations," *VT* 47 (1997): 310–15.

34 A convenient English translation of Shishak's historical inscription is available in *Ancient Near Eastern Texts Relating to the Old Testament* (ed. J. Pritchard; Princeton: Princeton University Press, 1955), pp. 263–64. Also see B. Mazar, "Pharaoh Shishak's Campaign to the Land of Israel," in *The Early Biblical Period* (Jerusalem: Israel Exploration Society, 1986), pp. 139–50.

35 This technique and relevant bibliography is described in M. Fishbane's *Biblical Interpretation in Ancient Israel* (Oxford: Oxford University Press, 1985), pp. 44–65.

Chapter 2

1 See Bengt Holbek, "What the Illiterate Think of Writing," in *Literacy and Society* (ed. K. Schousboe and M. Trolle-Larsen; Copenhagen: Akademisk Forlag, 1989), pp. 183–96.

2 See J. Black and A. Green, eds., *Gods, Demons, and Symbols of Ancient Mesopotamia: An Illustrated Dictionary* (Austin: University of Texas Press, 1992).

3 On Egyptian writing as magic and on the god Thoth, see R. Ritner, *The Mechanics of Ancient Egyptian Magical Practice* (Chicago: Oriental Institute, 1993), pp. 35–56.

4 From Ritner, *The Mechanics of Ancient Egyptian Magical Practice*, p. 100.

5 See E. Hornung, *The Ancient Egyptian Books of the Afterlife* (translated from German by D. Lorton; Ithaca: Cornell University Press, 1999), pp. 4–5.

6 See Ritner, *The Mechanics of Ancient Egyptian Magical Practice*, pp. 136–53.

Chapter 3

1 See J. Goody, *The Logic of Writing and the Organization of Society* (Cambridge: Cambridge University Press, 1986), pp. 53–56.

2 See, for example, H. Nissen, "The Emergence of Writing in the Ancient Near East," *Interdisciplinary Science Reviews* 10 (1985): 349–61; P. Michalowski, "Early Mesopotamian Communicative Systems: Art, Literature, and Writing," in *Investigating Artistic Environments in the Ancient Near East* (ed. A. Gunter; Washington, DC: Smithsonian Institution Press, 1990), pp. 53–69; M. Larsen, "What They Wrote on Clay," in *Literacy and Society* (ed. K. Schousboe and M. Trolle-Larsen; Copenhagen: Akademisk Forlag, 1989), pp. 121–48.

3 See G. R. Castellino, *Two Šulgi Hymns* (Rome, 1972), hymn B, line 11; see A. W. Sjöberg, "The Old Babylonian Eduba," in *Sumerological Studies in Honor of Thorkild Jacobsen* (Assyriological Studies, 20; Chicago: Oriental Institute, 1975), pp. 159–79.

4 See the summary by J. Baines, "Literacy," in *ABD*, vol. 4, pp. 333–37.

5 See S. Parpola, "The Royal Archives of Nineveh," in *Cuneiform Archives and Libraries: Papers Read at the 30e Rencontre Assyriologique Internationale, Leiden, 4–8 July, 1983* (ed. K. R. Veenhof; Istanbul, 1986), pp. 223–36.

6 Theorists correctly criticize the cliché that writing represents speech, particularly following the work of J. Derrida, *Of Grammatology* (Baltimore: Johns Hopkins University Press, 1974). Still, the invention of the alphabet clearly related the semiotics of writing with speech, even if they are not equated.

7 See J. Naveh, *Early History of the Alphabet: An Introduction to West Semitic Epigraphy and Palaeography* (2nd ed.; Jerusalem: Magnes, 1987), pp. 23–28.

8 One intriguing exception to this is the famous *Marzeah* Tablet, which apparently deals with a private association and was not written by a professional scribe. See the discussion by R. E. Friedman, "The *MRZḤ* Tablet from Ugarit," *MAARAV* 2, no. 2 (1979–80): 187–206.

9 A convenient translation of the Amarna Letters appears in W. Moran, *The Amarna Letters* (Baltimore: Johns Hopkins University Press, 1992). An exhaustive study of the Canaanite dialect of these documents is now available; see A. F. Rainey, *Canaanite in the Amarna Tablets: A Linguistic Analysis of the Mixed Dialect Used by the Scribes from Canaan*, 4 vols. (Leiden: Brill, 1996).

10 One recent and convenient translation and discussion is by K. A. D. Smelik in *The Context of Scripture*, vol. 2: *Monumental Inscriptions from the Biblical World* (ed. W. W. Hallo and K. L. Younger, Jr.; Leiden: Brill, 2000), pp. 137–38. Also see A. Lemaire, "'House of David' Restored in Moabite Inscription," *Biblical Archeology Review* 20, no. 3 (1994): 30–37.

11 S. Segert, "Die Sprache der Moabitischen Königsinschrift," *Archiv Orientalni* 29 (1961): 197–269.

12 See the original publication by A. Biran and J. Naveh, "An Aramaic Stele Fragment from Tel Dan," *IEJ* 43 (1993): 81–98. The translation here, however, is based on my article, Schniedewind, "Tel Dan Stela: New Light on Aramaic and Jehu's Revolt," *BASOR* 302 (1996): 75–90.

13 See the full discussion in my article, "Tel Dan Stela."

14 This was actually recognized by the Italian scholar G. Garbini. Remarkably, however, he did not see that this was a result of the pan-Levantine scribal schools and instead suggested that the Dan inscription had to be a forgery! The archaeological context of the 1995 excavations, however, completely destroyed the contention that this inscription was a modern forgery.

15 This is especially evident in the Amarna Letters; see Rainey, *Canaanite in the Amarna Tablets.* I will argue in a forthcoming book on the social history of Hebrew that this pan-Levantine scribal tradition continues until the eighth century B.C.E.

16 See. Y. Ikeda, "Solomon's Trade in Horses and Chariots in Its International Setting," in *Studies in the Period of David and Solomon and Other Essays* (ed. T. Ishida; Winona Lake, IN: Eisenbrauns, 1982), pp. 219–20.

17 The inscription is conveniently published in H. Donner and W. Röllig, *Kanaanäische und Aramäische Inschriften*, 3 vols. (Wiesbaden: Harrassowitz, 1968), §218.

18 See H. Tadmor, "The Aramaization of Assyria: Aspects of Western Impact," in *Mesopotamien und seine Nachbarn. Teil 2* (ed. H.-J. Nissen and J. Renger; Berlin: Dietrich Reimer, 1982), pp. 449–70.

19 Sometimes the use of Ugaritic can go too far, as it does in M. Dahood's brilliant but idiosyncratic three-volume commentary on the Psalms (Anchor Bible). See also Dahood, "Ugaritic-Hebrew Parallel Pairs," in *Ras Shamra Parallels I* (ed. L. Fisher; *AnOr*, 49; Rome, 1972), pp. 71–382; *Ras Shamra Parallels II* (ed. L. Fisher; *AnOr*, 50; Rome, 1975), pp. 1–39; *Ras Shamra Parallels III* (ed. S. Rummel; *AnOr* 51; Rome: Pontifical Biblical Institute, 1981), pp. 1–206.

20 U. Cassuto, "Biblical and Canaanite Literature," in *Biblical and Oriental Studies*, vol. 2: *Bible and Ancient Oriental Texts* (trans. Israel Abrahams; Jerusalem:

Magnes, 1975), p. 16; also see Y. Avishur, *Studies in Hebrew and Ugaritic Psalms* (Jerusalem: Magnes, 1989) [Hebrew].

21 Naveh, *Early History of the Alphabet*, pp. 89–112.

Chapter 4

1 See especially I. Finkelstein, *The Archaeology of the Israelite Settlement* (Jerusalem: Israel Exploration Society, 1988); I. Finkelstein and N. Na'aman, eds., *From Nomadism to Monarchy: Archaeological and Historical Aspects of Early Israel* (Jerusalem: Israel Exploration Society, 1994).

2 There is a voluminous literature on early Israel. Some more important recent works include Finkelstein and Na'aman, *From Nomadism to Monarchy*; R. Hess, "Early Israel in Canaan: A Survey of Recent Evidence and Interpretations," *PEQ* 125 (1993): 125–42; G. Ahlström, *Who Were the Israelites?* (Winona Lake, IN: Eisenbrauns, 1986); A. Frendo, "Five Recent Books on the Emergence of Ancient Israel: Review Article," *PEQ* 124 (1992): 145–51.

3 Translation from *ANET*, pp. 376–78.

4 See J. Allen, *Middle Egyptian: An Introduction to the Language and Culture of Hieroglyphs* (Cambridge: Cambridge University Press, 2000), §3.5.

5 M. Kochavi and A. Demsky, "An Israelite Village from the Days of the Judges," *BAR* 4, no. 3 (1978): 19–21.

6 As noted by H. Thackeray, "New Light on the Book of Jashar (A Study of 3 Regn. VIII 53b LXX)," *JTS* 11 (1910): 518–32.

7 See A. Hurvitz, "Originals and Imitations in Biblical Poetry: A Comparative Examination of 1 Sam 2:1–10 and Ps 113:5–9," in *Biblical and Related Studies Presented to Samuel Iwry* (ed. Ann Kort and Scott Morschauser; Winona Lake, IN: Eisenbrauns, 1986), pp. 115–21.

8 A classic analysis of this text was done by F. M. Cross and D. N. Freedman; see the second edition of *Studies in Ancient Yahwistic Poetry* (Biblical Resources Series; Grand Rapids: Eerdmans, 1997).

9 For the classic discussion of the archaic features of this text, see F. M. Cross, *Canaanite Myth and Hebrew Epic* (Cambridge, MA: Harvard University Press, 1974), pp. 121–44.

10 See S. Weitzman, *Song and Story in Biblical Narrative* (Bloomington: University of Indiana Press, 1997).

11 See D. Jamieson-Drake, who relies on Price's anthropological study of secondary state formation, *Scribes and Schools in Monarchic Judah* (Sheffield: JSOT, 1991).

12 Jamieson-Drake, *Scribes and Schools in Monarchic Judah*, p. 45. Mendenhall's and Gottwald's analyses were founded on Marxist social theory (namely, the revolting peasant theory) that recent excavations and survey data have completely undermined; see Finkelstein, *The Archaeology of the Israelite Settlement*, pp. 306–14.

13 See, for example, A. Mazar, *Archaeology of the Land of the Bible: 10,000–586 B.C.E.* (Garden City, NY: Doubleday, 1990), pp. 296ff.

14 See, for example, I. Finkelstein, "The Archaeology of the United Monarchy: An Alternative View," *Levant* 28 (1996): 177–87; T. Thompson, "Historiography of Ancient Palestine and Early Jewish Historiography: W. G. Dever and the Not So New Biblical Archaeology," in *The Origins of the Ancient Israelite States* (ed. V. Fritz and P. R. Davies; Sheffield: JSOT, 1996), pp. 26–43; W. Dever, "Histories and Nonhistories of Ancient Israel," *BASOR* 316 (1999): 89–106.

15 See D. Sivan, "The Gezer Calendar and Northwest Semitic Linguistics," *IEJ* 48 (1998): 101–5; W. F. Albright, "The Gezer Calendar," *BASOR* 92 (1943): 16–26.

16 Contra C. Rabin, "The Emergence of Classical Hebrew," in *The Age of the Monarchies: Culture and Society* (ed. A. Malamat; Jerusalem: Massada, 1979), pp. 71–78. Rabin is too dependent on the biblical presentation of David and Solomon. Although Rabin's socio-linguistic assumptions are valid, the later urbanization of the state in the eighth century better fits the data. Moreover, the inscriptional evidence of the late monarchy also accords well with the language of Classical Biblical Hebrew. S. Gogel points out that epigraphic Hebrew grammar is essentially the same as Classical Biblical Hebrew, but it must be noted that the corpus of epigraphic Hebrew is essentially late eighth through early sixth century B.C.E.; see Gogel, *A Grammar of Epigraphic Hebrew* (SBL Resources for Biblical Study, 23; Atlanta: Scholars, 1998).

17 Yahwistic theophoric elements (i.e., *-iah* or *Jeho-*) begin to appear in personal names in the tenth century but do not predominate until the ninth century. The use of these elements provides a rough gauge for the relative date of an Israelite personal name, with the Yahwistic theophoric elements emerging in the tenth century, becoming predominant in the late monarchy, and then beginning to disappear again in the post-exilic period. See further J. Tigay, *You Shall Have No Other Gods: Israelite Religion in the Light of Hebrew Inscriptions* (HSS, 31; Atlanta: Scholars, 1986); J. Fowler, *Theophoric Personal Names in Ancient Hebrew: A Comparative Study* (JSOTSS, 49; Sheffield: JSOT, 1988); N. Cohen, "Jewish Names as Cultural Indicators in Antiquity," *JSJ* 7 (1976–77): 97–128.

18 See the summary of the scholarly research by N. Fox, *In the Service of the King: Officialdom in Ancient Israel and Judah* (Monographs of the Hebrew Union College; Cincinnati: Hebrew Union College Press, 2000), pp. 110–21. See further T. Mettinger, *Solomonic State Officials* (Lund: CWK Gleerups, 1971), Y. Avishur and M. Heltzer, *Studies on the Royal Administration in Ancient Israel in Light of Epigraphic Sources* (Jerusalem: Academon, 1996); E. W. Heaton, *Solomon's New Men: The Emergence of Ancient Israel as a National State* (New York: Pica Press, 1974), pp. 47–60.

19 KB4, ad loc.

20 See Y. Avishur, "Administration," in *World History of the Jewish People*, vol. 4/2 (Jerusalem: Massada, 1979), p. 161.

21 On the Izbet Sartah abecedary, see A. Demsky, "A Proto-Canaanite Abecedary," *TA* 4 (1977): 14–27; M. Kochavi, "An Ostracon of the Period of Judges from Izbet Sartah," *TA* 4 (1977): 1–13.

22 See A. Biran, "The Tel Dan Inscription: A New Fragment," *IEJ* 45 (1995): pp. 1–18; W. Schniedewind, "Tel Dan Stela: New Light on Aramaic and Jehu's Revolt," *BASOR* 302 (1996): 75–90.

23 There is one very fragmentary monumental type inscription from the ninth century in Jerusalem; see M. Ben-Dov, "A Fragmentary Hebrew First Temple Period Inscription from the Ophel," in *Ancient Jerusalem Revealed* (ed. H. Geva; Jerusalem: Israel Exploration Society, 1994), pp. 73–75.

24 Fox, *In the Service of the King*, pp. 250–68; O. Goldwasser, "An Egyptian Scribe from Lachish and the Hieratic Tradition of the Hebrew Kingdoms," *TA* 18 (1991): 248–53.

25 Most recently, see R. E. Friedman, *The Hidden Book in the Bible* (New York: HarperCollins, 1998).

26 Recently Baruch Halpern has made a cogent argument for the antiquity of some of the David stories, *David's Secret Demons: Messiah, Murderer, Traitor, King* (Grand Rapids: Eerdmans, 2001).

Chapter 5

1 A. Millard, "The Uses of the Early Alphabets," in *Phoinikeia Grammata: Lire et écrire en Méditerranée* (ed. C. Baurain, C. Bonnet, and V. Krings; Namur: Société des Études Classiques, 1991), p. 105.

2 It is noteworthy that Shalmaneser III (r. 858–824 B.C.E.) fought frequently in the open field, which suggests a perceived parity between opponents. By the end of the eighth century, in contrast, Assyrian monarchs were more usually involved with siege warfare, suggesting their military superiority; cf. I. Eph'al, "On Warfare and Military Control in the Ancient Near Eastern Empires: A Research Outline," in *History, Historiography and Interpretation: Studies in Biblical and Cuneiform Literatures* (ed. H. Tadmor and M. Weinfeld; Jerusalem: Magnes Press, 1983), pp. 88–106.

3 See H. Kuhne, "The Urbanization of the Assyrian Provinces," in *Nuove Fondazioni Nel Vicino Oriente Antico: Relat e Ideologia* (ed. S. Mazzoni; Giardini, 1992), pp. 55–83.

4 See the discussion of "the people of the land" in my earlier book, *Society and the Promise to David: A Reception History of 2 Samuel 7:1–17* (New York: Oxford University Press, 1999), pp. 77–80.

5 O. Zimhoni, "Two Ceramic Assemblages from Lachish Levels III and II," *TA* 17 (1990): 49; also see N. Na'aman "The Kingdom of Judah under Josiah," *TA* 18 (1991): 3–71. A similar picture is also reflected at sites such as Timnah (Tel Batash) and Ekron (Tel Miqne) – all cities in the foothills west of Jerusalem and east of the coastal plain.

6 See B. Halpern, "Jerusalem and the Lineages in the Seventh Century BCE: Kinship and the Rise of Individual Moral Liability," in *Law and Ideology in Monarchic Israel* (ed. B. Halpern and D. W. Hobson; Sheffield: Sheffield Academic Press, 1991), pp. 11–107.

7 See the essays by J. Holladay, Jr., "The Kingdoms of Israel and Judah: Political and Economic Centralization in the Iron IIA-B (ca. 1000–750 BCE)," and W. Dever, "Social Structure in Palestine in the Iron II Period on the Eve of Destruction," in *The Archeology of Society in the Holy Land* (ed. T. Levy; New York: Facts on File, 1995), pp. 368–98, 416–31.

8 See N. Avigad, *Discovering Jerusalem* (Jerusalem: Israel Exploration Society, 1980), pp. 26–31.

9 M. Broshi, "The Expansion of Jerusalem in the Reigns of Hezekiah and Manasseh," *IEJ* 24 (1974): 21.

10 Translation from *ANET*, pp. 287–88.

11 I. Finkelstein, "The Archaeology of the Days of Manasseh," in *Scripture and Other Artifacts: Essays on the Bible and Archaeology in Honor of Philip J. King* (ed. M. Coogan, J. Cheryl Exum, and L. Stager; Louisville: Westminister John Knox, 1994), p. 173.

12 A short summary and bibliography of these jars and stamps can be found in D. Lance, "Stamps, Royal Judean," in *ABD*, vol. 6, pp. 184–85.

13 J. Cahill, "Rosette Stamped Handles," in *Excavations at the City of David*, vol. 6: *Inscriptions* (ed. A. Belfer-Cohen et al.; QEDEM, 41; Jerusalem: Institute of Archeology, Hebrew University of Jerusalem, 2000), pp. 85–108.

14 See Niditch's discussion and the literature cited there, S. Niditch, *Oral World and Written Word: Ancient Israelite Literature* (Library of Ancient Israel; Philadelphia: Westminster John Knox Press, 1966), pp. 54–55.

15 See S. Lancaster and G. Long, "Where They Met: Separations in the Rock Mass Near the Siloam Tunnel's Meeting Point," *BASOR* 315 (1999): 15–26;

A. Faust, "A Note on the Location of the Siloam Inscription and the Excavation of Hezekiah's Tunnel," in *New Studies on Jerusalem: Proceedings of the Second Conference November 28th 1996* (ed. A. Faust; Ramat Gan: Ingeborg Rennert Center for Jerusalem Studies, 1996), pp. 21–24.

16 See C. Clermont-Ganneau, "Les Tombreaux de David et rois de Juda et le tunnel-aqueduc de Siloe," *Recueil d'Archéologie orientale* 2 (1898): 254–94.

17 Recent surveys of the Jerusalem area have uncovered a number of eighth- through sixth-century settlements; see G. Edelstein and I. Milevski, "The Rural Settlement of Jerusalem Re-evaluated: Surveys and Excavations in the Reph'aim Valley and the Mevasseret Yerushalayim," *PEQ* 126 (1994): 2–11; S. Gibson and G. Edelstein, "Investigating Jerusalem's Rural Landscape," *Levant* 17 (1985): 139–55.

18 Ramat Rahel has been a problem for historical geography. It is often identified by Beth-Haccherem (Jer 6:1; Neh 3:14; Josh 15:59a [LXX]). G. Barkay makes a cogent case for its identification with the enigmatic *MMŠT* mentioned in the numerous *lmlk* stamps at the site; cf. "Ramat Rahel," in *NEAEHL*, pp. 1261–67.

19 See J. Pritchard, "Industry and Trade at Biblical Gibeon," *BA* 23 (1960): 23–29; S. Gitin, "Incense Altars from Ekron, Israel and Judah: Context and typology," *EI* 20 (1989): 52*–67*.

20 There was also a sudden expansion of settlement in the more arid regions of the Beersheba valley and the Judean desert; see Finkelstein, "The Archeology of the Days of Manasseh," pp. 175–76.

21 The percentages depend on the exact size of Jerusalem post-701 B.C.E. Finkelstein takes a conservative estimate of 60 hectares. This still would translate into an almost four-fold increase in Jerusalem's size and makes Jerusalem's population 23% of Judah's total population. Barkay argues cogently for a much larger Jerusalem of 100 hectares, which translates into about 34% (G. Barkay, "Northern and Western Jerusalem in the End of the Iron Age," Ph.D. diss., Tel Aviv University, 1985).

22 Despite efforts to completely dismiss the united monarchy, the evidence cannot support such attempts. See B. Halpern, "Erasing History," *Bible Review* 11 (1995): 27–35, 47.

23 See J. Black and W. Tait, "Archives and Libraries in the Ancient Near East," in *Civilizations of the Ancient Near East* (ed. J. Sasson; Simon & Schuster, 1995), pp. 2197–2209; O. Pedersén, *Archives and Libraries in the Ancient Near East, 1500–300 B.C.* (Bethesda, MD: CDL Press, 1998), pp. 158–64. More generally, see L. Casson, *Libraries in the Ancient World* (New Haven: Yale University Press, 2001).

24 See "Nabu," in *Gods, Demons and Symbols in Ancient Mesopotamia: An Illustrated Dictionary* (ed. J. Black and A. Green; Austin: University of Texas Press, 1992), pp. 133–34.

25 A. Loprieno, *La Pensée Et L'écriture: Pour Une Analyse Sémiotique De La Culture Égyptienne* (Paris: Cybele, 2001), p. 127 (see more generally Loprieno's observations on pp. 124–28).

26 See, for example, C. L. Seow, "Linguistic Evidence and the Dating of Qohelet," *JBL* 115 (1996): 643–66; Avi Hurvitz, "Review: *Qoheleth's Language: Re-evaluating its Nature and Date*, by Daniel C. Fredericks," *Hebrew Studies* 31 (1990): 144–54.

27 See M. Noth, *The Deuteronomistic History* (Sheffield: JSOT, 1991).

28 See my review of the recent literature, Schniedewind, "The Problem with Kings: Recent Study of the Deuteronomistic History," *RSR* 22, no. 1 (1995): 22–27.

29 I summarize this approach and support it in my lengthy review article, "The Problem with Kings." See this article for further bibliography.
30 A classic study on this formula in biblical literature was done by B. Childs, "A Study of the Formula 'Until This Day,'" *JBL* 82 (1963): 279–92.
31 This point is argued cogently and at length by M. Brettler, "Ideology, History and Theology in 2 Kings XVII 7–23," *VT* 39 (1989): 268–82.
32 I. Provan, *Hezekiah in the Book of Kings* (BZAW, 172; Berlin: de Gryter, 1988), pp. 116–17. Also see R. E. Friedman, "From Egypt to Egypt in Dtr 1 and Dtr 2," in *Traditions in Transformations: Turning Points in Biblical Faith* (ed. B. Halpern and J. D. Levenson; Winona Lake, IN: Eisenbrauns, 1981), pp. 171–73; E. Eynikel, *The Reform of King Josiah and the Composition of the Deuteronomistic History* (OTS, 33; Leiden: Brill, 1996), pp. 107–11.
33 Another example may be Psalm 78; see R. Clifford, "In Zion and David a New Beginning: An Interpretation of Psalm 78," in *Traditions in Transformations: Turning Points in Biblical Faith* (ed. B. Halpern and J. D. Levenson; Winona Lake, IN: Eisenbrauns, 1981), pp. 121–41.
34 See, for example, Avi Hurvitz, "The Evidence of Language in Dating the Priestly Code," *RB* 81 (1974): 24–57; A. Hurvitz, *A Linguistic Study of the Relationship between the Priestly Source and the Book of Ezekiel: A New Approach to an Old Problem* (Paris: Gabalda, 1982).
35 For example, Frank H. Polak, "Epic Formulas in Biblical Narrative – Frequency and Distribution," in *Acts du Second Colloque International Bible et Informatique: Méthodes, outils, résultats* (Paris: Champion, 1989), pp. 437–89. Interestingly enough, the genre of literature does not seem to have impacted this shift from oral to chancellery style. Thus, Esther is strikingly more scribal in its style than the patriarchal narratives.
36 Most notably, Moshe Weinfeld, *Deuteronomy and the Deuteronomic School* (reprint, Eisenbrauns, 1992 ed.; Oxford: Clarendon Press, 1972); H. L. Ginsberg, *The Israelian Heritage of Judaism* (New York: Jewish Theological Seminary, 1982); M. Haran, *Temples and Temple Service in Ancient Israel* (Oxford: Clarendon Press, 1985).
37 Most forcefully, Israel Knohl, *The Sanctuary of Silence: The Priestly Torah and the Holiness School* (Philadephia: Fortress, 1995).
38 D. N. Freedman, "Headings in Books of Eighth-Century Prophets," *Andrews University Seminary Studies* 25 (1987): 22.
39 See the extensive discussion in my earlier book, *Society and the Promise to David*, chap. 4.
40 D. N. Freedman, *Amos* (AB; New York: Doubleday, 1989); S. Paul, *Amos, A Commentary on the Book of Amos* (Hermeunia; Philadephia: Fortress, 1991).
41 It is also noteworthy that Gath is missing from the list of Philistine cities mentioned in Amos 1:6–8. Its fate is apparently summed up in the words of the prophet Micah, "Tell it not in Gath" (Mic 1:10).
42 For example, Harper, *Amos*, pp. 195–96; Driver, *Amos*, pp. 119–24.
43 Contra R. E. Clements, who – for reasons that are unclear – ascribes this verse to a late-seventh-century editor. See Clements, *Isaiah and the Deliverance of Jerusalem: A Study of the Interpretation of Prophecy in the Old Testament* (JSOTSS, 13; Sheffield: JSOT, 1980), p. 60.

Chapter 6

1 This point is nicely made by A. Loprieno, "Von der Stimme zur Schrift," in *Was ist der Mensch? Zwischen Affe und Robot* (ed. Andreas Münkel; München: Beck,

2003). Also see Loprieno, *La Pensée Et L'écriture: Pour Une Analyse Sémiotique De La Culture Égyptienne* (Paris: Cybele, 2001), pp. 124–28.

2 E. Havelock's book, *The Muse Learns to Write: Reflections on Orality and Literacy from Antiquity to the Present* (New Haven: Yale University Press, 1986), is a popularization and summary of his research. Havelock's seminal book was *Preface to Plato* (Cambridge, MA: Harvard University Press, 1963); also see Havelock, *The Literate Revolution in Greece and Its Cultural Consequences* (Princeton: Princeton University Press, 1982). Also see W. Ong, *Orality and Literacy: The Technologizing of the World* (London: Routledge, 1982).

3 See O. Andersen, "The Significance of Writing in Early Greece – A Critical Appraisal," in *Literacy and Society* (ed. K. Schousboe and M. Trolle-Larsen; Copenhagen: Akademisk Forlag, 1989), pp. 73–90.

4 See Harris's critique in *The Origin of Writing* (London, 1986).

5 In any case, vowel letters were already in limited use in Hebrew by the seventh century. They seem to reflect the spread of writing outside the closed circles of scribal schools; see my article, W. M. Schniedewind,"Sociolinguistic Reflections on the Letter of a 'Literate' Soldier (Lachish 3)," *ZAH* 13 (2000): 157–67.

6 See W. M. Schniedewind, "The Geopolitical History of Philistine Gath," *BASOR* 309 (1998): 69–78; S. Gitin, "The Effects of Urbanization on a Philistine City-State: Tel Miqne-Ekron in the Iron Age II Period," in *Proceedings of the World Congress of Jewish Studies, Jerusalem, August 16–24, 1989. Division A: The Bible and Its World* (Jerusalem: World Union of Jewish Studies, 1990), pp. 277–84.

7 See W. M. Schniedewind, "History and Interpretation: The Religion of Ahab and Manasseh in the Book of Kings," *CBQ* 55 (1993): 657–60.

8 For a similar interpretation, see H. G. M. Williamson, *1 and 2 Chronicles* (NCBC; Grand Rapids: Eerdmans, 1982), p. 361; also note S. Talmon's interpretation of Hezekiah in his essay, "The Cult and Calendar Reform of Jeroboam I," in *King, Cult, and Calendar in Ancient Israel: Collected Studies* (Jerusalem: Magnes, 1986), pp. 123–30.

9 I. Finkelstein, "The Archeology of the Days of Manasseh," in *Scripture and Other Artifacts: Essays on the Bible and Archeology in Honor of Philip J. King* (ed. M. Coogan, J. Cheryl Exum, and L. Stager; Louisville: Westminister John Knox, 1994), p. 173.

10 For a classic study of the role of the temple in the economy, see J. Weinberg, *The Citizen-Temple Community* (trans. D. Smith-Christopher; Sheffield: JSOT, 1992).

11 This point is developed particularly by M. Haran, *Temples and Temple Service in Ancient Israel* (Oxford: Clarendon, 1985).

12 See, for example, W. Claburn, "The Fiscal Basis of Josiah's Reforms," *JBL* 92 (1973): 11–22; N. Steinberg, "The Deuteronomic Law Code and the Politics of Centralization," in *The Bible and the Politics of Exegesis* (ed. D. Jobling et al.; Cleveland: Pilgrim, 1991), pp. 161–70; M. Heltzer, "Some Questions Concerning the Economic Policy of Josiah, King of Judah," *IEJ* 50 (2000): 105–8.

13 Y. Aharoni, *Arad Inscriptions* (Jerusalem: Israel Exploration Society, 1981).

14 P. Bordreuil, F. Israel, and D. Pardee, "King's Command and Widow's Plea: Two New Hebrew Ostraca of the Biblical Period," *Near Eastern Archaeology* 61 (1998): 2–13. The name of the king is somewhat problematic. As it stands, the text seems to refer to an unknown Judean king named 'Ashyahu; the original editors (Bordreuil, Israel, and Pardee) argue cogently that it is a variant of the name Josiah. The fact that the ostracon is unprovenenced makes the interpretation of this artifact much more complex and uncertain.

15 See N. Avigad, *Corpus of West Semitic Stamp Seals* (revised and completed by B. Sass, ed.; Jerusalem: Israel Exploration Society, 1997), pp. 49–61.

16 See H.-J. Martin, *The History and Power of Writing* (trans. Lydia G. Cochrane; Chicago: University of Chicago Press, 1994).

17 This observation has been acknowledged by many scholars, especially during the last few years in the light of new archaeological developments. I lectured on this topic at the 1998 meeting of the SBL in San Francisco. See also the recent arguments by M. Coogan, "Literacy and the Formation of Biblical Literature," in *Realia Dei: Essays in Archaeology and Biblical Interpretation* (ed. P. Williams and T. Hiebert; Atlanta: Scholars, 1999), pp. 47–61, as well as the popular book by I. Finkelstein and N. Silberman, *The Bible Unearthed* (New York: Free Press, 2001).

18 E. Stern, *Archaeology of the Land of the Bible*, vol. 2 (New York: Doubleday, 2001), p. 169.

19 Avigad, *Corpus of West Semitic Stamp Seals*.

20 These seals have been the subject of extensive discussion. See, for example, D. Ussishkin, "Royal Judean Storage Jars and Private Seal Impressions," *BASOR* 223 (1976): 1–13; A. F. Rainey, "Wine from the Royal Vineyards," *BASOR* 245 (1982): 57–62.

21 Yair Shoham, "A Hebrew Seals and Seal Impressions," in *Excavations at the City of David*, vol. 6: *Inscriptions* (ed. A. Belfer-Cohen et al.; QEDEM, 41; Jerusalem: Institute of Archaeology, Hebrew University of Jerusalem, 2000), pp. 29–57.

22 N. Avigad, *Hebrew Bullae from the Time of Jeremiah* (Jerusalem: Magnes, 1986), p. 121.

23 A. Millard, "The Uses of the Early Alphabets," in *Phoinikeia Grammata: Lire et écrire en Méditerranée* (ed. C. Baurain, C. Bonnet, and V. Krings; Namur: Société des Études Classiques, 1991), p. 106.

24 R. Deutsch and M. Heltzer, *New Epigraphic Evidence from the Biblical Period* (Tel Aviv: Archaeological Center, 1995), pp. 92–103.

25 See R. Kletter, *Economic Keystones: The Weight System of the Kingdom of Judah* (JSOTSS, 276; Sheffield: Sheffield Academic Press, 1998).

26 The *editio princeps* was done by H. Torczyner, *Lachish I. The Lachish Letters* (Oxford: Oxford University Press, 1938). The present discussion draws upon my article, Schniedewind, "Sociolinguistic Reflections on the Letter of a 'Literate' Soldier (Lachish 3)," pp. 157–67.

27 B. Isserlin, "Epigraphically attested Judean Hebrew, and the question of upper class (Official) and popular speech variants in Judea during the eighth-sixth centuries B.C.," *Australian Journal of Biblical Archeology* 2 (1972): 197; I. Young, *Diversity in Pre-Exilic Hebrew* (Tübingen: J.C.B. Mohr, 1993), p. 110.

28 Schniedewind, "Sociolinguistic Reflections on the Letter of a 'Literate' Soldier (Lachish 3)," pp. 157–67.

29 The original publication was by J. Naveh, "A Hebrew Letter from the Seventh Century B.C.," *IEJ* 10 (1960): 129–39. Also see J. Naveh, "Some Notes on the Reading of the Meṣad Hashavyahu Letter," *IEJ* 14 (1964): 158–59; S. Talmon, "The New Hebrew Letter from the Seventh Century B.C. in Historical Perspective," *BASOR* 176 (1964): 29–38.

30 This inscription was initially published by W. Dever, "Iron Age Epigraphic Material from the Area of Khirbet el-Kôm," *HUCA* 40–41 (1970): 139–204.

31 The tombs date to the end of the Judean monarchy, despite some suggestions that they might be later; cf. J. Naveh, "Old Hebrew Inscriptions in a Burial Cave," *IEJ* 13 (1963): 74–92; A. Lemaire, "Prières en temps de crise: Les inscriptions de Khirbet Beit Lei," *RB* 83 (1976): 558–68.

32 Originally published by G. Barkay, "The Priestly Benediction on Silver Plaques from Ketef Hinnom in Jerusalem," *TA* 19 (1992): 139–91.

33 The paleographic dating of the amulets has been the subject of some discussion. Unfortunately, much of the earlier discussion was based on early photographs and consequently inaccurate drawings; see G. Barkay, M. Lundberg Vaughn, and B. Zuckerman, "The Amulets from Ketef Hinnom: A New Edition and Evalvation," *Near Eastern Archeology* forthcoming.
34 See also M. Fishbane, "Form and Reformulation of the Biblical Priestly Blessing," *JAOS* 103 (1983): 115–21.
35 There is no consensus on the exact identification of Bozkath, although it was apparently located in the Judean foothills near Lachish (cf. Josh. 15:39).
36 For a good summary of the literature, see J. Healy, "Am Ha'aretz," in *ABD*, vol. 1, pp. 168–69.
37 On Josiah's reforms, see E. Eynikel, *The Reform of King Josiah and the Composition of the Deuteronomistic History* (OTS, 33; Leiden: Brill, 1996); N. Lohfink, "The Cult Reform of Josiah of Judah: 2 Kings 22–23 as a Source for the History of Israelite Religion," in *Ancient Israelite Religion: Essays in Honor of Frank Moore Cross* (ed. P. D. Miller, P. Hanson, and S. D. McBride; Philadephia: Fortress, 1987), pp. 459–76; M. Sweeney, *King Josiah of Judah: The Lost Messiah of Israel* (Oxford: Oxford University Press, 2001); W. M. Schniedewind, "History and Interpretation: The Religion of Ahab and Manasseh in the Book of Kings," *CBQ* 55 (1993): 649–61.
38 J. Goody, *The Domestication of the Savage Mind* (Cambridge: Cambridge University Press, 1977), p. 37.
39 See M. Brettler, "The Structure of 1 Kings 1–11," *JSOT* 49 (1991): 87–97. For a broad account of the concept of ancient Israelite kingship and its representation in Deuteronomy and the Deuteronomistic History, see B. Levinson, "The Reconceptualization of Kingship in Deuteornomy and the Deuteronomistic History's Transformation of Torah," *VT* 51 (2001): 511–34.
40 Levinson ("The Reconceptualization of Kingship") and Gary Knoppers ("Rethinking the Relationship between Deuteronomy and the Deuteronomistic History," *CBQ* 63 (2001): 393–415), both recognize the tension between Deuteronomy and the DtrH, especially over the role of the king. I believe that Deuteronomy must be regarded as encapsulating the traditions of "the people of the land," whereas DtrH is the work of the royal scribes.
41 See B. Levinson, *Deuteronomy and the Hermeneutics of Legal Innovation* (New York: Oxford University Press, 1997).
42 E. Nicholson, *Jeremiah 1–25* (Cambridge: Cambridge University Press, 1973), p. 86.
43 For a popular account of P, see R. E. Friedman, *Who Wrote the Bible?* (San Francisco: Harper & Row, 1987), pp. 188–206.
44 See my earlier book, Schniedewind, *The Word of God in Transition: From Prophet to Exegete in the Second Temple Period* (Sheffield: JSOT, 1995), pp. 130–38; also S. Mowinckel, "'The Spirit' and the 'Word' in the Pre-exilic Reforming Prophets," *JBL* 53 (1934): 199–227.
45 See my article, Schniedewind, "The Chronicler as an Interpreter of Scripture," in *The Chronicler as Author: Studies in Text and Texture* (ed. M. P. Graham and S. L. McKenzie; Sheffield: Sheffield Academic Press, 1999), pp. 172–78.

Chapter 7

1 M. Weinfeld, "Deuteronomy, Book of" in *ABD* vol. 2, p. 175. See further, Weinfeld, *Deuteronomy and the Deuteronomic School* (reprint; Winona Lake, IN: Eisenbrauns, 1992), pp. 158–70.

2 See B. Sommer, "Revelation at Sinai in the Hebrew Bible and in Jewish Theology," *Journal of Religion* 79 (1999): 428–29.

3 Whether the four traditional strands of Pentateuchal criticism (JEDP) even have their own individual accounts of the act of writing down torah will depend on how we assign the sources. There is obviously a great deal of disagreement here. There should also be some question about the role of writing in each source, and this should be correlated to some extent to the dating of the various strands, which is itself a topic of some disagreement (e.g., contrast the recent work of Blum, van Seters, and Knohl). I, for example, would follow Haran, Hurvitz, Weinfeld, Knohl and others in dating P earlier; therefore, I am not surprised that the so-called Priestly Source does not have a substantial account of writing Torah. The priests will become interested in a written Torah only in the later post-exilic times, when they will claim part of their authority from their role as scribes, teachers, and guardians of the Torah.

One major problem with analyzing the role of writing in the various Pentateuchal strands is the lack of agreement on the assignment of critical texts. So, for example, classical source criticism might assign a description of writing down material revealed at Sinai to each of the strands in Exodus (J: 34:27; E: 24:4; P: 31:18, 34:29), but debate remains on the assignment of these sources. For example, 24:4 has often been assigned to D (where it parallels Deut 31:9). Exodus 31:18 is often divided into parts, though it must be related to the earlier 24:12 to which it explicitly refers. The issue of the different views of what is written down and who did the writing has not been sufficiently explored by scholars.

4 Most recently Exodus 19–24 was the subject of a Zürich dissertation by Wolfgang Oswald, *Israel am Gottesberg. Eine Untersuchung zur Literargeschichte der vordern Sinaiperikope Ex 19–24 und deren historischen Hintergrund* (OBO, 159; Fribourg: Vandenhoeck & Ruprecht, 1998). For a review of literature and some representative approaches, see L. Perlitt, *Bundestheologie in Alten Testament* (WMANT, 36; Neukirchen-Vlyun: Neukirchen Verlag, 1969), pp. 156–238; H. H. Schmid, *Der sogenannte Jahwist: Beobachtungen und Fragen zur Pentateuchforschung* (Zürich: Theologischer Verlag, 1976), pp. 83–93; J. van Seters, *The Life of Moses: The Yahwist as Historian in Exodus-Numbers* (Louisville: Westminster John Knox Press, 1994), pp. 247–360.

5 On the phenomenon of explicative scribal comments more generally, see M. Fishbane, *Biblical Interpretation in Ancient Israel* (Oxford: Clarendon, 1985), pp. 44–88.

6 On the repetition in Deuteronomy 31 and Joshua 1, see Fishbane, *Biblical Interpretation in Ancient Israel*, pp. 384–85.

7 The "tablets of stone" are described as "the *Torah* and the commandment that God has given to teach them" in Exodus 24:12. As many have noted, the Hebrew syntax of "also, the law [*tôrah*] and the commandment [*mitzvah*]" in verse 12 is particularly difficult. For example, B. Childs notes, "The *waw* ... before the word *tôrāh* can be translated" either as a conjunction or as an explicative; Childs, *Exodus* (OTL; Louisville: Westminster John Knox Press, 1972), p. 499. For this reason, already a century ago, S. R. Driver suggested that the words *torah* and *mitzvah* must be a Deuteronomic redactor's gloss; Driver, *Exodus* (Cambridge: Cambridge University Press, 1918), p. 255.

8 Targum Neophiti was published by A. Dîez Macho, *Neophyti I: Targum Palestinese Ms de la Biblioteca Vaticana* (Madrid, 1970). On the dating of the Targum Neophiti, see A. Díez Macho, "The Recently Discovered Palestinian Targum: Its Antiquity and Relationship with the Other Targums," *VTSup* 7 (1959): 222–45.

9 On the antiquity of the tabernacle, see F. M. Cross, "The Tabernacle," *BA* 10 (1947): 45–68. This may be supplemented by more recent articles by Cross, "The Early Priestly Tabernacle in Light of Recent Research," in *Temples and High Places in Biblical Times* (ed. A. Biran; Jerusalem: Magnes Press, 1981), pp. 169–80; K. A. Kitchen, "The Tabernacle – A Bronze Age Artifact," *EI* 24 (1993): pp 119*–129*.

10 See discussion and references W. Harvey, "Torah," in *Encyclopedia Judaica*, vol. 15, (Jerusalem: Keter, 1972), cols. 1236–38.

11 The Golden Calf story (Exod 32–34) interrupts the revelation of the tabernacle and its construction (Exod 25–31, 35–40). The chronological disjunction of this material is highlighted by the fact that the Golden Calf narrative assumes that the tabernacle had already been built (cf. Exod 33:7–11).

12 B. Schwartz argues that P's account does not include the tablets at all, "The Priestly Account of the Theophany and Lawgiving at Sinai," in *Texts, Temples, and Traditions: A Tribute to Menahem Haran* (ed. M. V. Fox et al.; Winona Lake, IN: Eisenbrauns, 1996), pp. 126–27. I would argue that the priestly narratives see the tablets as giving the divine plans for the tabernacle.

13 Both the ark and the tabernacle are named after the tablets of the *'edut* (Exod 31:18; cf. Exod 25:16, 21, 22; 38:21; Num 1:50, etc.). In other words, the tablets give definition to the ark and the tabernacle.

14 See R. E. Friedman, "The Tabernacle in the Temple," *BA* 43 (1980): 241–48. Later Jewish tradition continues to note the connection between the tabernacle and the Temple. Josephus notes the similarity of the two and says that the tabernacle was brought to the Temple (*Ant* 8.101–106). The Babylonian Talmud reports that the tabernacle was stored in the crypts of the Solomonic Temple (*b. Soṭa* 9a).

15 See discussions of sacred time and space by J. Z. Smith, *To Take Place: Toward Theory in Ritual* (Chicago: University of Chicago Press, 1987) as well as M. Eliade, *The Sacred and the Profane* (trans. Willard Trask; New York: Harcourt Brace, 1959). B. Sommer discusses these theoretical studies with relation to the Israelite Temple and tabernacle, "Conflicting Constructions of Divine Presence in the Priestly Tabernacle," *Biblical Interpretation* 9 (2001): 41–63.

16 Several biblical texts pick up on this association between the Sabbath and the tabernacle (e.g., Lev 19:30; 26:2). See A. Toeg, *Lawgiving at Sinai* (Jerusalem: Magnes, 1977), p. 146 [Hebrew]; Toeg, "Genesis 1 and the Sabbath," *BethM* 50 (1972): 288–96 [Hebrew].

17 One of the most remarkable textual transformations must be the Sabbath Law in Exodus 20:8–11 and Deuteronomy 5:12–15. How is it that something supposedly written by "the finger of God" (in Deuteronomy's interpretation) is so radically different in Exodus and Deuteronomy? See further the article by G. Hasel on "Sabbath" in *ABD*, vol. 5, pp. 849–56, and the bibliography cited there.

18 See M. Haran, "The Disappearance of the Ark," *IEJ* 13 (1963): 46–58.

19 The title comes from the Greek title, *to deuteronomion* (Latin, *Deuteronomium*), which draws upon the Hebrew description, *Mishneh Torah* "second/repeated law" (based on Deut 17:18; Josh 8:32). The Hebrew undoubtedly reflects the fact that Deuteronomy repeats sections of the law and narrative from the first four books of the Pentateuch; cf. Nahmanides to Deut 1:1 and Ibn Ezra to Deut 1:5.

20 On Deuteronomy as a commentary on Exodus, see Sommer, "Revelation at Sinai," pp. 432–35.

21 Some scholars have claimed that Deuteronomy relies on fourteenth–thirteenth century B.C.E. Hittite treaties more than on the neo-Assyrian treaties; see, for example, the classic articulation of this by G. Mendenhall, "Covenant Forms in Israelite Tradition," *BA* 17 (1954): 50–76.

22 M. Weinfeld argues (correctly, in my opinion) that Deuteronomy marks a turning point in Israelite religion and gives several examples of this. One important point is that Deuteronomy separates law from the realm of magic; see Weinfeld, *Deuteronomy 1-11* (AB; New York: Doubleday, 1991), p. 44. To Weinfeld's observations I would add that Deuteronomy separates the treaty from the realm of myth and magic. This is critical to the assertion of a textual authority that was not based on the magical power of writing itself.
23 For the Assyrian covenantal ceremony, see R. Frankena, "The Vassal-Treaties of Esarhaddon and the Dating of Deuteronomy," *OTS* 14 (1965): 122–54; M. Weinfeld, "The Loyalty Oath in the Ancient Near East," *UF* 8 (1976): 392–93. For the Sefire treaty, see J. Fitzmyer, *The Aramaic Inseriptions from Sefire* (Rome: PBI, 1995).
24 See particularly the study by B. Levinson, *Deuteronomy and the Hermeneutics of Legal Innovation* (New York: Oxford University Press, 1997).
25 Weinfeld, "Deuteronomy, Book of," in *ABD*, vol. 2, p. 175.
26 See introduction to and translation of Jubilees by O. S. Wintermute in *The Old Testament Pseudepigrapha*, vol. 2 (ed. J. Charlesworth; Garden City, NY: Doubleday, 1985), pp. 35–142.
27 A new critical edition of the Temple Scroll (replacing Y. Yadin's original edition) was done by E. Qimron, *The Temple Scroll: A Critical Edition with Extensive Reconstructions* (Beersheba: Ben-Gurion; Jerusalem: Israel Exploration Society, 1996). A good, convenient translation with brief introduction may be found in G. Vermes, *The Complete Dead Sea Scrolls in English* (New York: Penguin, 1997).

Chapter 8

1 J. Barton, "Wellhausen's Prolegomena to the History of Israel: Influences and Effects," in *Text and Experience: Toward a Cultural Exegesis of the Bible* (ed. D. Smith-Christopher; Sheffield: Sheffield Academic Press, 1995), p. 328. Also see D. Smith-Christopher's essay that cites Barton approvingly, "Reassessing the Historical and Sociological Impact of the Babylonian Exile (597/587–539 BCE)," in *Exile: Old Testament, Jewish, and Christian Conceptions* (ed. J. M. Scott; Leiden: Brill, 1997), pp. 7–36.
2 See, for example, A. Hurvitz, *The Transition Period in Biblical Hebrew* (Jerusalem: Bialik, 1972) [Hebrew]; Y. Kutscher, *A History of the Hebrew Language* (Jerusalem: Magnes Press, 1982); A. Sáenz-Badillos, *A History of the Hebrew Language* (ET; Cambridge: Cambridge University Press, 1993).
3 P. Ackroyd, *Exile and Restoration: A Study of Hebrew Thought in the Sixth Century* (Louisville: Westminster John Knox Press, 1968).
4 See S. N. Eisenstadt, ed., *The Origins and Diversity of Axial Age Civilizations* (New York: State University of New York Press, 1986).
5 Ackroyd, *Exile and Restoration*, p. 7.
6 C. C. Torrey, *Ezra Studies* (Chicago: University of Chicago Press, 1910), p. 289.
7 H. Barstad, *The Myth of the Empty Land: A Study in the History and Archaeology of Judah during the "Exilic" Period* (Oslo: Scandinavian University Press, 1996).
8 R. Carroll, "Exile! What Exile?" in *Leading Captivity Captive: "The Exile" as Ideology and History* (ed. L. Grabbe; Sheffield: Sheffield Academic Press, 1998), p. 77.
9 E. Stern, *Archaeology of the Land of the Bible*, vol. 2: *The Assyrian, Babylonian, and Persian Periods (732–332 B.C.E.)* (Anchor Bible Reference Library; New York: Doubleday, 2001), p. 303.

10 Recent trends to downplay the exile have been conveniently discussed by D. Smith-Christopher, *A Biblical Theology of Exile* (Minneapolis: Augsburg Fortress, 2002), pp. 30–34, 45–74. Also see I. Finkelstein and N. A. Silberman (*The Bible Unearthed* [New York: Free Press, 2001], p. 306), suggest that 75 percent of the people remained in the land after the exiles; however, as Stager and King ask, "where are the archaeological remains?" (*Life in Biblical Israel*, p. 257). See the complete survey in O. Lipschitz and J. Blenkinsopp, eds., *Judah and Judeans in the Neo-Babylonian Period* (Winona Lake, IN: Eisenbrauns, 2003).
11 J. Zorn, "Mizpah: Newly Discovered Stratum Reveals Judah's Other Capital," *BAR* 23, no. 5 (1997): 28–38, 66; H. J. Stipp, "Gedalja und die Kolonie von Mizpa," *ZAR* 6 (2000): 155–71.
12 On the Babylonian administration of Judah, see D. Vanderhooft, *The Neo-Babylonian Empire and Babylon in the Latter Prophets* (HSM, 59; Atlanta: Scholars Press, 1999), pp. 104–10.
13 Barstad, *Myth of the Empty Land*, pp. 18–19.
14 R. Carroll, "Israel, History of. Post-Monarchic Period," in *ABD*, vol. 3, pp. 567–576.
15 H. Barstad, "On the History and Archaeology of Judah during the Exilic Period: A Reminder," *OLP* 19 (1988): 25–36.
16 See, for example, D. Jamieson-Drake, *Scribes and Schools in Monarchic Judah* (Sheffield: Sheffield Academic Press, 1991), p. 60; Stern, *Archaeology of the Land of the Bible*, pp. 421–26.
17 See D. Smith, *The Religion of the Landless: The Social Context of the Babylonian Exile* (Bloomington, IN: Meyer-Stone Book, 1989); Smith-Christopher, "Reassessing the Historical and Sociological Impact of the Babylonian Exile, pp. 7–36, and Smith-Christopher, *A Biblical Theology of Exile.*
18 For a popular account, see L. Stager, "The Fury of Babylon," *BAR* 22 (1996): 56–69, 76–77.
19 See Vanderhooft, *The Neo-Babylonian Empire*, pp. 61–114.
20 These statistics follow Jamieson-Drake, *Scribes and Schools in Monarchic Judah*, p. 62. Although this data is now slightly dated, the more recent data compiled by C. Carter follow the similar trends; see Carter, *The Emergence of Yehud in the Persian Period* (JSOTSS, 294; Sheffield: Sheffield Academic Press, 1999), pp. 114–213.
21 See the summary by A. Mazar, *Archaeology of the Land of the Bible, 1000–586 B.C.E.* (Garden City, NY: Doubleday, 1990), pp. 458–60.
22 See Carter, *The Emergence of Yehud in the Persian Periods*, pp. 119–34.
23 G. Lehmann, "Trends in the Local Pottery Development of the Late Iron Age and Persian Period in Syria and Lebanon, ca. 700 to 300 B.C.," *BASOR* 311 (1998), pp. 21–32. Lehmann's work utilizes the new archaeological data to update Ephraim Stern's classic work that had pointed to some continuity in the material culture between the Iron and Persian periods; cf. Stern, *Material Culture of the Land of the Bible in the Persian Period, 538–332 BCE* (Warminster: Aris & Phillips, 1982), p. 229.
24 Vanderhooft, *The Neo-Babylonian Empire*, pp. 61–114.
25 The arguments by Barstad (and earlier J. N. Graham) suggesting Babylonian economic development of this region have been shown by recent archaeological and historical investigations to be completely unfounded; see Vanderhooft, *The Neo-Babylonian Empire*, pp. 104–12.
26 If we look at the borders of Persian Yehud, we see a territory confined to the hill country; cf. C. Carter, "The Province of Yehud in the Post-Exilic Period: Soundings in Site Distribution and Demography," in *Second Temple Studies*,

vol. 2: *Temple and Community in the Persian Period* (ed. T. C. Eskenazi and K. H. Richards; *JSOTS*, 175; Sheffield: Sheffield Academic Press, 1994), pp. 106–45; Carter, *The Emergence of Yehud in the Persian Period.*

27 Charts in the appendices to D. Jamieson-Drake, *Scribes and Schools in Monarchic Judah*, conveniently quantify the precipitous decline.

28 Note the four supposedly Babylonian seals discussed by Carter, *The Emergence of Yehud in the Persian Period*, pp. 125, 169. It is just as likely that they date to the Persian period.

29 To be fair, there has been scholarly debate over whether a few Hebrew inscriptions might possibly date to the Babylonian period. For example, several inscriptions were found in a burial cave at Khirbet Beit Lei, in the hills west of Jerusalem. The inscriptions were apparently scrawled on the cave walls by refugees hiding from either the Assyrians or Babylonians. They are dated variously from the late eighth century to the mid-sixth century. Even if the later dating were correct, the inscriptions would still be the legacy of the late Judean monarchy. See the general discussion by A. Lemaire, "Palestinian Funerary Inscriptions," *ABD*, vol. 5, pp. 126–35; also F. M. Cross, "The Cave Inscriptions from Khirbet Beit Lei," in *Near Eastern Archeology in the Twentieth Century* (ed. J. A. Sanders; Garden City, NY: Doubleday, 1970), pp. 299–306.

30 Naveh dates them to the fourth century (*The Development of the Aramaic Script*, pp. 61–62). Cross dates them to the late sixth and early fifth centuries, and Stern dates them to the neo-Babylonian period (*Archaeology of the Land of the Bible*, p. 336) as does J. Zorn (cf. Zorn et al., "The m(w)sh Stamp Impressions and the Neo-Babylonian Period," *IEJ* 44 [1994]: pp. 161–83). Carter dates them to the Persian period (*The Emergence of Yehud in the Persian Period*, pp. 266–67).

31 See the discussion by Smith-Christopher, *A Biblical Theology of Exile*, p. 66.

32 Cited by Smith-Christopher; see M. Noth, *History of Israel* (ET; London: SCM, 1958), p. 296.

33 Dandamaev, "Social Stratification in Babylonia, Seventh to Fourth Centuries BC," *Acta Antiqua* 22 (1974): 437; "Free Hired Labor in Babylonia during the Sixth through Fourth Centuries BC," in *Labor in the Ancient Near East* (ed. M. Powell; AOS, 68; New Haven: American Oriental Society, 1987), pp. 271–79.

34 Cited, for example, by B. Oded, "Judah and the Exile," in *Israelite and Judean History* (ed. J. Hayes and M. Miller; London: SCM, 1977), p. 483. See the discussion Smith-Christopher, *A Biblical Theology of Exile*, pp. 69–71.

35 Stolper, "Murashû, the Archive of," in *ABD*, vol. 4, pp. 927–28. See further M. D. Coogan, *West Semitic Personal Names in The Murashû Documents* (HSM 7; Missoula: Scholars, 1976); Stolper, *Entrepreneurs and Empire: The Murashû Archive, the Murashû Firm, and Persian Rule in Babylonia* (Uitgaven van het Nederlands Historisch-Archaeologisch Instituut te Istanbul 54; Leiden: Brill, 1985).

36 See F. Joannes and A. Lemaire, "Trois tablettes cunéiformes a onomastique ouest-sémitique (collection Sh. Moussaieff) (Pls. I–II)," *Transeuphrates* 17 (1996): 27; see the discussion by Smith-Christopher, *A Biblical Theology of Exile*, p. 68.

37 See, for example, Y. Zakovitch, *"And You Shall Tell Your Son . . .": The Concept of the Exodus in the Bible* (Jerusalem: Magnes, 1991); S. Loewenstamm, *The Evolution of the Exodus Tradition* (translated from Hebrew ed.; Jerusalem: Magnes, 1992).

38 See D. Hillers, "Lamentations, Book of," in *ABD*, vol. 4, pp. 137–41.

39 This gap has not been lost on all scholars. Thomas Thompson, for example, observes, "We have, in fact, no narrative about the exile in the Bible" ("The Exile in History and Myth," in *Leading Captivity Captive*, p. 111). He notes the contrast

with the earlier and later periods. We have narratives of the earlier history of Israel (in the books of Joshua, Judges, Samuel, and Kings) and of the post-exilic period (in the books of Ezra and Nehemiah). However, Thompson comes to the rather strange conclusion that there was no exile. This bizarre conclusion can be dismissed on the weight of archaeological and literary evidence.

40 E. Weidner, "Jojachin, König von Juda," in *Mélanges Syriens offerts a M. René Dussaud*, vol. 2 (Paris: Geuthner, 1939), pp. 923–28; W. F. Albright, "King Jehoiachin in Exile," *BA* 5 (1942): 49–55. The neo-Babylonian archives, including this particular archive, are discussed by O. Pedersén, *Archives and Libraries in the Ancient Near East, 1500–300 B.C.* (Bethesda, MD: CDL Press, 1998), pp. 183–84.

41 The exact amount of Jehoiachin's oil ration is variously translated. Weidner originally transcribed the text as 1/2 PI (*ban*), which would have been 3 *sila* (= 3 liters) according to the neo-Babylonian measurement system. Oppenheim (*ANET*, p. 205) correctly read the text as 1 PI, but used the early Babylonian standard (1 *ban* = 10 *sila*). Relying on Powell's work on neo-Babylonian measurements, I assume that 1 *ban* = 6 *sila* (cf. Powell, "Masse und Gewichte," in *Realexikon der Assyriologie und Vorderasiatischen Archäologie*, vol. 7 [Berlin, 1987–90], p. 494).

42 As suggested by J. Berridge, "Jehoiachin," in *ABD*, vol. 3, pp. 661–63; also see Albright, "King Joiachin in Exile," 49–55.

43 M. Cogan and H. Tadmor, *II Kings* (New York: Doubleday, 1988), p. 320.

44 See E. Tov, "The Literary History of the Book of Jeremiah in Light of Its Textual History," in *Empirical Models for Biblical Criticism* (ed. J. Tigay; Philadephia: University of Pennsylvania Press, 1985), pp. 211–38.

45 Naturally, this explanation is also incorporated into the description of Manasseh's reign itself by means of a later interpolation (2 Kgs 21:11–17). See my article, Schniedewind, "History and Interpretation: The Religion of Ahab and Manasseh in the Book of Kings," *CBQ* 55 (1993): 649–61.

46 On the theme of Manasseh's sins in the exilic redaction of the Book of Kings, see Schniedewind, "History and Interpretation," pp. 649–61.

47 On the use of repetition as an editorial device, see M. Fishbane, *Biblical Interpretation in Ancient Israel* (Oxford: Oxford University Press, 1985), pp. 44–65, and the related discussion in Chapter 1.

48 See, for instance, L. Boadt, "Ezekiel, The Book of," in *ABD*, vol. 2, pp. 711–22.

49 Morton Smith has pointed out that Ezekiel 8 seems to refer to the sins of Manasseh; Smith, "The Veracity of Ezekiel, the Sins of Manasseh, and Jeremiah," *ZAW* 87 (1975): 11–16.

50 These genealogies are not without discrepancies; see M. Ben-Yashar, "On the Problem of Sheshbazzar and Zerubbabel," *BethM* 88 (1981): 46–56 [Hebrew].

51 Translation by Coogan, *The Context of Scripture*, vol. 2, pp. 314–15.

52 In my book, *Society and the Promise to David*, I show that 2 Samuel 7 was a "constitutional" text in ancient Israel. That is, it was one of the best known and most often interpreted texts within the biblical corpus.

53 Although there is a consensus that it is an early post-exilic prose narrative, Ezra 1–6 has been incorporated into a wholly different and later narrative composition. Scholars are divided on the relationship of Ezra 1–6 to the composition of the Book of Chronicles, the Greek 1–2 Esdras, and the canonical Ezra-Nehemiah; for some views, see D. N. Freedman, "The Chronicler's Purpose," *CBQ* 23 (1961): 436–42; F. M. Cross, "A Reconstruction of the Judean Restoration," *JBL* 94 (1975): 4–18; T. Eskenazi, "The Chronicler and the Composition of 1 Esdras," *JBL* 48 (1986): 39–61; R. Klein, "Chronicles, the Book of," in *ABD*, vol. 1, pp. 992–1002.

54 See the discussion by C. Meyers and E. Meyers, *Haggai, Zechariah 1–8* (Anchor Bible; Garden City, NY: Doubleday, 1987), pp. 9–15.
55 See Carter, *The Emergence of Yehud in the Persian Period*, pp. 75–113.
56 See, for example, Neh 1:3; 2:3; 5:2–5.

Chapter 9

1 G. Garbini, "Hebrew Literature in the Persian Period," in *Second Temple Studies*, vol. 2: *Temple and Community in the Persian Period* (ed. T. C. Eskenazi and K. H. Richards; *JSOTSS*, 175; Sheffield: Sheffield Academic Press, 1994), p. 188.
2 See, for example, I. Eph'al, "Changes in Palestine during the Persian Period," *IEJ* 48 (1998): 106–19 (note especially his comments on p. 116).
3 Some have argued (including myself) that the first edition of the Book of Chronicles was originally composed in the late sixth century; see especially F. M. Cross, "A Reconstruction of the Judean Restoration," *JBL* 94 (1975): 4–18. Others have dated it to the fourth century B.C.E., for example, S. Japhet, *I & II Chronicles: A Commentary* (OTL; Louisville: Westminister John Knox Press, 1993), pp. 23–28. The Book of Chronicles in its canonical form is certainly a product of the late Persian period.
4 The dating of Ecclesiastes and Song of Songs has been controversial; see, for example, A. Hurvitz, "Review: Qoheleth's Language: Re-evaluating Its Nature and Date, by Daniel C. Fredericks," *Hebrew Studies* 31 (1990): 144–54; C. L. Seow, "Linguistic Evidence and the Dating of Qohelet," *JBL* 115 (1996): 643–66; M. Pope, *Song of Songs* (Anchor Bible; Garden City, NY: Doubleday, 2000), p. 27. Both Ecclesiastes and Song of Songs have several Aramaisms. Although Aramaisms do not definitively make a book late (cf. A. Hurvitz, "The Chronological Significance of 'Aramaisms' in Biblical Hebrew," *IEJ* 18 [1968]: 234–40), one has to come up with a special explanation (e.g., dialect, genre) to account for the peculiarities.
5 Mark S. Smith, "The Levitical Compilation of the Psalter," *ZAW* 103 (1991): 258–63. See further the survey by J. Limburg, "Psalms, Book of," in *ABD*, vol. 5, pp. 522–36. The problem of the canonical development of Psalms was most sharply raised by the Dead Sea Scroll Psalms scroll; see J. Sanders, *The Psalms Scroll of Qumran Cave 11* (DJD, IV; Oxford: Clarendon Press, 1965).
6 See A. Hurvitz, "The Date of the Prose-Tale of Job Linguistically Reconsidered," *HTR* 67 (1975): 17–34.
7 See M. Haran, "Book Scrolls at the Beginning of the Second Temple Period," *EI* 16 (1982): 86–92; Haran, "More Concerning Book-Scrolls in Pre-Exilic Times," *JJS* 35 (1984): 84–85.
8 These minor prophetic "books" came to be copied on one scroll in Hebrew manuscripts. The order was fairly consistent in Hebrew, but Greek translations and lists varied within the Twelve. Codices B (Vaticanus) and A (Alexandrinus) put Amos and Micah after Hosea and before Joel.
9 The strongest early advocate was C. C. Torrey, *Ezra Studies* (Chicago: University of Chicago Press, 1910).
10 See, for example, N. P. Lemche, "The Old Testament – A Hellenistic Book?" *SJOT* 7 (1993): 163–93; this inspired a collection of essays edited by L. Grabbe, *Did Moses Speak Attic? Jewish Historiography and Scripture in the Hellenistic Period* (JSOTSS, 317; Sheffield: Sheffield Academic Press, 2001). See the stinging review of Lemche by E. Gruen, *JBL* 121 (2002): 359–61.

11 For a survey of these assertions about the "invention" of ancient Israel, see J. Barr, *History and Ideology in the Old Testament: Biblical Studies at the End of a Millennium* (Hensley Henson Lectures for 1997 delivered to the University of Oxford; Oxford: Oxford University Press, 2000), pp. 59–101.
12 See B. Halpern, "Erasing History," *Bible Review* 11 (1995): 27–35, 47.
13 Barr, *History and Ideology*, p. 99.
14 Barr, *History and Ideology*, p. 134. For a more polemical critique, see I. Provan, "Ideologies, Literary and Critical: Reflections on Recent Writing on the History of Israel," *JBL* 114 (1995): 585–606.
15 Carter, *The Emergence of Yehud in the Persian Period*, p. 226.
16 Carter, *The Emergence of Yehud in the Persian Period*, p. 201.
17 *Greek and Latin Authors on Jews and Judaism*, vol. 1: *From Herodotus to Plutarch* (ed. M. Stern; Jerusalem: Israel Academy of Sciences and Humanities, 1974), pp. 27–28.
18 *Greek and Latin Authors on Jews and Judaism*, p. 28.
19 Carter, *The Emergence of Yehud in the Persian Period*, p. 259.
20 See Carter, *The Emergence of Yehud in the Persian Period*, pp. 288–89.
21 E. Stern, *Archaeology of the Land of the Bible*, vol. 2: *The Assyrian, Babylorian, and Persian Periods (732–332 B.C.E.)* (Anchor Bible Reference Library; New York: Doubleday, 2001), p. 581.
22 This is especially discussed by K. Hoglund, *Achaemenid Imperial Administration in Syria-Palestine and the Missions of Ezra and Nehemiah* (SBLDS, 125; Atlanta: Scholars, 1992), and J. Berquist, *Judaism in Persia's Shadow: A Social and Historical Approach* (Minneapolis: Augsburg, 1995).
23 Carter, *The Emergence of Yehud in the Persian Period*, p. 285.
24 P. Davies, *Scribes and Schools: The Canonization of the Hebrew Scriptures* (Louisville: Westminster John Knox Press, 1998), p. 79.
25 A. Saldarini, "Scribes," in *ABD*, vol. 5, p. 1013.
26 C. Meyers and E. Meyers, *Haggai, Zechariah 1–8* (Anchor Bible; Garden City, NY: Doubleday, 1987), pp. 9–15.
27 *Greek and Latin Authors on Jews and Judaism*, p. 28.
28 See P. Machinist, "The First Coins of Judah and Samaria: Numismatics and History in the Achaemenid and Early Hellenistic Periods," in *Achaemenid History*, vol. 8: *Continuity and Change* (ed. H. Sancisi-Weerdenbur et al.; Leiden: Nederlands Instituut Voor Het Nabije Oosten, 1994), pp. 375–76; J. Betylon, "The Provincial Government of Persian Period Judea and the Yehud Coins," *JBL* 105 (1986): 633–42.
29 Eph'al, "Changes in Palestine during the Persian Period," p. 116.
30 For an analysis Jewish coins, see Ya'akov Meshorer, *Ancient Jewish Coinage*, 2 vols. (Dix Hills, NY: Amphora Books, 1982). Also noteworthy is an ostracon dating to about 300 B.C.E. from the City of David excavations, which is written with Aramaic letters and uses the Aramaic plural ending but uses Hebrew vocabulary (*City of David*, vol. 6: *Inscriptions* [ed. D. Ariel; QEDEM, 41; Jerusalem: IES, 2000], pp. 9–10).
31 See, for example, E. Kutscher, *A History of the Hebrew Language* (Jerusalem: Magnes, 1982), pp. 105–6; S. Weitzman, "Why Did the Qumran Community Write in Hebrew?" *JAOS* 119 (1999): 35–45.
32 Carter, *The Emergence of Yehud in the Persian Period*, pp. 279–80.
33 Paleo-Hebrew is stylized on the basis of the Lachish ostraca (about 600 B.C.E.) and the Aramaic based on the Elephantine papyri (late fifth century B.C.E.). On these scripts, see J. Naveh, *The Early History of the Alphabet: An Introduction to West Semitic Epigraphy and Palaeography* (2nd ed.; Jerusalem: Magnes, 1987).

34 M. H. Segal, *A Grammar of Mishnaic Hebrew* (Oxford: Clarendon, 1927), p. 6.

35 H. Tadmor, "The Aramaization of Assyria: Aspects of Western Impact," in *Mesopotamien und seine Nachbarn. Teil 2* (ed. H.-J. Nissen and J. Renger; Berlin: Dietrich Reimer, 1982), pp. 449–70. As a result, isolated Aramaisms cannot be used to argue that a biblical text is late; cf. A. Hurvitz, "Hebrew and Aramaic in the Bible: The Problem of 'Aramaicisms' in the Research of Biblical Hebrew," in *Studies in the Hebrew Language and in Languages of the Jews* (ed. M. Bar-Asher; Jerusalem: Bialik, 1996), pp. 79–94.

36 J. Barr, *Comparative Philology and the Text of the Old Testament* (Oxford: Clarendon, 1968), pp. 328–72. Emanuel Tov concurs ("Did the Septuagint Translators Always Understand Their Hebrew Text?" in *De Septuaginta: FS J. Wevers* [ed. A. Pietersma and C. Cox; Mississauga, Ontario: Benben Publications, 1984], pp. 53–70).

37 J. Joosten, "The Knowledge and Use of Hebrew in the Hellenistic Period Qumran and Septuagint," in *Diggers at the Well: Proceedings of a Third International Symposium on the Hebrew of the Dead Sea Scrolls and Ben Sira* (ed. T. Muraoka and J. F. Elwolde; Leiden: Brill, 2000), p. 122.

38 A. Sáenz-Badillos, *A History of the Hebrew Language* (ET; Cambridge: Cambridge University Press, 1993), p. 115.

39 See, for example, G. Landes, "A Case for the Sixth-Century BCE Dating for the Book of Jonah," in *Realia Dei: Essays in Archaeology and Biblical Interpretation* (ed. P. Williams and T. Hiebert; Atlanta: Scholars Press, 1999), pp. 100–16.

40 The exact placement of these books within the Persian period is a matter of scholarly debate. I have argued, following Frank Moore Cross, that the Book of Chronicles was composed in at least two stages. The first stage would have been in the late sixth century, but the final form of the book derives from the fourth century B.C.E.; Schniedewind, *Society and the Promise to David: A Reception History of 2 Samuel 7: 1–17* (New York: Oxford University Press, 1999), pp. 125–28. The Book of Ezra-Nehemiah is also usually seen as coming together in stages during the Persian period with its canonical form coming together in the fourth century B.C.E.; see J. Blenkinsopp, *Ezra-Nehemiah* (OTL; Louisville: Westminister John Knox Press, 1988), pp. 41–47.

41 See, for example, J. G. Gammie, "The Classification, Stages of Growth and Changing Intentions in the Book of Daniel," *JBL* 93 (1976): 356–85.

42 See A. Hurvitz's extensive review of Daniel Fredericks's book, *Qoheleth's Language: Re-evaluating Its Nature and Date*, in *Hebrew Studies* 31 (1990): 144–54. Hurvitz notes the difficulty of reaching an unequivocal decision about the dating of the Book of Ecclesiastes.

43 See J. Schaper, "Hebrew and Its Study in the Persian Period," in *Hebrew Study from Ezra to Ben-Yehuda* (ed. W. Horbury; Edinburgh: T & T Clark, 1999), p. 15.

44 C. Rabin's contention ("The Historical Background of Qumran Hebrew," *ScrHier* 4 [1958]: 144–61) that Persian period Jews were trilingual, knowing Aramaic as well as both a late colloquial Hebrew dialect and the classical biblical literary idiom is untenable (as Schaper points out, "Hebrew and Its Study in the Persian Period," pp. 16–18).

45 Berquist, *Judaism in Persia's Shadow*, p. 137.

46 See *Antiquities* 3.1.7; 5.1.17; 10.4.2.

47 This has been nicely outlined by T. Eskenazi, "Ezra–Nehemiah: From Text to Actuality," in *Signs and Wonders: Biblical Texts in Literary Focus* (ed. J. C. Exum; Atlanta: Scholars Press, 1989), pp. 165–98. I appreciate Professor Eskenazi's pointing me to this article and her incisive reading of a draft of this manuscript that sharpened my own perceptions of textualization in the Persian period.

48 See R. Braun, "The Message of Chronicles: Rally 'Round the Temple," *CTM* 42 (1971): 502–14; Braun, "Solomon, The Chosen Temple Builder: The Significance of 1 Chronicles 22, 28, and 29 for the Theology of Chronicles," *JBL* 95 (1976): 581–90. There may be an older literary work dating to the time of Zerubbabel (ca. 515 B.C.E.) lying behind the canonical Book of Chronicles, but it is difficult to recover it with any certainty; see F. M. Cross, "A Reconstruction of the Judean Restoration," *JBL* 94 (1975): 4–18.

49 Also note 2 Chr 23:18 "according to that which was written in the *Torah* of Moses (ככתוב בתורת משה)," 25:4 "according to that which was written in the *Torah* in the book of Moses (ככתוב בחודת בספר משה)," 2 Chr 31:3 and 35:6 "according to that which was written in the *Torah* of YHWH (ככתוב בתוות יהוה)."

50 H. J. Martin, *The History and Power of Writing* (trans. Lydia G. Cochrane; Chicago: University of Chicago Press, 1994), pp. 86–87.

51 This is discussed at length in my book, Schniedewind, *The Word of God in Transition: From Prophet to Exegete in the Second Temple Period* (JSOTSS, 197; Sheffield: JSOT, 1995), pp. 130–38.

52 The only case where it might be found used in this way is Deut 5:5. However, there is considerable textual variation between the "words of YHWH" and the "word of YHWH" evident in the manuscripts. This probably reflects later confusion that merged Mosiac revelation with prophetic speech; see Schniedewind, *The Word of God in Transition*, pp. 131–32.

53 On the problem of the end of prophecy, see Frederick Greenspahn, "Why Prophecy Ceased," *JBL* 108 (1989): 37–49; Benjamin Sommer, "Did Prophecy Cease? Evaluating a Reevaluation," *JBL* 115 (1996): 31–47.

54 M. Fishbane, "Torah," in *Encyclopedia Miqra'it*, vol. 8 (Jerusalem: Bialik, 1982), col. 469–83 [Hebrew].

55 See, for example, Ezr 3:2, 4; 6:18; Neh 8:15; 10:34, 36; 2 Chr 23:18; 25:4; 30:5, 18.

Chapter 10

1 For a survey of the development of canon, see D. Carr, "Canonization in the Context of the Community; An Outline of the Formation of Tanakh and the Christian Canon," in *A Gift of God in Season: Essays on Scripture and Community in Honor of James A. Sanders* (ed. R. Weis and D. Carr; Sheffield: Sheffield Academic Press, 1996), 22–64.

2 See MMT C10 (4Q397 frag. 14–21, line 10). For a critique of the tripartite canon in MMT, see E. Ulrich, "The Non-attestation of a Tripartite Canon in 4QMMT," *CBQ* 65 (2003): 202–14.

3 See the general discussion in L. Casson, *Libraries in the Ancient World* (New Haven: Yale University Press, 2001), pp. 124–35.

4 W. Graham, *Beyond the Written Word: Oral Aspects of Scripture in the History of Religion* (Cambridge: Cambridge University Press, 1987), p. 5.

5 For an exhaustive discussion of the ancient synagogue, see L. Levine, *The Ancient Synagogue: The First Thousand Years* (New Haven: Yale University Press, 2000). Critical discussion of the origin and development of the synagogue in antiquity may be found in *Ancient Synagogues: Historical Analysis and Archaeological Discovery* (ed. P. Flesher and D. Urman; Leiden: Brill, 1995).

6 See Casson, *Libraries in the Ancient World*, pp. 32–33.

7 This is cogently argued by Steven Fraade in several articles, including "The Early Rabbinic Sage," in *The Sage in Israel and the Ancient Near East* (ed. J. Gammie

and L. Perdue; Winona Lake, IN: Eisenbrauns, 1990), pp. 417–36. I also wish to thank Professor Fraade for giving me a copy of his unpublished paper, "Priests, Scribes and Sages in Second Temple Times," which develops this argument in more detail.

8 Fragments of the original Hebrew work have been discovered among the Cairo Geniza manuscripts; see H. Rüger, *Text und Textform im hebräischen Sirach* (BZAW, 112; Berlin: de Gruyer, 1970).

9 On the Hebrew language of Ben-Sira, see A. Hurvitz, "The Linguistic Status of Ben Sira as a Link Between Biblical and Mishnaic Hebrew: Lexicographical Aspects," in *The Hebrew of the Dead Sea Scrolls and Ben Sira* (ed. T. Muraoka and J. F. Elwolde; Leiden: Brill, 1997), pp. 72–86; and, "Further Comments on the Linguistic Profile of Ben Sira: Syntactic Affinities with Late Biblical Hebrew," in *Sirach, Scrolls, and Sages* (ed. T. Muraoka and J. F. Elwolde; Leiden: Brill, 1999), pp. 132–45.

10 Steven Fraade points out that the Mishnah conflates this practice with the law of the king in Deuteronomy 17:20 ("Priests, Scribes and Sages in Second Temple Times"). Not only does the Mishnah Sota 7:8 (also Sifre Deut ‘160) follow Deuteronomy 17:20, but these texts all also follow the example of 2 Kings 22:16, where it suggests that King Josiah had read the book of the Torah.

11 See Fraade, "The Early Rabbinic Sage," pp. 420–21.

12 Fraade, "The Early Rabbinic Sage," p. 421.

13 See A. Saldarini, *Pharisees, Scribes and Sadducees in Palestinian Society* (Wilmington, DE: Michael Glazier, 1988), pp. 39–43.

14 See Josephus, *War* §2.8.6.136, 142, 159; Community Rule vi, 6–7.

15 4QFlorilegium.

16 See the general discussion by J. VanderKam, *The Dead Sea Scrolls Today* (Grand Rapids: Eerdmans, 1994), pp. 71–120.

17 L. Schiffman, *Reclaiming the Dead Sea Scrolls* (New York: Doubleday, 1994).

18 Adiel Schremer applies a modern analogy from Orthodox Judaism for the Qumran tendency to base religious praxis on written texts rather than on living tradition; see "'[T]he[y] Did Not Read in the Sealed Book': Qumran Halakhic Revolution and the Emergence of Torah Study in Second Temple Judaism," in *Historical Perspectives: From the Hasmoneans to Bar Kokhba in Light of the Dead Sea Scrolls (Proceedings of the Fourth International Symposium of the Orion Center, 27–31 January 1999)* (ed. D. Goodblatt, A. Pinnick, and D. Schwartz; STDJ, 37; Leiden: Brill, 2001), pp. 105–26. Azzan Yadin shows how the Qumran reliance on scriptural authority continues into the school of Rabbi Ishmael, against R. Akiva; "4QMMT, Rabbi Ishmael, and the Origins of Legal Midrash," *DSD* 10 (2003): 130–49.

19 For a summary of scholarly literature on the Pharisees, see Saldarini, *Pharisees, Scribes and Sadducees in Palestinian Society: A Sociological Approach*, or more conveniently, Saldarini's article, "Pharisees," in *ABD*, vol. 5, pp. 289–303.

20 M. Jaffee, *Torah in the Mouth*, p. 39.

21 Fraade, "The Early Rabbinic Sage," p. 417.

22 As M. Jaffee points out (*Torah in the Mouth*), this is a quite different state of affairs than is reflected in Charles's monumental translation of *The Apocrypha and Pseudepigrapha of the Old Testament* (1913), published almost a century ago. At that time, many works were routinely ascribed to the Pharisees, including the Zadokite fragments from the Cairo Geniza that are now known from the Dead Sea Scrolls as the "Damascus Document."

23 Jaffee, *Torah in the Mouth*, p. 85.

24 M. Jaffee, "Oral-Cultural Context of the Yerushalmi: Greco-Roman Rhetorical Paideia, Discipleship, and the Concept of Oral Torah," in *Transmitting Jewish Tradition: Orality, Textuality, and Cultural Diffusion* (ed. Y. Elman and I. Gersoni; New Haven: Yale University Press, 2000), p. 53.

25 I accept the arguments of J. Murphy-O'Connor for the Pauline authorship of 2 Timothy; cf. Murphy-O'Connor, *Paul: A Critical Life* (New York: Oxford University Press, 1997), pp. 358–59.

26 W. Kelber, *The Oral and the Written Gospel: The Hermeneutics of Writing and Speaking in the Synoptic Tradition, Mark, Paul, and Q* (Bloomington: University of Indiana Press, 1977). For "gospel," see W. Bauer and W. Gingrich, *A Greek-English Lexicon of the New Testament and Other Early Christian Literature* (3rd ed.; revised and edited by F. W. Danker; Chicago: University of Chicago Press, 2000), ad loc.

27 B. Gerhardsson, *Memory and Manuscript: Oral Tradition and Written Transmission in Rabbinic Judaism and Early Christianity* (Lund: CWK Gleerup, 1961; reprint, Grand Rapids: Eerdmans, 1998), pp. 12–13.

28 J. D. Crossan and J. Reed, *Excavating Jesus: Beneath the Stones, Behind the Texts* (San Francisco: Harper, 2001), pp. 30–31.

29 See C. Hezser, *Jewish Literacy in Roman Palestine* (TSAJ, 81; Tübingen: Mohr-Siebeck, 2001), who critiques earlier studies that argued from rather extensive literacy among Jewish males in Roman Palestine. It is important to note that the very ideology of orality limited the spread of high-level literacy. Alan Millard, in contrast, argues for rather extensive literacy among Jews in the Roman world at the time of Jesus; see Millard, *Reading and Writing in the Time of Jesus* (Sheffield: Sheffield Academic Press, 2001).

Index

Lightning Source UK Ltd.
Milton Keynes UK
UKOW01f1346140617
303240UK00021B/637/P

9 780521 536226